TURf

It's your space.
Build what you want.

EAGLE

TURf

It's your space. Build what you want.

anthony garay

HOW BOOKS
www.howdesign.com
Cincinnati, Ohio

[READ THIS IMPORTANT SAFETY NOTICE]

To prevent accidents, keep safety in mind while you work. Use the safety guards installed on power equipment; they are for your protection. When working on power equipment, keep fingers away from saw blades, wear safety goggles to prevent injuries from flying wood chips and sawdust, wear hearing protection and consider installing a dust vacuum to reduce the amount of airborne sawdust in your woodshop. Don't wear loose clothing, such as neckties or loose sleeves, or jewelry, such as rings, necklaces or bracelets, when working on power equipment. Tie back long hair to prevent it from getting caught in your equipment. People who are sensitive to certain chemicals should check the chemical content of any product before using it. The author and editors who compiled this book have tried to make the contents as accurate and correct as possible. Plans, illustrations, photographs and text have been carefully checked. All instructions, plans and projects should be carefully read, studied and understood before beginning construction. Due to the variability of local conditions, construction materials, skill levels, etc., neither the author nor HOW Books assumes any responsibility for any accidents, injuries, damages or other losses incurred resulting from the material presented in this book. Prices listed for supplies and equipment were current at the time of publication and are subject to change. Glass shelving should have all edges polished and must be tempered. Untempered glass shelves may shatter and can cause serious bodily injury. Tempered shelves are very strong and if they break will just crumble, minimizing personal injury.

 Published by HOW Books, an imprint of F+W Publications, Inc., 4700 East Galbraith Road, Cincinnati, Ohio, 45236. First edition.

Distributed in Canada by Fraser Direct
100 Armstrong Avenue
Georgetown, Ontario L7G 5S4
Canada

Distributed in the U.K. and Europe by David & Charles
Brunel House
Newton Abbot
Devon TQ12 4PU
England
Tel: (+44) 1626 323200
Fax: (+44) 1626 323319
E-mail: mail@davidandcharles.co.uk

Distributed in Australia by Capricorn Link
P.O. Box 704
Windsor, NSW 2756
Australia

Other fine HOW Books are available from your local bookstore or direct from the publisher (see www.howdesign.com).

09 08 07 06 05 5 4 3 2 1

Library of Congress Cataloging-in-Publication Data

Garay, Anthony, 1981-
Turf: it's your space, build what you want/Anthony Garay.
p. cm.
Includes index.
ISBN 1-55870-761-1 (pbk.: alk. paper)
1. Furniture making--Amateurs' manuals. 2. House furnishings--Recycling. I. Title.
TT195.G37 2005
684.1--dc22
2005006246

ACQUISITIONS EDITOR: Jim Stack
EDITOR: Amy Hattersley
DESIGNER: Brian Roeth
PRODUCTION COORDINATOR: Jennifer Wagner
PROJECT PHOTOGRAPHERS: Tim Grondin and Greg Grosse
COVER PHOTOGRAPHER: Brian Steege
STEP-BY-STEP PHOTOGRAPHER: Jim Stack
STEP-BY-STEP ILLUSTRATOR: Anthony Garay

fw
F+W PUBLICATIONS, INC.

[ABOUT THE AUTHOR]

Anthony Garay was born and raised in Cincinnati, Ohio. In 2004 he graduated from the University of Cincinnati's College of Design, Architecture, Art & Planning (DAAP) with a bachelor of science degree in industrial design. (UC's DAAP college was named the #1 public design school in the world by *I.D.* magazine in October 2002.) Through his college career, Anthony worked as a student co-op for different companies and design studios throughout the country, completing a full 18 months of professional practice. While living in Minneapolis, Minnesota, and working for a prestigious contemporary furniture design company, he began to realize his love for modern furniture design. Anthony continues to be an enthusiastic student of design, always searching for another big design challenge and his next great adventure!

[TO ALL OF MY FAMILY AND FRIENDS: THANK YOU FOR YOUR ENDLESS LOVE AND SUPPORT. THIS BOOK IS FOR EACH AND EVERY ONE OF YOU. TURF IS DEDICATED TO CALLISTA. XXOO]

ACKNOWLEDGEMENTS

Thank you, Amy, for this opportunity. This book never would have happened if it wasn't for you.

Jim, you are terrific. Thank you, thank you! I never could have done all of this without your selfless help.

Thank you Brian, Tricia and the rest of the F+W team for making this happen.

Thank you Hayes and Chris for helping out with supplies.

Thank you Michelle for the all the fabric help (and some painting).

Thank you to my brother, Joe, for lots of finishing help.

Thank you Mom, Dad, Joe, Greg, Matt, Mike and the girls for the moral support.

Thank you to all my teachers and mentors throughout the years, especially those from DAAP.

Section 2 and ID04: Friends forever! You've all contributed to my learning and my accomplishments.

SPECIAL THANKS

Special thanks to all the good-looking kids we used as "models" for the room shots: Medinah Abernathy, Amy Hattersley, Josh Hill, Jessica Schultz and Hayes Shanesy.

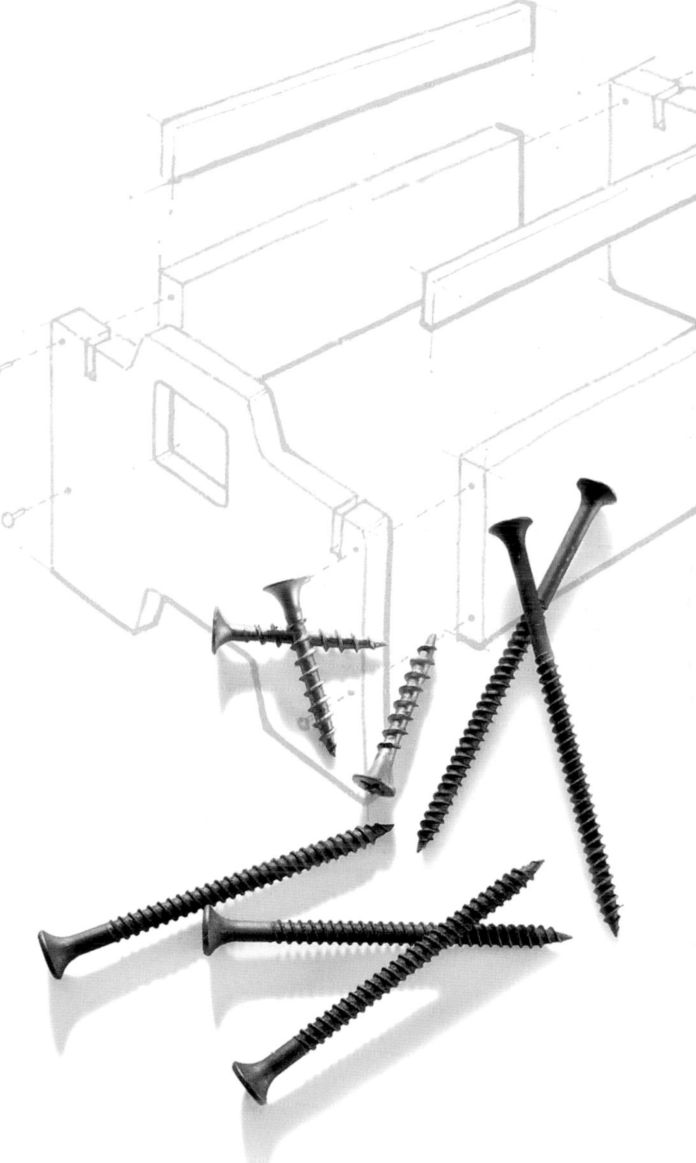

[TABLE OF]

CONTENTS

work space

kitchen

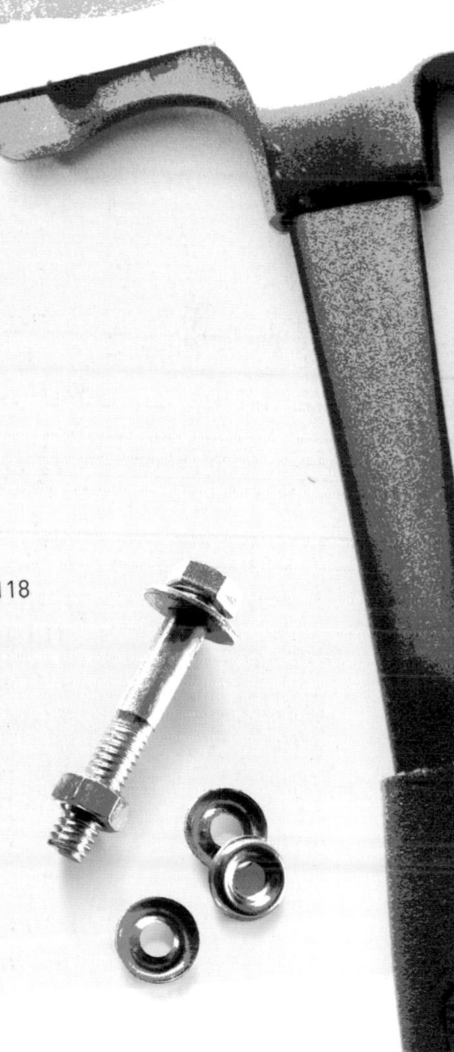

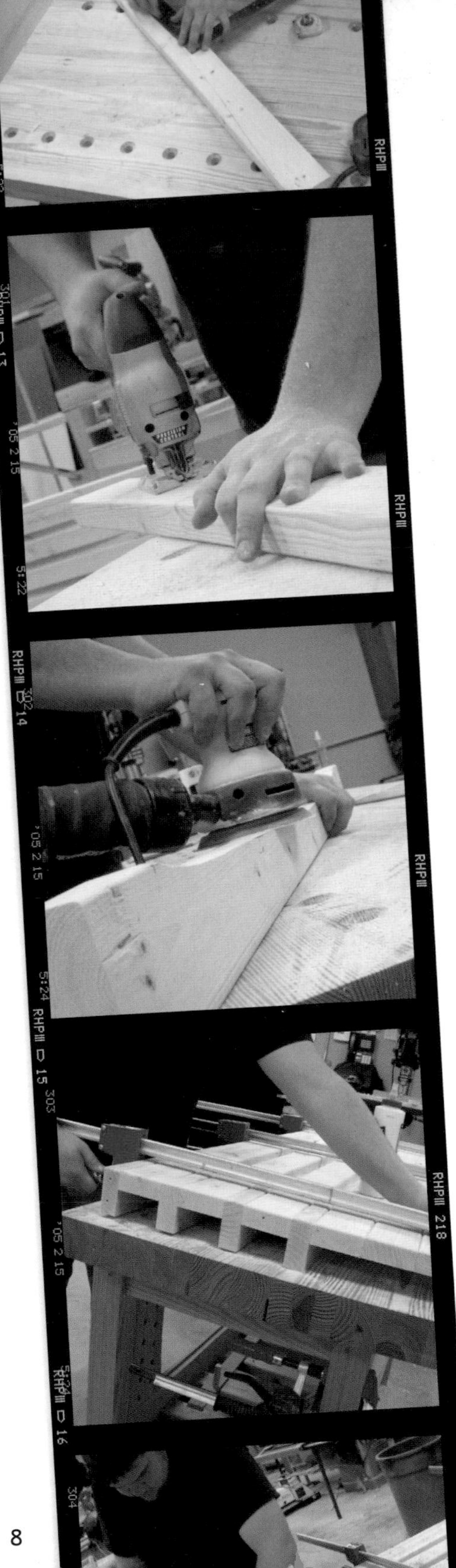

HELLO, FRIENDS!

[INTRODUCTION]

MY NAME IS ANTHONY GARAY. I HAVE BEEN A STUDENT OF DESIGN AND A FURNITURE ENTHUSIAST FOR MANY YEARS. DURING MY COLLEGE CAREER, I HAD THE OPPORTUNITY TO WORK WITH AND LEARN FROM MANY INFLUENTIAL FURNITURE DESIGNERS FROM ALL OVER THE WORLD. IT WAS DURING THIS TIME IN MY LIFE THAT I REALLY LEARNED TO APPRECIATE AND LOVE MODERN FURNITURE DESIGN.

AFTER MY COLLEGE YEARS, I STILL DIDN'T HAVE THE INCOME TO AFFORD THE EXPENSIVE DESIGNER PIECES THAT I COULD SEE IN MANY CATALOGS AND SHOWROOMS. TO HAVE ULTRAHIP DESIGNER FURNITURE IN MY APARTMENT, I DECIDED THAT I SHOULD DESIGN AND BUILD IT MYSELF!

THIS BOOK IS A COMPILATION OF PROJECTS THAT YOU CAN CREATE YOURSELF, WITH LITTLE SHOP OR TOOL KNOWLEDGE. **ALL THE PIECES CAN BE CREATED FOR NEXT TO NOTHING, SOME EVEN FREE,** IF YOU HAVE ACCESS TO THE RIGHT HARDWARE AND MATERIALS.

THIS BOOK IS REALLY INTENDED FOR THE TRUE DESIGNER AND DO-IT-YOURSELFER. I URGE YOU TO THINK OF THE PROJECTS IN THIS BOOK AS STARTING POINTS FOR WHAT YOU CAN DO WITH YOUR OWN PIECES. I HOPE THAT YOU WILL INTRODUCE YOUR OWN SKILLS AND KNOWLEDGE, AS WELL AS PAINTS, FABRICS AND MATERIALS THAT WILL MAKE EACH PROJECT UNIQUELY YOUR OWN.

MOST IMPORTANTLY, HAVE A BUNCH OF FUN!

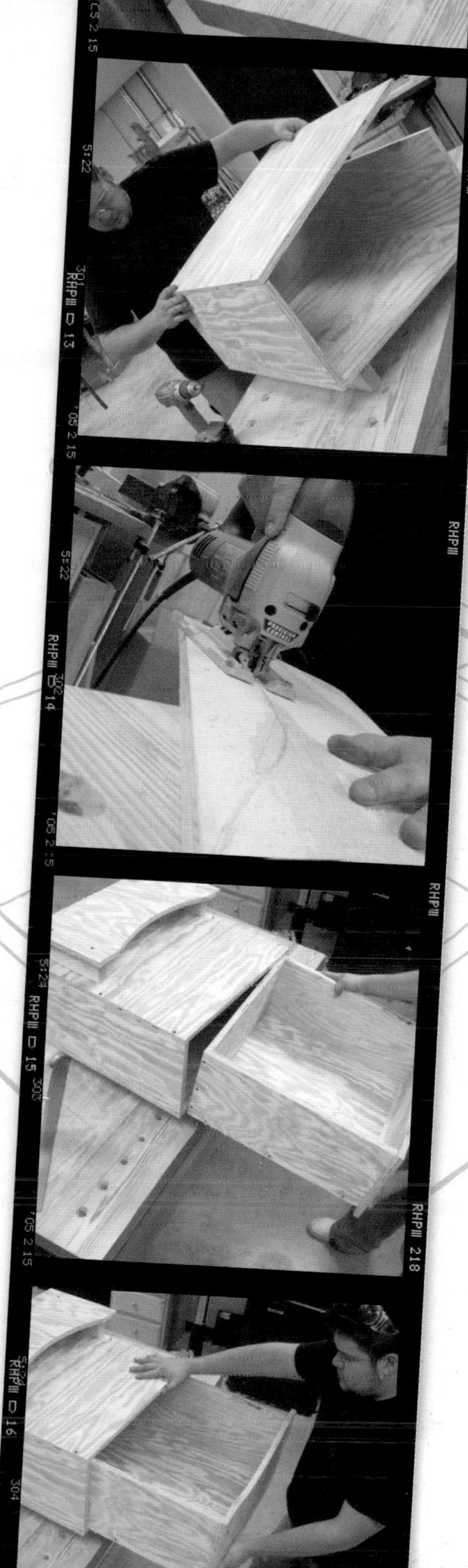

HOW TO USE TOOLS

THE PROJECTS IN THIS BOOK WERE DESIGNED SO THAT THE AVERAGE JOE OR JANE COULD GRAB A FEW THINGS AND PUT THEM TOGETHER WITHOUT A LOT OF HEADACHE. YOU DON'T NEED A TABLE SAW, DRILL PRESS OR TRIM ROUTER TO COMPLETE THESE PROJECTS AND MAKE THEM LOOK GREAT. EACH PROJECT CAN BE FABRICATED WITH NOTHING MORE THAN A JIGSAW AND A DRILL/DRIVER. IF YOU DO HAVE ACCESS TO MORE-ADVANCED TOOLS, THEN OF COURSE YOU SHOULD USE THEM. THE FOLLOWING LIST OF TOOLS AND MATERIALS YOU MIGHT COME ACROSS WHILE BUILDING THESE PROJECTS INCLUDES SOME SIMPLE TIPS FOR USING THEM CORRECTLY.

SAFETY FIRST! THAT IS THE MOST IMPORTANT RULE. DON'T BE STUPID WITH THE TOOLS! PLEASE DON'T USE THE TOOLS IF YOU'RE DIZZY, YOU HAVEN'T SLEPT FOR THREE DAYS, OR YOU JUST GOT DUMPED AND CAN'T STOP CRYING. IF YOU ARE UNFAMILIAR WITH CERTAIN TOOLS, ASK SOMEBODY WHO KNOWS HOW TO USE THEM TO TEACH YOU.

SAFETY GOGGLES

Safety goggles are important, especially when you're using high-powered tools. Get into the habit of using safety goggles when you're building, and it won't be a big deal after too long. You may think that they look dorky or that only squares wear them, but eye patches aren't exactly the hottest thing going, either!

CORDLESS DRILL/DRIVER

What an awesome tool! Cordless drills are so versatile and work so well that you should get one just to have one! Most of these tools have two drive settings (if not more). The first is a lower-speed, higher-torque setting for driving screws, and the second is a higher-speed setting for drilling. Find out which is which and use them accordingly. Most drills have variable speeds, too. These speeds are handy for driving different types of screws without stripping them out.

The hardest things to learn how to do when using the drill/driver for the first time are drilling holes square to your material and driving screws without stripping them. Have a friend watch as you practice drilling holes. They can tell you when the drill is square to your material. You'll get the feel of it in no time. So, make sure your settings are correct, and just take it slowly!

DRILL BITS

I used a variety of standard and specialty bits (such as Forstner bits) to complete the projects in this book. You can usually find individual specialty bits at the hardware store. They're worth every penny to have with your drill/driver.

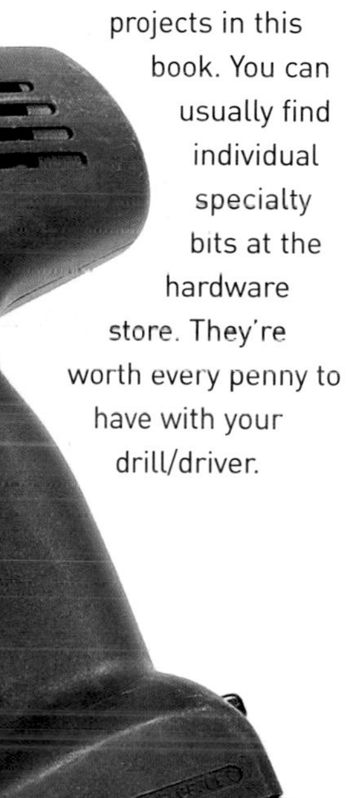

STANDARD BITS

Standard twist bits are used to drill little holes into things. Make pilot holes for screws with these. Hardened-steel twist bits will drill through metal. When drilling, plunge into your workpiece, then retract the bit some and repeat. This will allow sawdust or other waste to leave from the flutes in the bit. Clear flutes will create better cuts!

SPECIALTY BITS

A countersink bit is a conical bit that creates a round chamfer inside a pilot hole. Use this before driving wood screws into a workpiece and you'll be able to drive the head of the screw flush into the panel.

To drill a big through-hole, you could use a variety of bits, including spade bits, Forstner bits, or hole saw bits. Find out which is best for your application. It's important with these bits to use a spoil board — a board underneath your workpiece to minimize blowout around the hole when you poke through.

JIGSAW

A really great jigsaw has variable speeds, adjustable blade action and an adjustable footplate for cutting angles. Learn about your particular saw and what settings and blades are right for cuttings woods, metals, plastics and other materials. For the projects in this book, it would probably be good to have a couple of nice wood blades and a few metal-cuttiing blades on hand, too.

For making long, straight cuts through boards, a jigsaw isn't the optimal tool, but if it's all you've got, you have to make do. Try clamping a metal straightedge or a straight piece of wood to your workpiece and run the jigsaw footplate against it.

If you are cutting a material you have never cut before, try to cut off a practice corner before cutting into your workpiece. Always make sure your workpiece is well stabilized before you cut, as the saw will create a lot of vibration. Also, make sure that the path the blade is going to travel is clear and that you're not going to be cutting any tables in half!

TABLE SAW & OTHER CUTTING TOOLS

Of course, a jigsaw isn't the only tool you can use to cut your material to size. Quite a lot of other options are out there. A circular saw or a table saw will yield a nicer plank than a jigsaw. A band saw would be better than a jigsaw if you want to cut faster and make cleaner cuts. If you have access to better tools and the knowledge to use them, you definitely should use them.

Many hardware stores and lumberyards have some of the more industrial tools on-site, and usually, if you buy the stock from them, they'll gladly cut it down to the size you need. Some stores will give you only a certain number of cuts before they start charging you, but take your dimensions with you when you go to get stuff. It's worth asking.

TAPE MEASURE

Probably one of the best tools to have on hand during any of these these projects is a tape measure. An old plastic 12" grade school ruler just won't do it. Get yourself a nice tape measure that's at least 12' (3.65m) in length. Also, learn to read the tape measure correctly. It just takes a little practice to learn which marks are $\frac{1}{8}$" (or cm) marks versus $\frac{1}{16}$" (or mm) marks. Then you won't ever have to tell anyone to measure "19 inches and five little marks!"

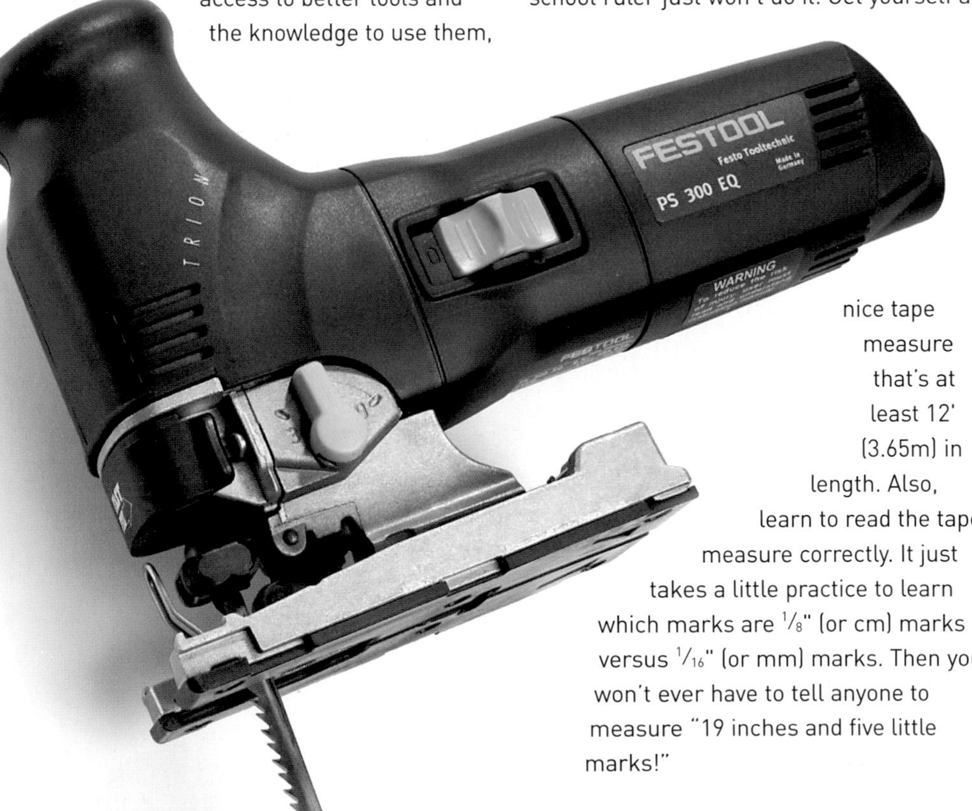

STRAIGHT-EDGE & SQUARE

A lot of the projects in this book, like a lot of things in our world, utilize right angles and straight lines. It's worth the investment to have a tool or two that will help you achieve these things.

A long steel straightedge, anything from 18" to 36", is a pretty good start. For longer lines, you may still need to measure marks and connect the dots, though.

To create square edges, a carpenter's combination square and a framing square are both handy tools. A framing square is a large flat metal right angle that could also double as your straightedge. The carpenter's combination square has an adjustable right-angle head that slides along a steel ruler of about 8" or 12". The combination square is a versatile tool to have around, as it can be used as a square, straightedge, depth gauge, scribe and many other things!

UTILITY KNIFE

Sometimes you'll need to just pick up a blade and get some cutting done. Your standard hardware store utility knife will do the trick. Many new fancy varieties are available if you'd like to splurge, but you really just need something with a sharp blade and a handle you can really get a hold of.

For doing nice clean cuts, a sharp blade

is important; keep an eye on that cutting edge, and change it when it starts to show wear.

For cutting most materials, keep the knife low to the surface with a constant, controlled pressure on the blade, and recognize that some materials will take a few passes to cut through.

GLUES & EPOXY

There's not a lot of fine wood joinery going on in the projects of this book. In fact, most of the wood joints in this book are butt joints, where you press one flat surface against the other. Wood glue will come in handy to help strengthen these joints. Use a liberal amount of glue when joining the pieces, and then clamp them or screw them together, cleaning up the excess glue with a damp rag when it squeezes out. Most wood glue needs to set up 30 minutes to an hour before the workpiece is messed with and will fully cure within 24 hours.

For gluing other materials together, have a two-part epoxy or some superglue on hand. Superglue will take care of small quick jobs that will not be under a lot of stress. A two-part, general-purpose epoxy requires mixing but will provide a strong bond between many different materials.

Each of these adhesives has an archenemy that will dilute it or destroy its bond. It might be good to know about those agents just in case you end up with a finger glued inside a nose or something. Read the labels on the adhesives' packaging.

SANDPAPER

The first step in the finishing process of all of these projects is to sand them. This will remove any tool marks, pencil lines, dirt and uneven surfaces, and it'll get the workpiece ready for some paint or stain. Sandpaper is classified by how coarse the grit of the paper is. Sandpaper with a lower grit number, like 80, is much coarser than a piece of 220-grit sandpaper. In fact, you won't need to venture out from the range between 80 and 220 for any of these projects.

The idea with sandpaper is to start with a heavy grit and work your way to the lighter grits. For sanding big broad panels, wrap or glue some sandpaper to a wood block. This same block can be used to give the edges of your boards a nice bevel: Just keep the block at a constant angle to the surface and work it back and forth over the edges. For a roundover, let the block roll over each edge.

Remember to always sand in the direction of the grain to prevent scratching or splintering.

PAINT BUCKET

For covering large areas of material with one color, nothing's easier than a can of paint and a new brush. Latex paint is probably the easiest to use for most people without a lot of painting experience, and the color palette is virtually limitless. Work the paint calmly. The latex may not cover the material fully with the first coat. Rather than trying to get the whole gallon on the workpiece at one time, give three or four coats the chance to build up to a nice finish. The best thing about latex is that it cleans up easily with some warm soapy water!

When you go to get the paint for a project, get a decent paintbrush, too. Cheap paintbrushes will lose bristles easily, messing up your painted surface and causing more headaches in the long run. When you're done painting, clean your nice brush thoroughly so it'll be ready to go the next time you need it.

SPRAY PAINT

For trickier assemblies and more-unique materials, a lacquer or acrylic spray paint is a terrific color solution. Spray paint is especially useful for metals and plastics. A standard spray can is the best bet for beginners, and color selection is pretty good.

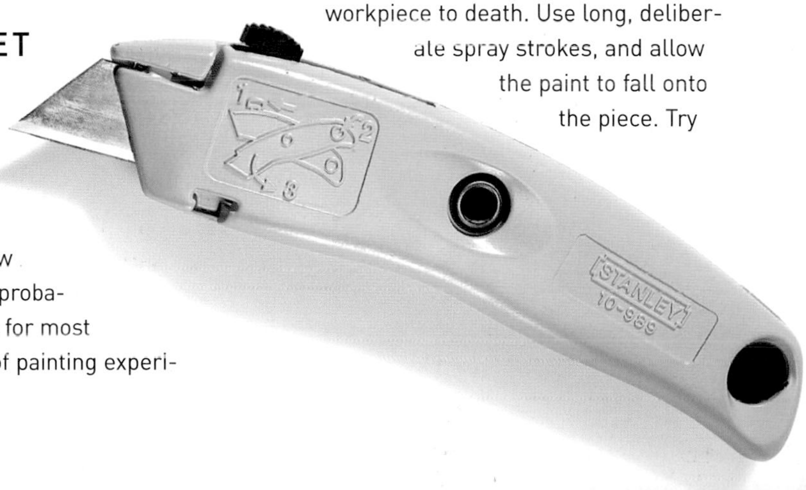

Shake the can really well; let that little ball inside talk to you for a good minute or so before you spray. The idea with spray paint is to slowly build up to complete coverage of the full color, not drown your workpiece to death. Use long, deliberate spray strokes, and allow the paint to fall onto the piece. Try not to start and stop or turn directions of the spray in the middle of the piece. A good pass will leave the piece looking wet but not dripping.

Always make sure you use spray cans in a well-ventilated area. The fumes don't have a pleasant smell, and they might make you feel funny in the head if you inhale them too much!

WOOD STAIN

Wood stain accents the natural features of the wood. Even though a lot of these projects don't use fine hardwoods, the plywood you choose might be veneered in pine, birch or even oak. A stain will have just as nice an effect on these veneers as on any hardwood.

The easiest stain for a beginner to use is an oil-based stain. You can use a brush or rag to evenly apply a liberal amount of the stain to your workpiece, and then after a few minutes remove the excess with a clean cloth or sponge. Most stains can be reapplied a few times on most woods. Try your stain out on a test piece of your project's wood. Cover the entire test piece with the first coat, three-quarters of the strip with the second coat, and half with the third. Then you can see the difference between coats and decide on a color that suits you.

An oil-based stain does not seal the wood, though, so you may still want to coat the piece with a urethane, shellac or varnish. To make your life much easier, some all-in-one stains that have the urethane finish already mixed in and are available at paint and hardware stores.

FABRIC

A couple of the projects in this book use fabric in their designs. Much like we have different building materials we can use, we have many choices when it comes to fabrics. None of the projects call for anything too specific, so the materials and the colors will be left to your discretion. If you don't know a lot about fabrics and aren't familiar with the many different kinds, just visit a fabric store. Just like the hardware store might have a nice old guy behind the counter, it seems like the fabric store always has a sweet old lady at the cutting table. Explain the project to her, and ask her for help and advice. (Just don't call her an old lady.)

In a couple of instances, the fabrics need to be stitched together for the project. A simple hand-sewn, needle-and-thread stitch is all that's required. If you have access to and experience with a sewing machine, it could come in handy, too!

HARDWARE

The projects in this book call for many different types of hardware. At the hardware store, you may be amazed at all the different types of screws and bolts. Each of those pieces are slightly different, though, and intended for a special purpose.

Just as it's important to have the right tool for the job, it's important to have the right hardware for the job, too. If you are unclear about which piece of hardware is which, ask someone at the store for a hand, or ask people who have a lot of experience with hardware. You're going to see things out there that you've never even dreamed of! With so many possibilities, hardware store employees expect that some people will be confused.

HARDWARE STORE GUY

One of the greatest resources you might discover as you build the projects in this book is the old guy behind the counter at your local hardware store. Share your projects with him. Ask him questions about using the tools. See if he has ever built a plywood chair. You'll also be surprised to see how well stocked a little neighborhood store really is. The greatest benefit of patronizing these independent stores is getting to talk to a real person who will help you find what you need, make suggestions for the projects, and even ask you the next time you visit how things turned out! Nothing's wrong with the superstore hardware chains, but don't forget about the local outfits, either.

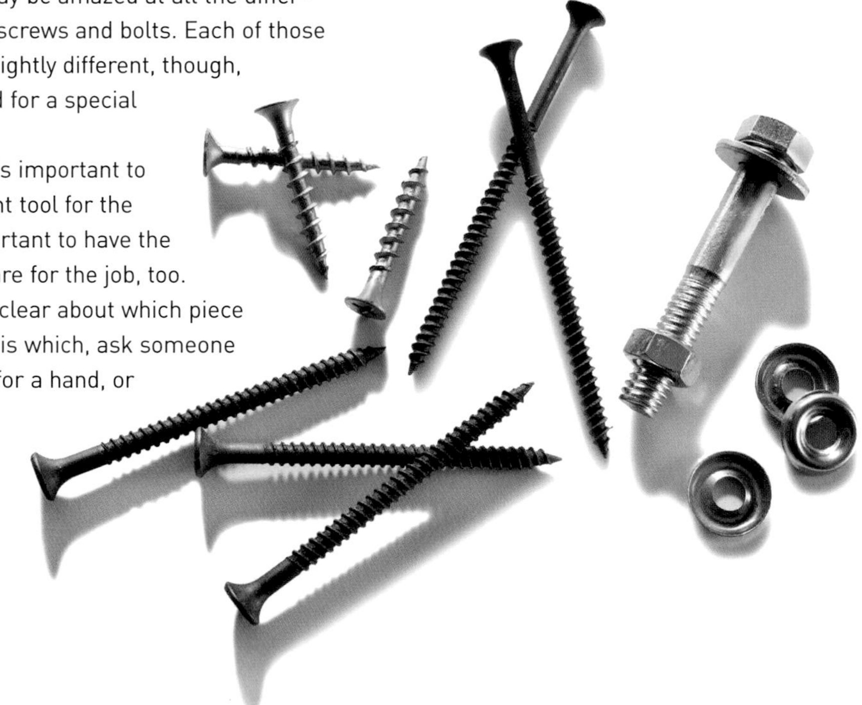

HOW TO USE THIS BOOK

THIS IS *THE* PAGE YOU NEED WHEN YOU WANT TO BUILD ONE OF THE FABULOUS PROJECTS IN THIS BOOK. IF YOU'RE THINKING, "HUH?", THEN DEFINITELY READ ON...

This is all the stuff you'll need to build the project. Take this list with you to the store!

This drawing is called an EXPLODED VIEW. Using this, you can see how all the parts fit together. Parts that need to be cut to a specific size have a reference letter (A,B,C,etc.) that corresponds to the cutting list below.

The cutting list gives you the EXACT DIMENSIONS (inches for the USA [and some others] and metric for the rest of the world) for each part that needs to be cut. It also tells you how many are needed and the type of material, or *stock*, if you want to get all technical.

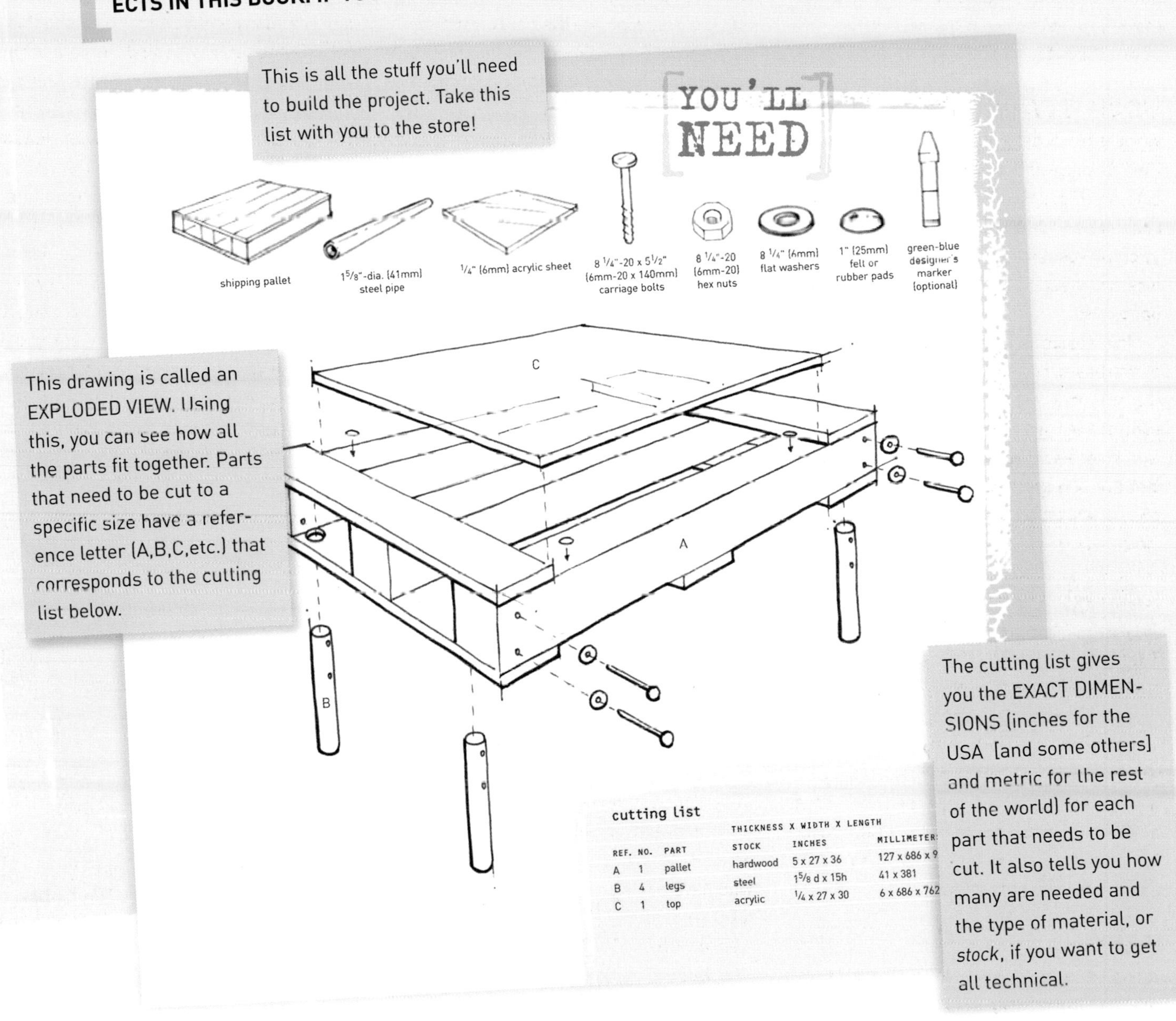

cutting list

REF.	NO.	PART	STOCK	THICKNESS X WIDTH X LENGTH INCHES	MILLIMETER:
A	1	pallet	hardwood	5 x 27 x 36	127 x 686 x 9
B	4	legs	steel	1 5/8 d x 15h	41 x 381
C	1	top	acrylic	1/4 x 27 x 30	6 x 686 x 762

START
HOME

[LIVING ROOM]

THIS IS WHERE IT ALL GOES DOWN. THERE'S NO BETTER PLACE TO HANG OUT WITH ALL YOUR FRIENDS. **PIZZA AND A BEVERAGE OF CHOICE. VIDEO GAMES. MOVIE NIGHTS. BOY-GIRL MIXERS!** IT ALL HAPPENS IN THE LIVING ROOM. TO ACCOMMODATE ALL THESE CRAZY EVENTS, YOU'RE GOING TO NEED A SPACE WITH ALL THE RIGHT GEAR: PLACES TO SIT, A PLACE FOR YOUR TV AND ALL THAT MULTIMEDIA GEAR, **AND DON'T FORGET A TABLE FOR THE CHIPS AND DIP.** EVEN IF YOU DON'T HAVE ANY FRIENDS, PUT THE PROJECTS IN THIS CHAPTER TOGETHER; KIDS WILL BE BEGGING TO HANG WITH YOU IN THE BEST-DRESSED LIVING ROOM ON THE BLOCK. JUST DON'T FORGET A COPY OF "STAIRWAY TO HEAVEN" FOR THE LAST SLOW DANCE OF THE EVENING!

CHAIR AND OTTOMAN

[throne]

Everyone should have that one chair in the living room. You know the one — the one that's just for you that you come home to after a long day and crash into in front of the TV, the one that you lounge in and yell at your favorite sports team from, the one that you fall asleep in during the late movie, the one piece of furniture that you love. The throne is that chair!

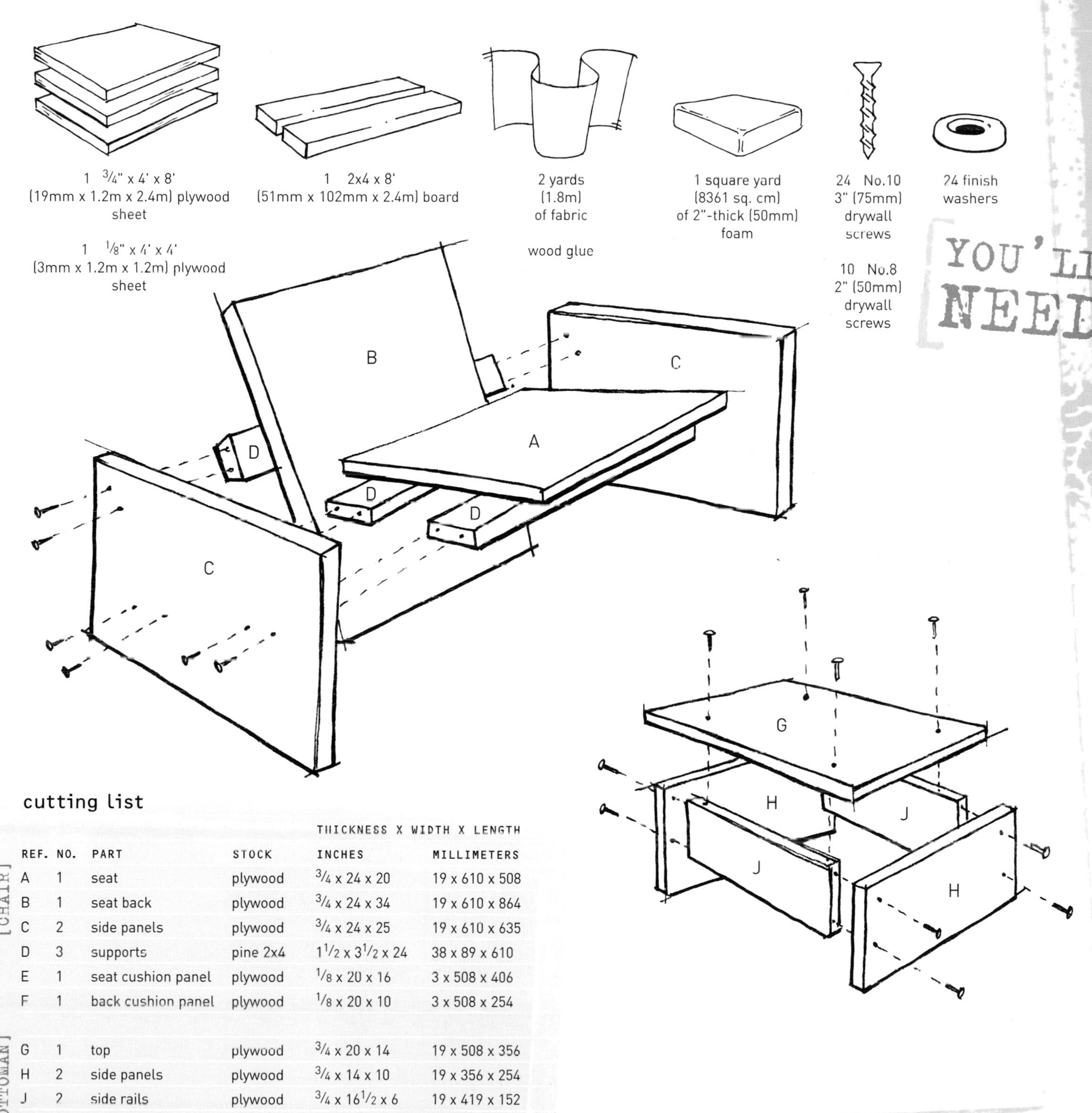

cutting list

	REF.	NO.	PART	STOCK	INCHES (THICKNESS X WIDTH X LENGTH)	MILLIMETERS (THICKNESS X WIDTH X LENGTH)
[CHAIR]	A	1	seat	plywood	3/4 x 24 x 20	19 x 610 x 508
	B	1	seat back	plywood	3/4 x 24 x 34	19 x 610 x 864
	C	2	side panels	plywood	3/4 x 24 x 25	19 x 610 x 635
	D	3	supports	pine 2x4	1 1/2 x 3 1/2 x 24	38 x 89 x 610
	E	1	seat cushion panel	plywood	1/8 x 20 x 16	3 x 508 x 406
	F	1	back cushion panel	plywood	1/8 x 20 x 10	3 x 508 x 254
[OTTOMAN]	G	1	top	plywood	3/4 x 20 x 14	19 x 508 x 356
	H	2	side panels	plywood	3/4 x 14 x 10	19 x 356 x 254
	J	2	side rails	plywood	3/4 x 16 1/2 x 6	19 x 419 x 152
	K	1	cushion panel	plywood	1/8 x 16 x 10	3 x 406 x 254

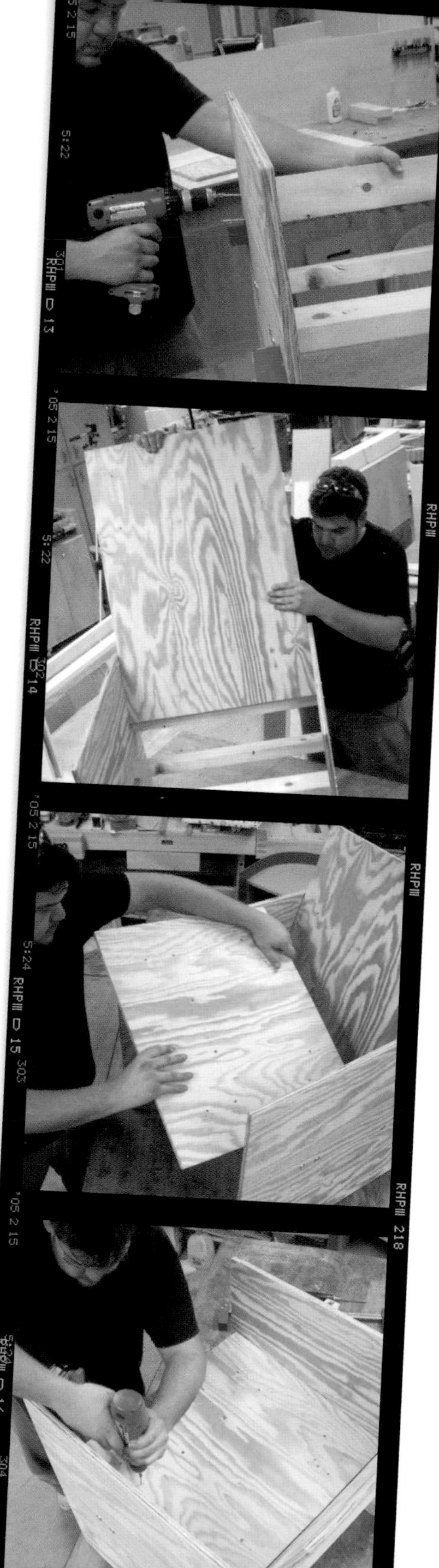

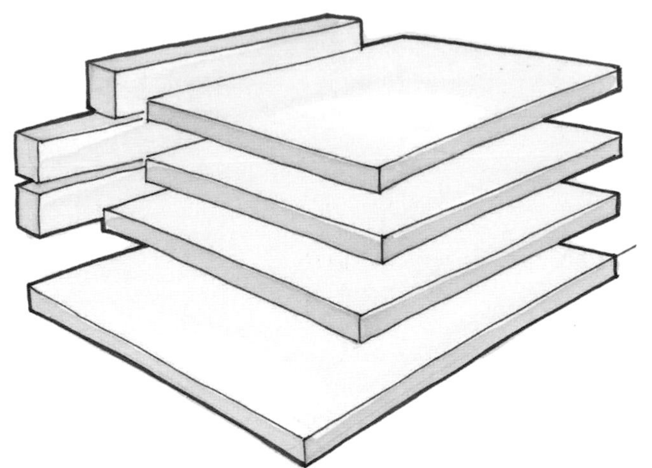

[1] Grab some plywood and a 2x4 from the hardware store. Have them cut the boards to the dimensions given in the cutting list. You'll leave the store with a stack of planks and beams. Almost like a box of furniture parts!

[2] Plot these dimensions on the side panels of the chair, and drill pilot holes to receive the 2x4 supports.

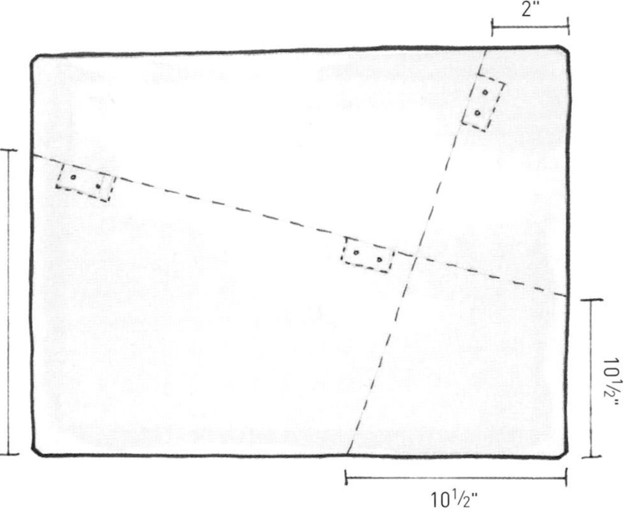

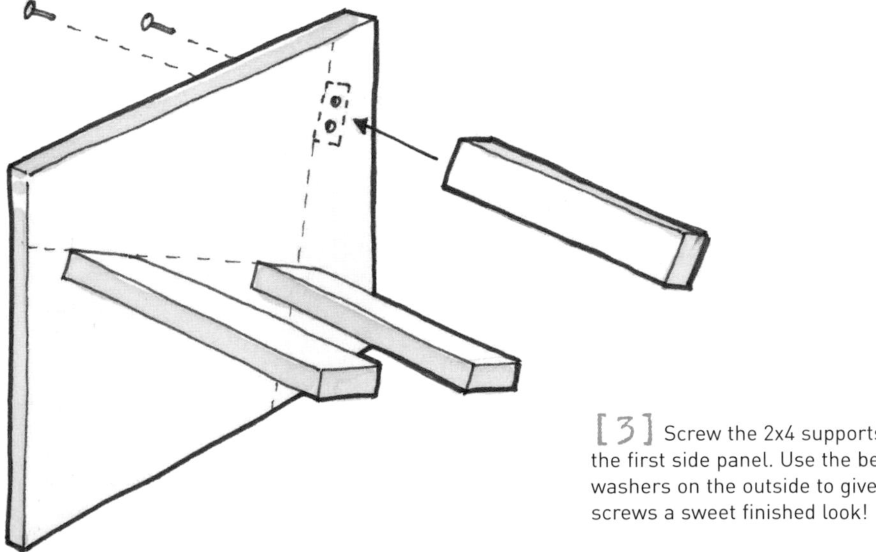

[3] Screw the 2x4 supports to the first side panel. Use the bevel washers on the outside to give the screws a sweet finished look!

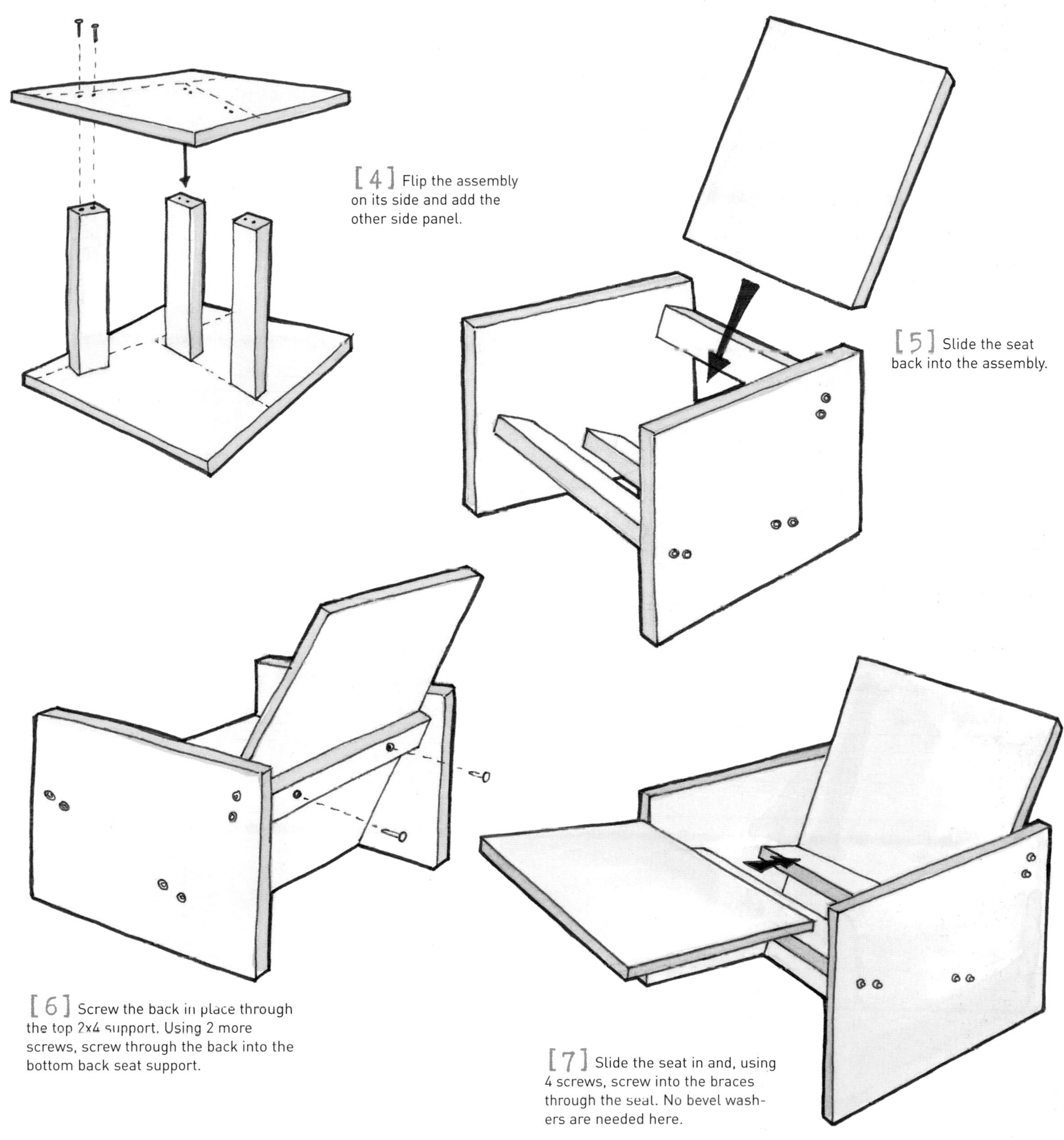

[4] Flip the assembly on its side and add the other side panel.

[5] Slide the seat back into the assembly.

[6] Screw the back in place through the top 2x4 support. Using 2 more screws, screw through the back into the bottom back seat support.

[7] Slide the seat in and, using 4 screws, screw into the braces through the seat. No bevel washers are needed here.

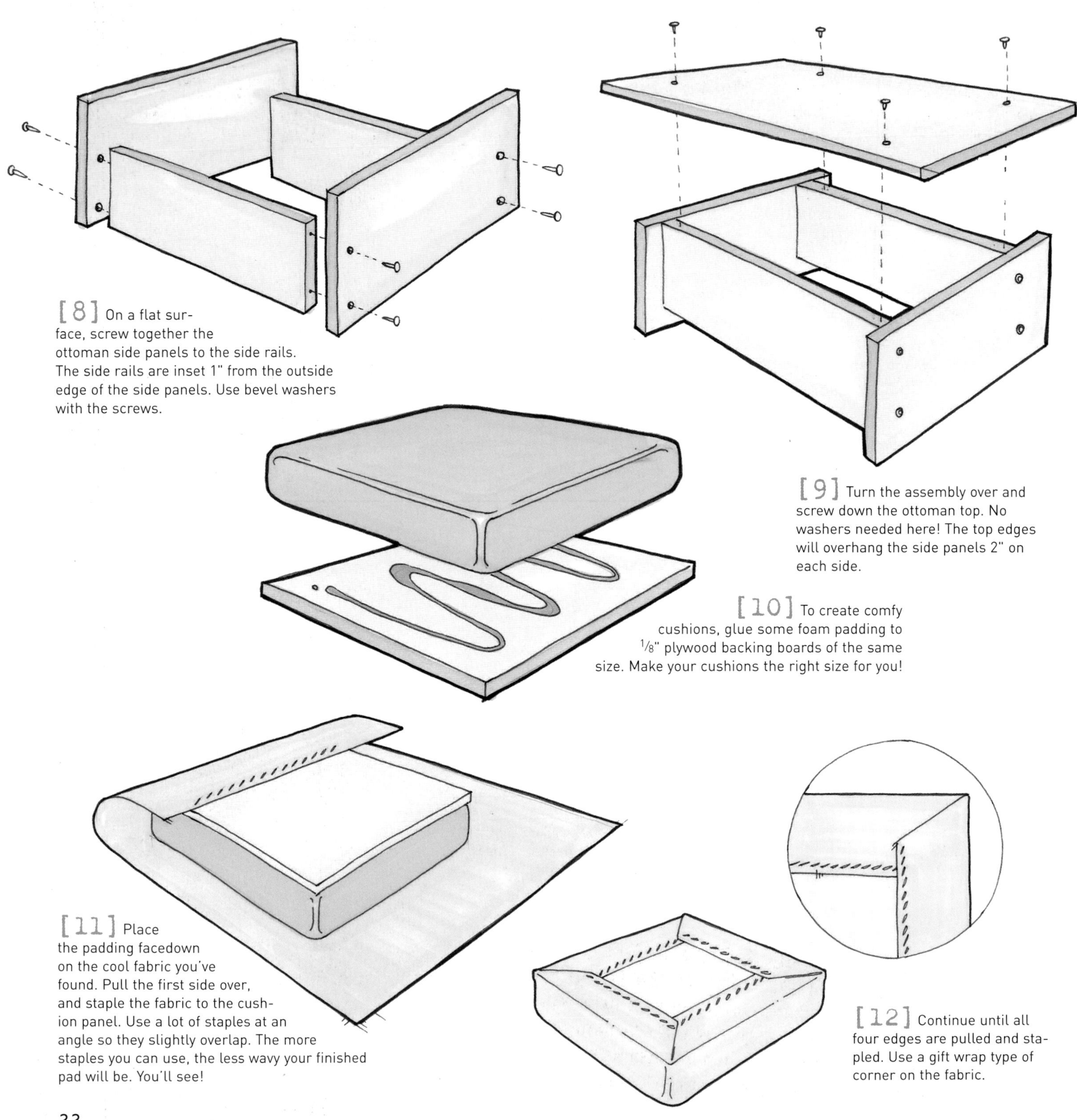

[8] On a flat surface, screw together the ottoman side panels to the side rails. The side rails are inset 1" from the outside edge of the side panels. Use bevel washers with the screws.

[9] Turn the assembly over and screw down the ottoman top. No washers needed here! The top edges will overhang the side panels 2" on each side.

[10] To create comfy cushions, glue some foam padding to 1/8" plywood backing boards of the same size. Make your cushions the right size for you!

[11] Place the padding facedown on the cool fabric you've found. Pull the first side over, and staple the fabric to the cushion panel. Use a lot of staples at an angle so they slightly overlap. The more staples you can use, the less wavy your finished pad will be. You'll see!

[12] Continue until all four edges are pulled and stapled. Use a gift wrap type of corner on the fabric.

[13] From the bottom up, drill into the corners of the cushion and attach it with 1" screws. Make sure the screws aren't too long or they'll be poking you!

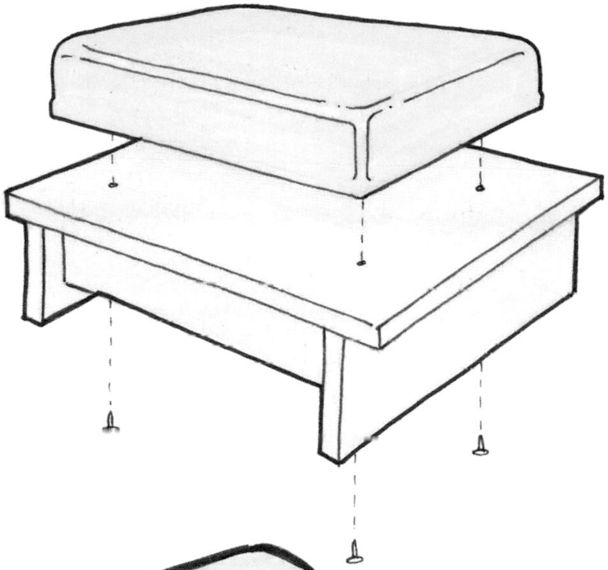

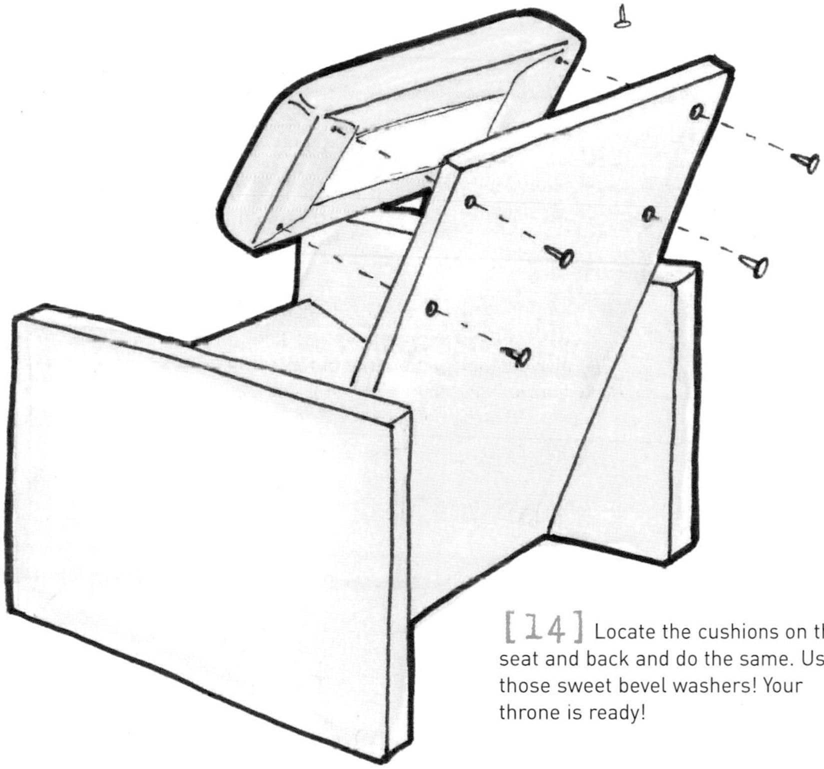

[14] Locate the cushions on the seat and back and do the same. Use those sweet bevel washers! Your throne is ready!

HAVE SOME FUN AND PICK A FABRIC THAT MATCHES YOUR SHOES OR YOUR DRAPES. YOU CAN GIVE THE PLANKS A NICE FINISH USING STAIN OR POLYURETHANE. PAINT THEM ALL BLUE IF YOU THINK THAT'S COOL. ALSO, DON'T BE AFRAID TO CUT LITTLE FEET OUT OF THE SIDE PANELS OR EVEN CHANGE THE DIMENSIONS TO CREATE A SNUGGLY SEAT FOR TWO! THAT'S IT! NOW YOU'RE READY FOR SOME SERIOUS LOUNGING.

[felt fine] STOOL

This little guy is the perfect companion to any room — he's so cool and useful. You can throw your feet up on it or pull it out when an extra friend drops by to hang out. It's basically just a few yards of some heavy-duty industrial felt, some funky fabric and plywood!

YOU'LL NEED

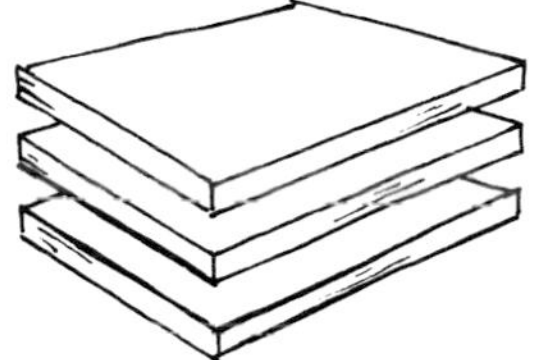

5 3/4" x 24" x 24" (19mm x 610mm 610mm) pieces of plywood

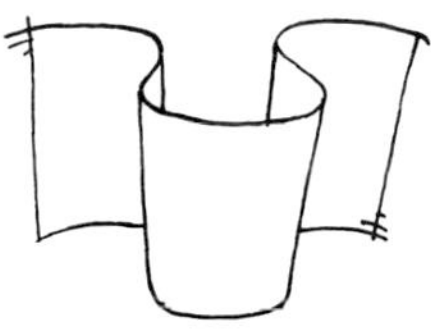

1 yard (91cm) of industrial felt & 1/2 yard (46cm) of fabric

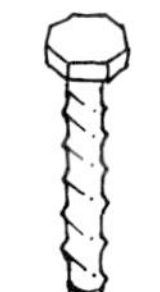

8 3/8"-16 x 2" (10mm x 50mm) hex-head bolts

16 3/8" (10mm) fender washers

8 3/8"-16 (10mm) hex nuts

6 3" (75mm) drywall screws

4 1 5/8" (40mm) drywall screws

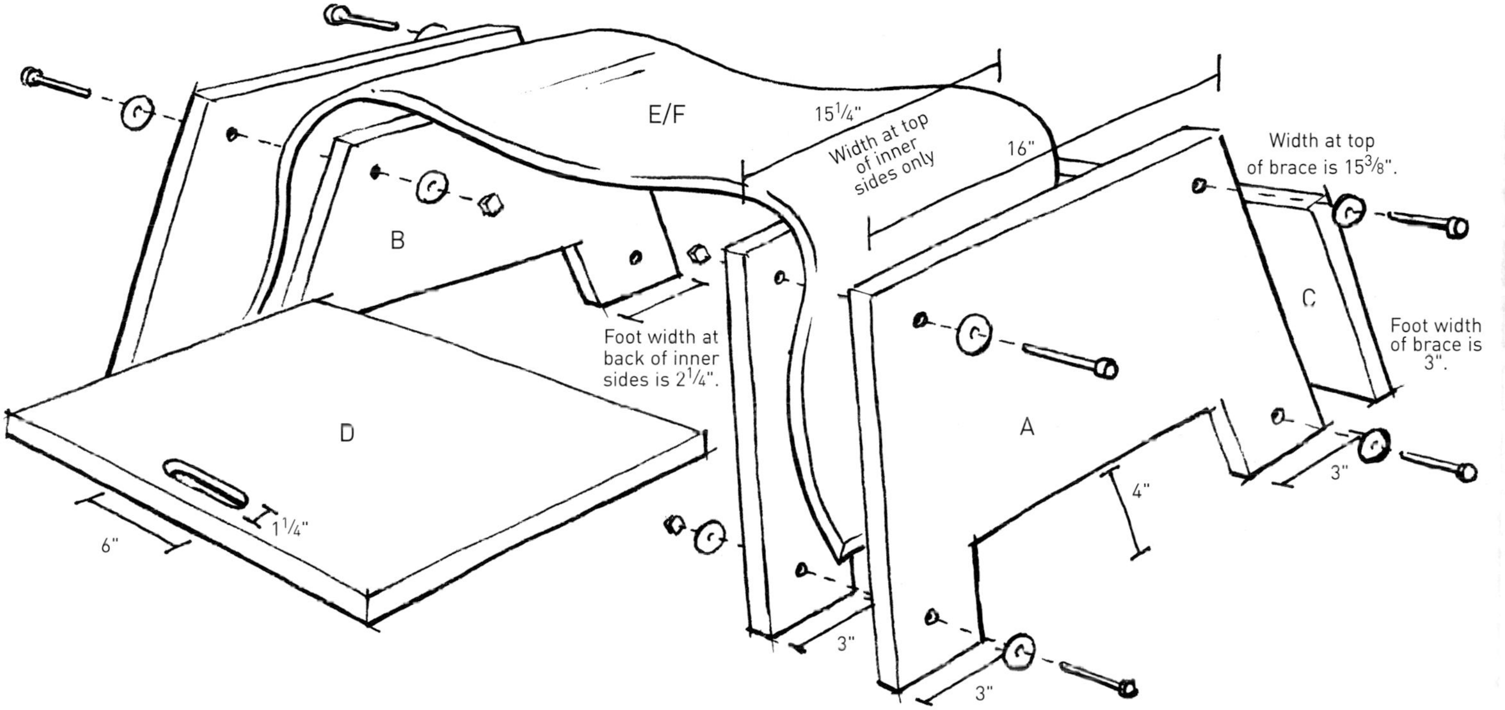

E/F
15 1/4"
Width at top of inner sides only
16"
Width at top of brace is 15 3/8".
B
C
Foot width at back of inner sides is 2 1/4".
Foot width of brace is 3".
D
A
6"
1 1/4"
4"
3"
3"
3"

cutting list

REF.	NO.	PART	STOCK	THICKNESS X WIDTH X LENGTH INCHES	MILLIMETERS
A	2	outer sides	plywood	3/4 x 18 x 20	19 x 457 x 508
B	2	inner sides	plywood	3/4 x 18 x 19 1/4	19 x 457 x 489
C	1	brace	plywood	3/4 x 14 x 18 1/2	19 x 356 x 470
D	1	shelf	plywood	3/4 x 16 3/4 x 15	19 x 426 x 381
E	2	seat material	felt	18 x 52	457 x 1321
F	1	seat material	fabric	18 x 52	457 x 1321

[1] Use a jigsaw to cut all the sides to shape. Cut the shelf to size and drill two 1¼"-diameter holes and "connect" them with the jigsaw to create the handle. Screw the inner sides to the shelf. The side panels need to angle in slightly from bottom to top. To help hold the sides at the correct angle, you can attach the brace now if you like. See detail on page 27.

[2] Lay all your felt and fabric together and cut out the pattern shown. You can trace the outside panels for help. It's a square, 15¼"-wide straight shot between the sides for the seat.

[3] Drape your fabric stack over the stool assembly.

[**PAY ATTENTION TO HOW ALL THE PIECES FIT AND LAP TOGETHER. A DRY RUN FOR THIS ONE WITH ALL THE LITTLE ANGLES COMING TOGETHER IS A REALLY GREAT IDEA. ONCE IT'S ALL TOGETHER, YOU'RE GOING TO FALL IN LOVE WITH THIS STOOL! AFTER SITTING IN IT, YOUR FRIENDS WILL SAY IT "FELT FINE!"**]

[4] Place the outer sides against the assembly. Use a few clamps to trap and keep the fabric from moving. Bore the holes and lock it all together with the nuts, washers and bolts in one fell swoop!

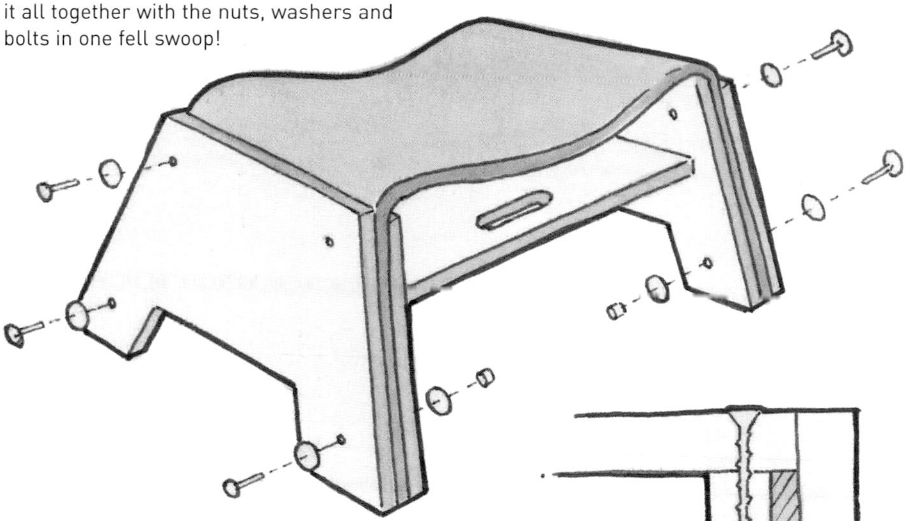

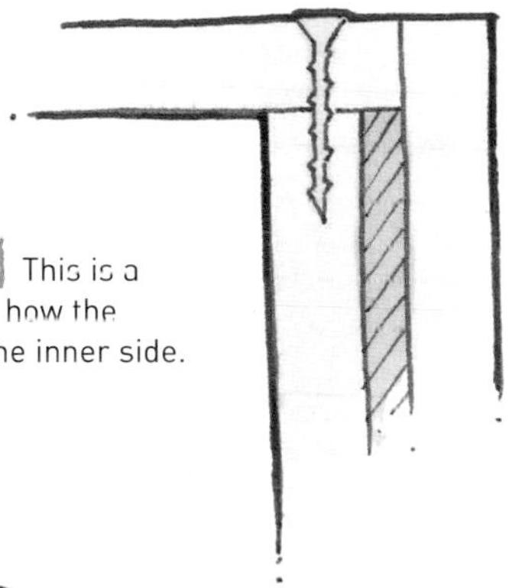

[detail] This is a top view showing how the brace laps over the inner side.

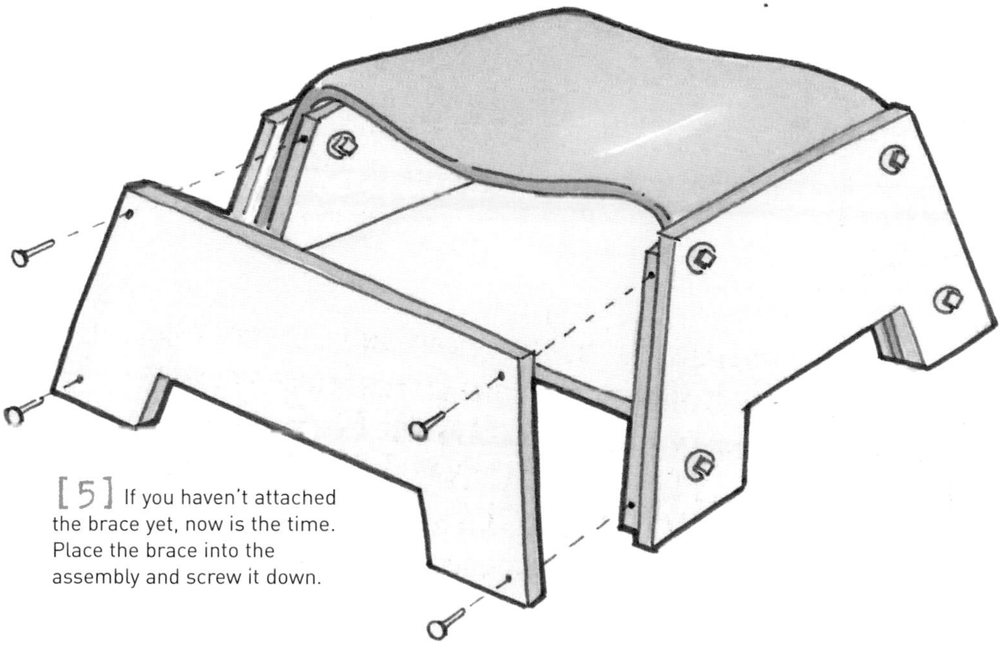

[5] If you haven't attached the brace yet, now is the time. Place the brace into the assembly and screw it down.

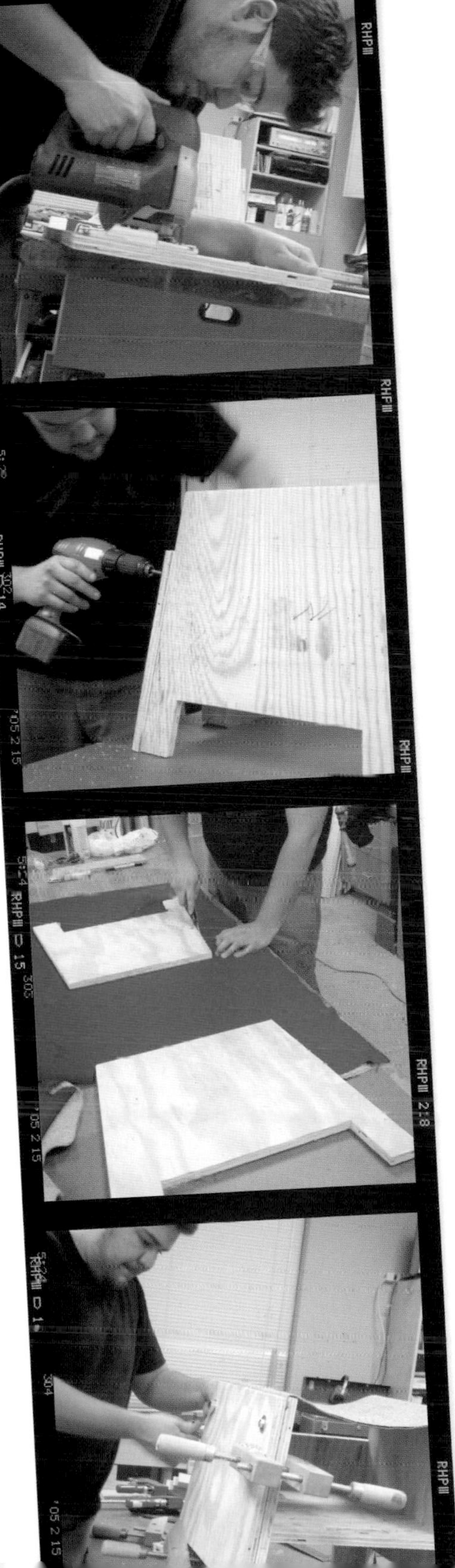

[coffee pal]

COFFEE TABLE

One of the coolest pieces of furniture in a living room is a sweet coffee table, and, oh, so useful! Kick your feet up on it, place your design book in sight to impress your visitors, or put the pizza box there when you're just kickin' it. You can put this fancy little guy together cheap and superquick, and what's best of all is that it looks ultrahip!

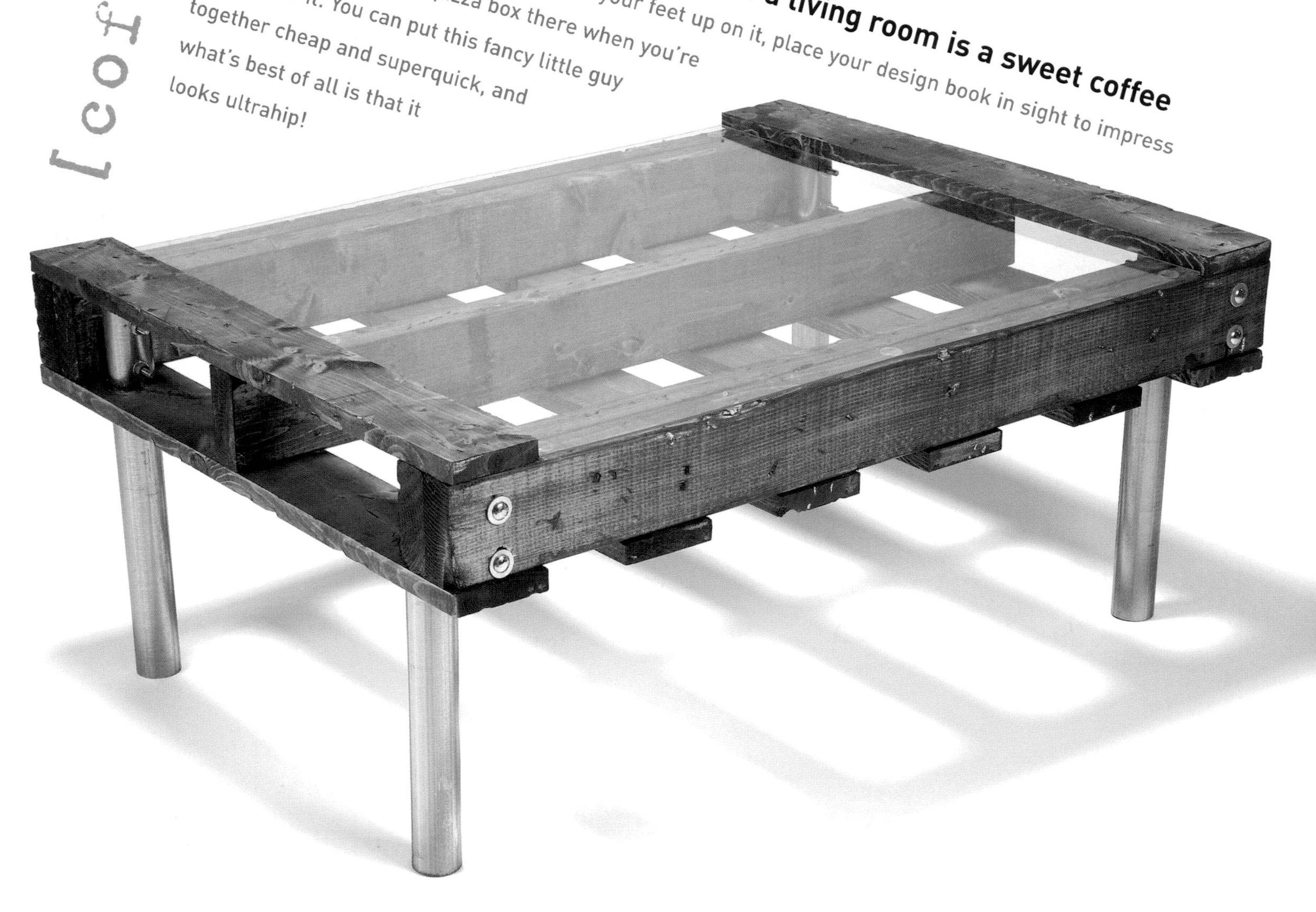

YOU'LL NEED

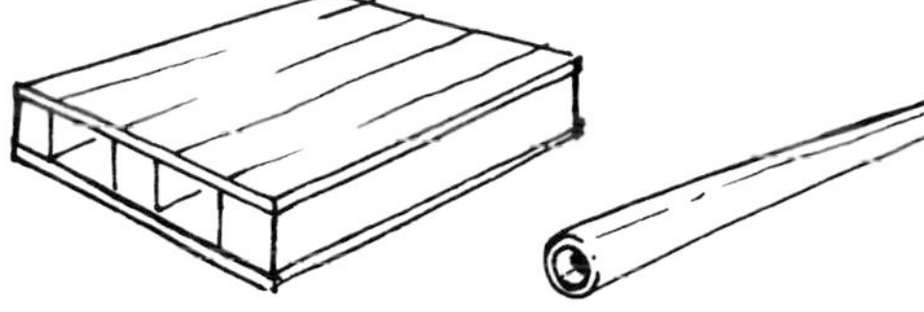
shipping pallet

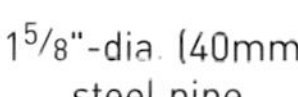
1 5/8"-dia. (40mm) steel pipe

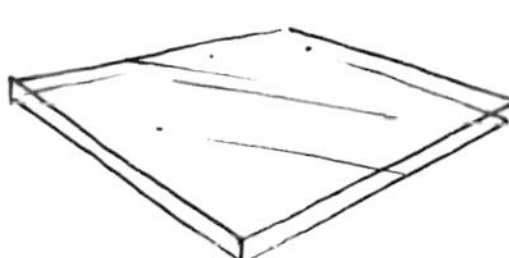
1/4"-thick (6mm) acrylic sheet

8 1/4"-20 x 5 1/2" (6mm x 140mm) carriage bolts

8 1/4"-20 (6mm) hex nuts

8 1/4" (6mm) flat washers

1" (25mm)-diameter felt or rubber pads

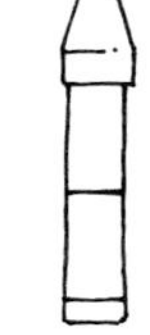
green-blue designer's marker (optional)

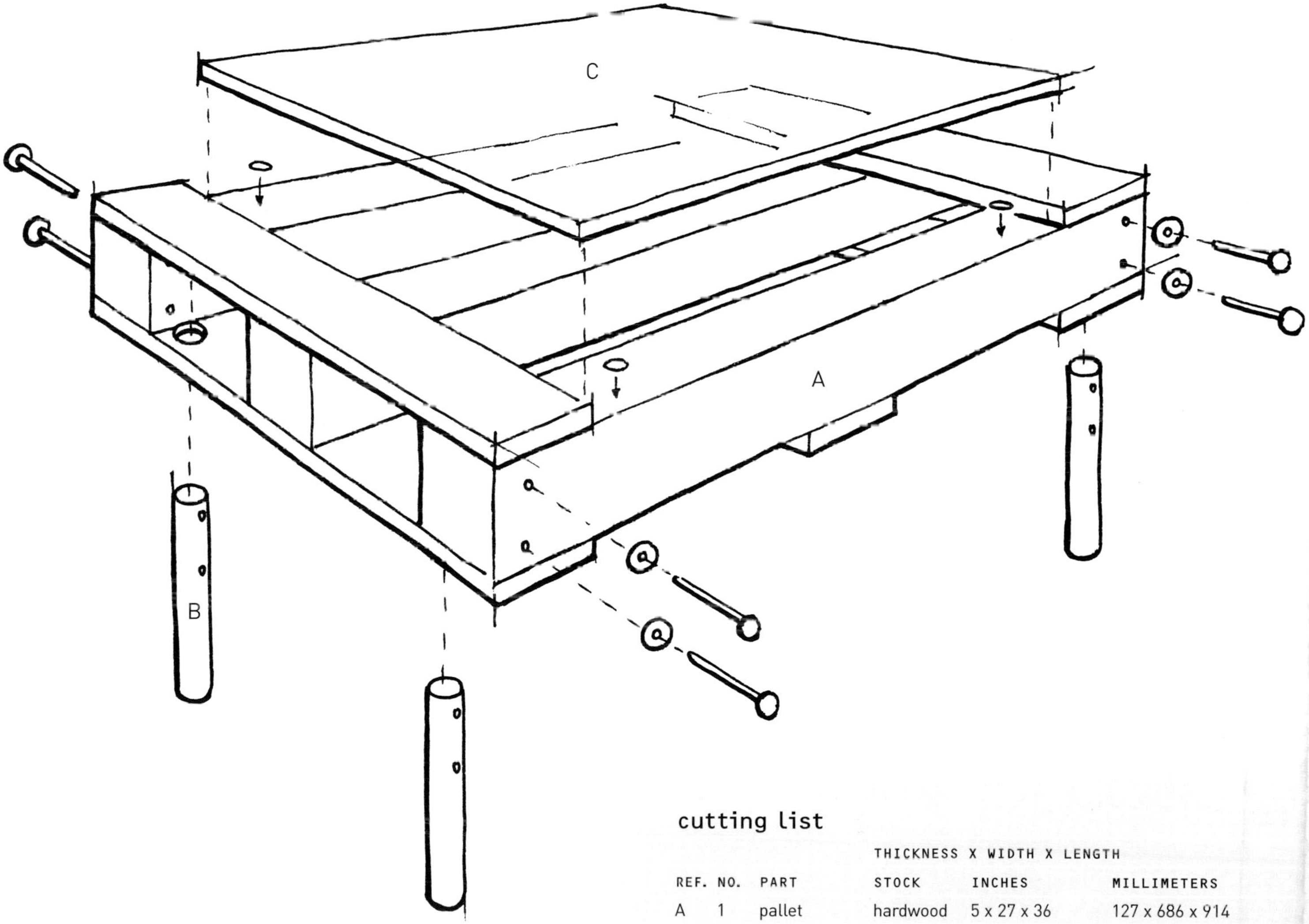

cutting list

				THICKNESS X WIDTH X LENGTH	
REF.	NO.	PART	STOCK	INCHES	MILLIMETERS
A	1	pallet	hardwood	5 x 27 x 36	127 x 686 x 914
B	4	legs	steel	1 5/8 d x 15h	41 x 381
C	1	top	acrylic	1/4 x 27 x 30	6 x 686 x 762

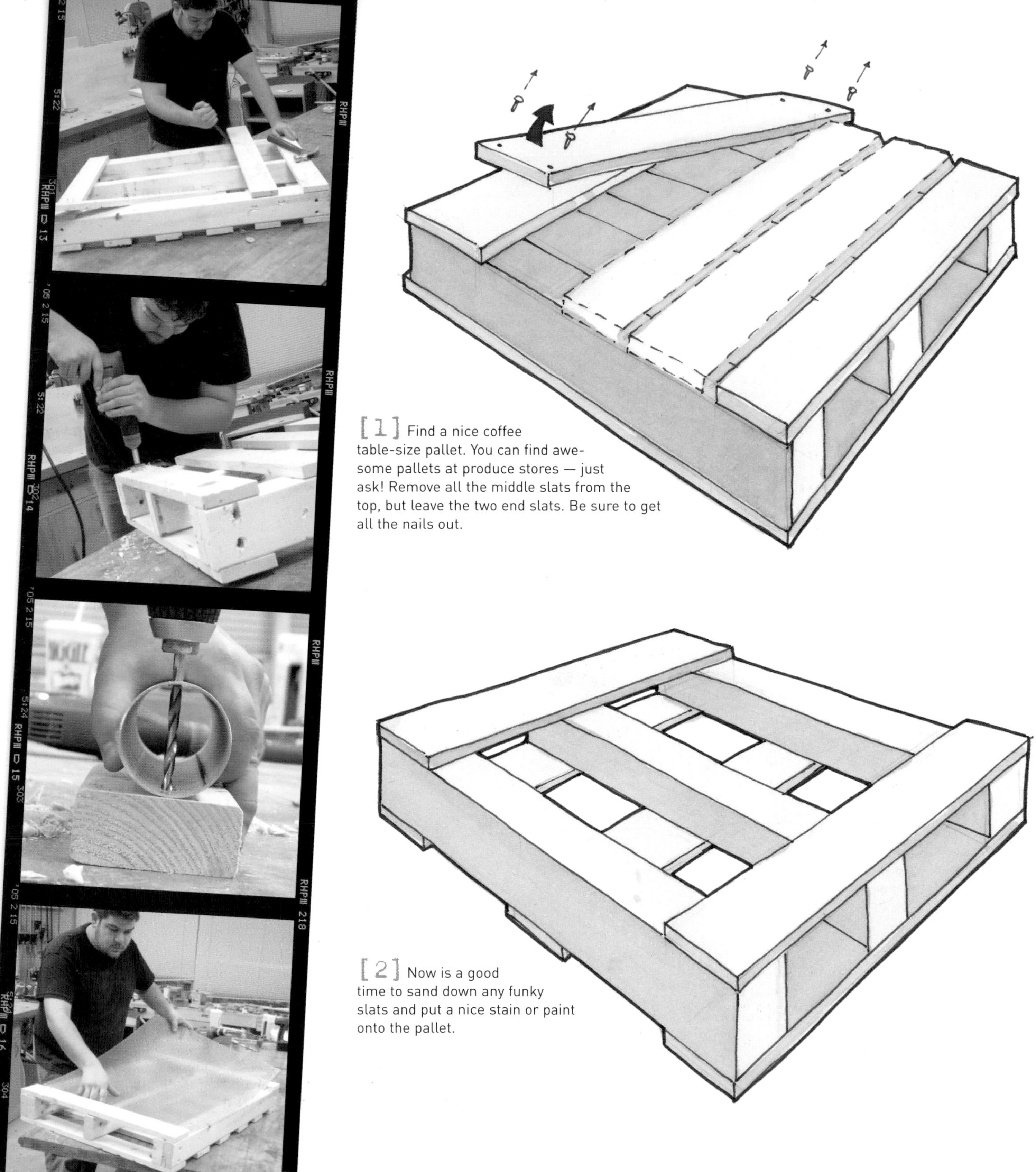

[1] Find a nice coffee table-size pallet. You can find awesome pallets at produce stores — just ask! Remove all the middle slats from the top, but leave the two end slats. Be sure to get all the nails out.

[2] Now is a good time to sand down any funky slats and put a nice stain or paint onto the pallet.

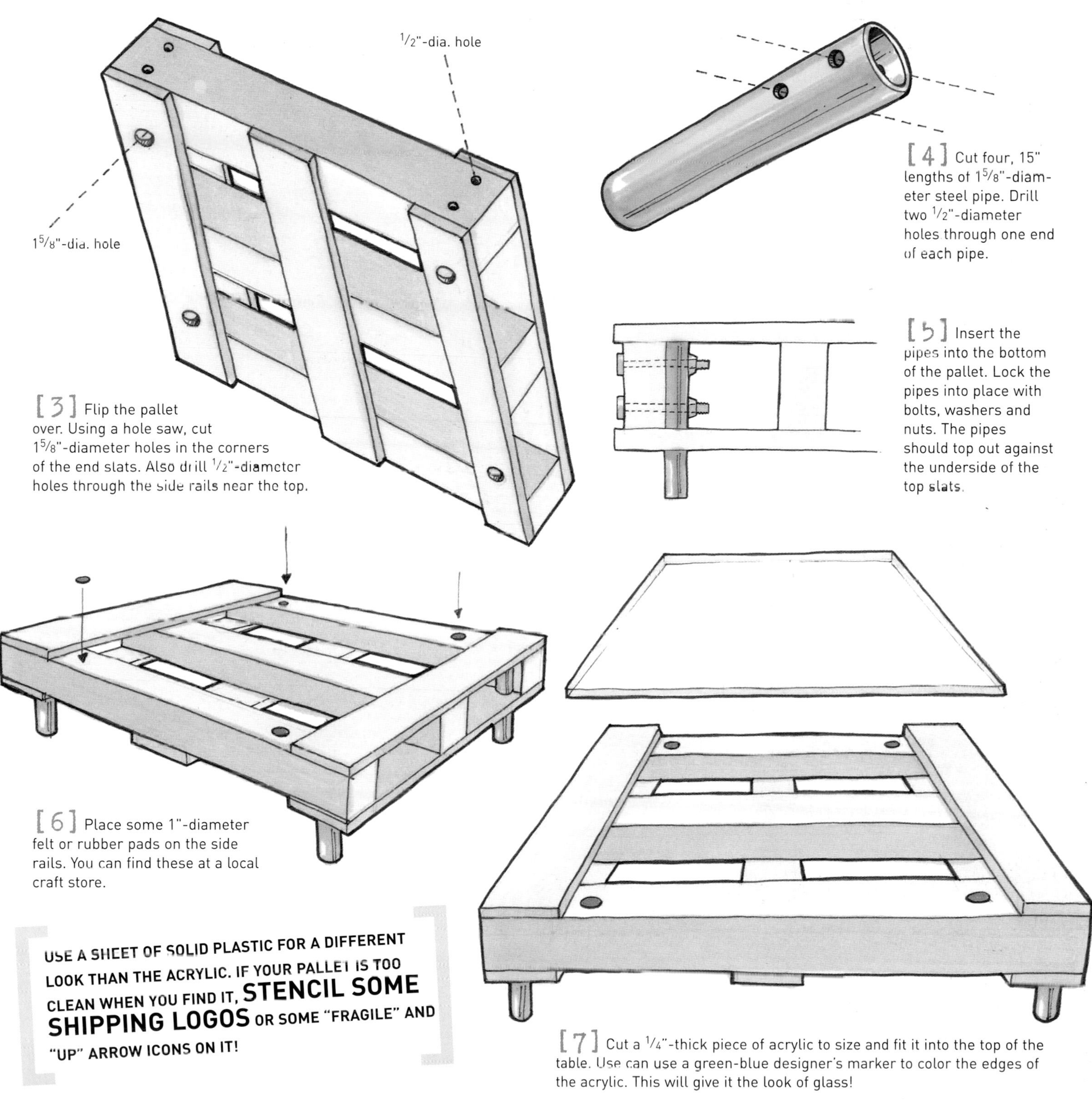

[3] Flip the pallet over. Using a hole saw, cut $1^5/_8$"-diameter holes in the corners of the end slats. Also drill $^1/_2$"-diameter holes through the side rails near the top.

[4] Cut four, 15" lengths of $1^5/_8$"-diameter steel pipe. Drill two $^1/_2$"-diameter holes through one end of each pipe.

[5] Insert the pipes into the bottom of the pallet. Lock the pipes into place with bolts, washers and nuts. The pipes should top out against the underside of the top slats.

[6] Place some 1"-diameter felt or rubber pads on the side rails. You can find these at a local craft store.

[7] Cut a $^1/_4$"-thick piece of acrylic to size and fit it into the top of the table. Use can use a green-blue designer's marker to color the edges of the acrylic. This will give it the look of glass!

[USE A SHEET OF SOLID PLASTIC FOR A DIFFERENT LOOK THAN THE ACRYLIC. IF YOUR PALLET IS TOO CLEAN WHEN YOU FIND IT, **STENCIL SOME SHIPPING LOGOS** OR SOME "FRAGILE" AND "UP" ARROW ICONS ON IT!]

This is truly a top-shelf design for a bunch of bottoms to sit on! Benches are a cool modern seating option that not a lot of people can obtain. (Designer benches retail for thousands of dollars.) This unique piece will really impress your guests and give them plenty of space to chill.

[bottom shelf] BENCH

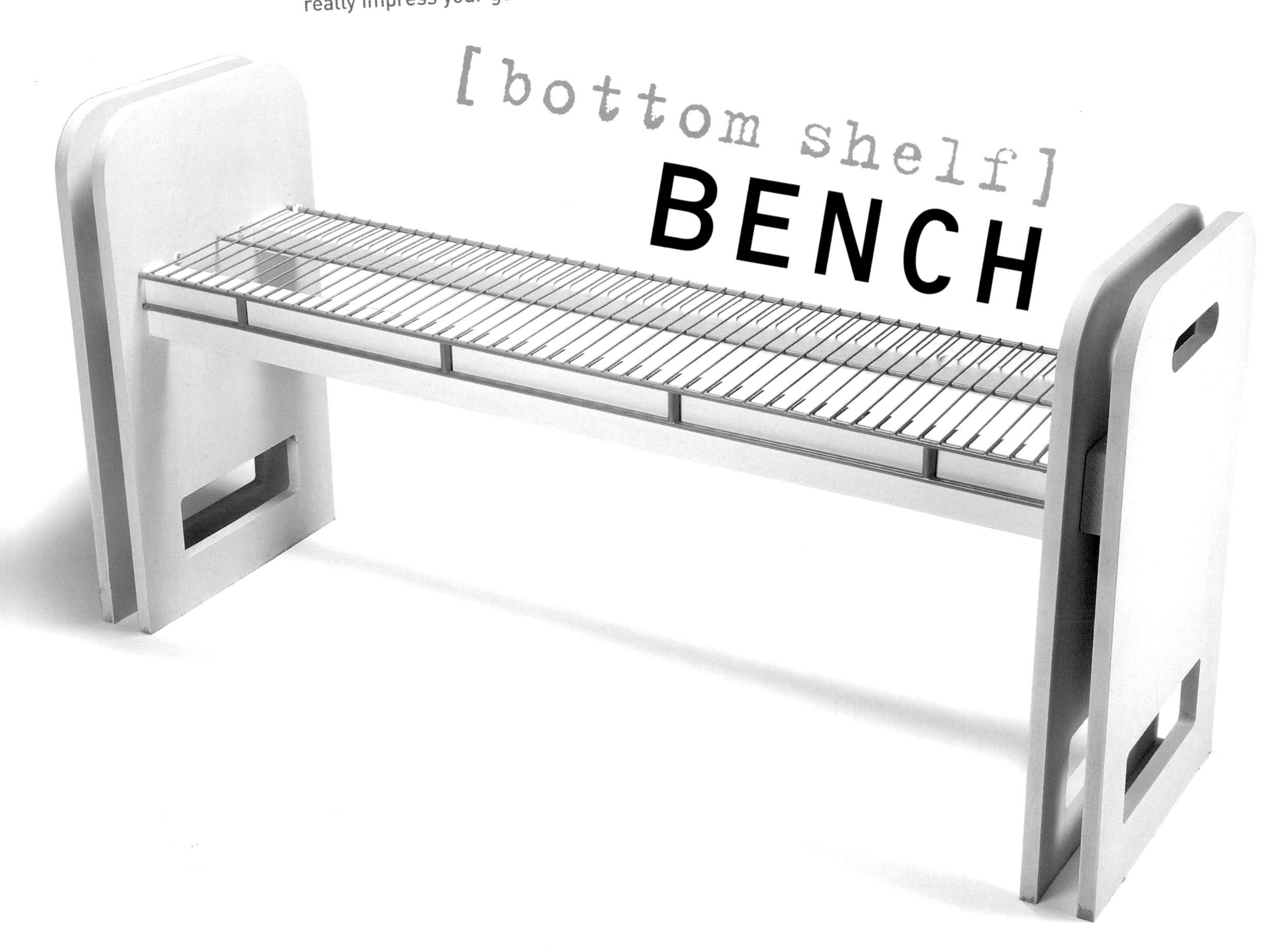

YOU'LL NEED

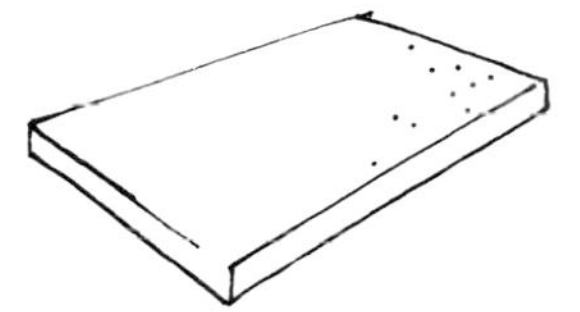
$^3/_4$" x 4' x 4'
(19mm x 1.2m x 1.2m)
MDF board

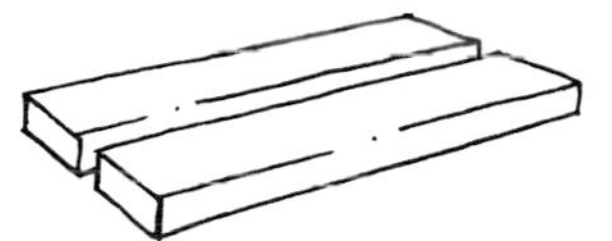
1 8'
(2.4m)
pine 2x4

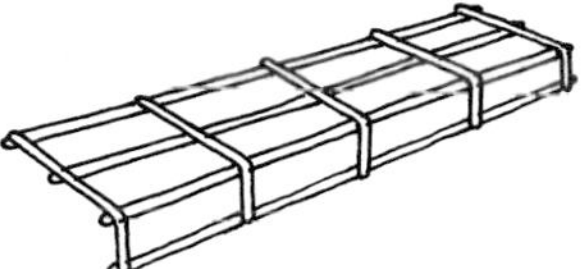
12" x 6'
(305mm x 1.8m)
length of closet shelving

8 No.10 x 3"
(75mm)
wood screws

4 2"
(50mm)
wood screws

4 $2^1/_2$"
(65mm)
wood screws

2
coaxial cable
staples

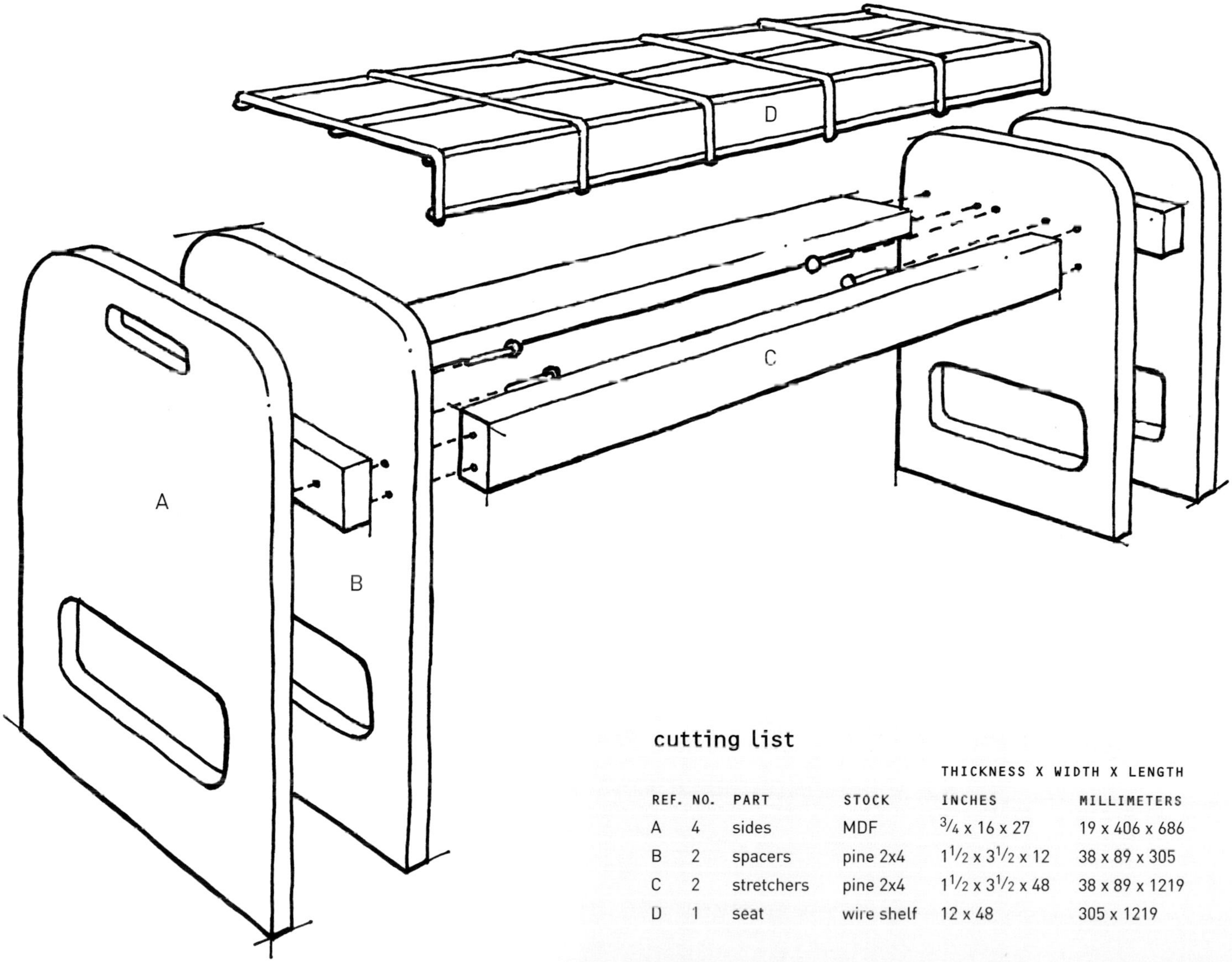

cutting list

REF.	NO.	PART	STOCK	THICKNESS X WIDTH X LENGTH INCHES	MILLIMETERS
A	4	sides	MDF	$^3/_4$ x 16 x 27	19 x 406 x 686
B	2	spacers	pine 2x4	$1^1/_2$ x $3^1/_2$ x 12	38 x 89 x 305
C	2	stretchers	pine 2x4	$1^1/_2$ x $3^1/_2$ x 48	38 x 89 x 1219
D	1	seat	wire shelf	12 x 48	305 x 1219

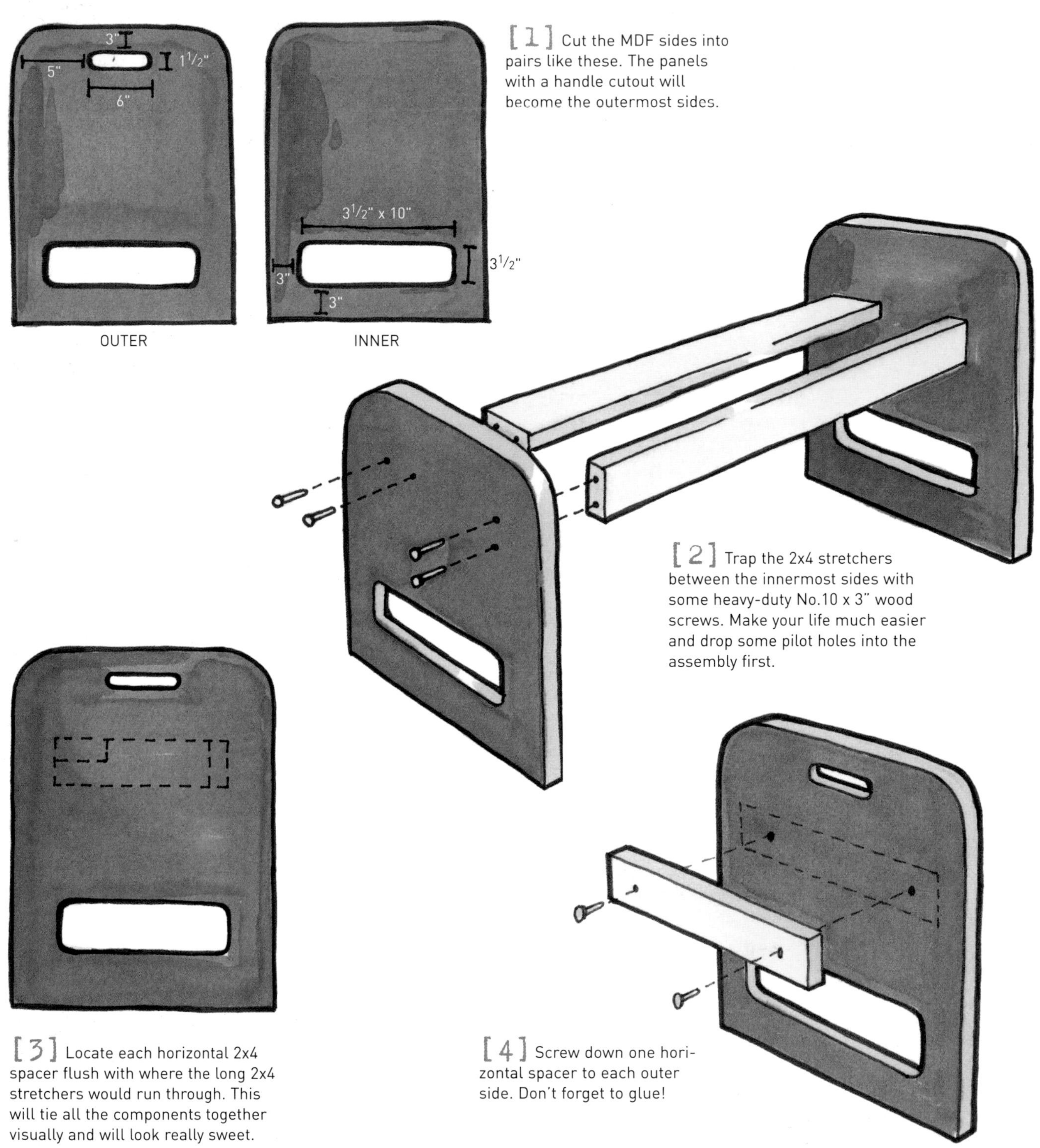

[1] Cut the MDF sides into pairs like these. The panels with a handle cutout will become the outermost sides.

[2] Trap the 2x4 stretchers between the innermost sides with some heavy-duty No.10 x 3" wood screws. Make your life much easier and drop some pilot holes into the assembly first.

[3] Locate each horizontal 2x4 spacer flush with where the long 2x4 stretchers would run through. This will tie all the components together visually and will look really sweet.

[4] Screw down one horizontal spacer to each outer side. Don't forget to glue!

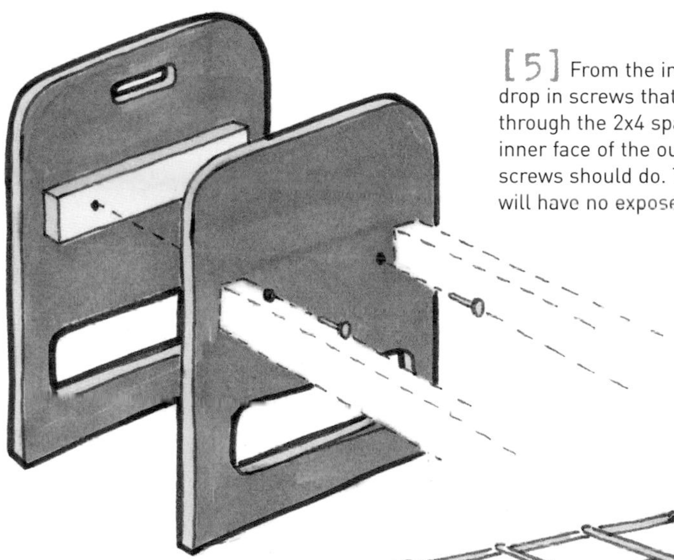

[5] From the inside of the assembly, drop in screws that will bite all the way through the 2x4 spacer and just into the inner face of the outer side; $2^{1}/_{2}$" wood screws should do. This way, the bench will have no exposed hardware.

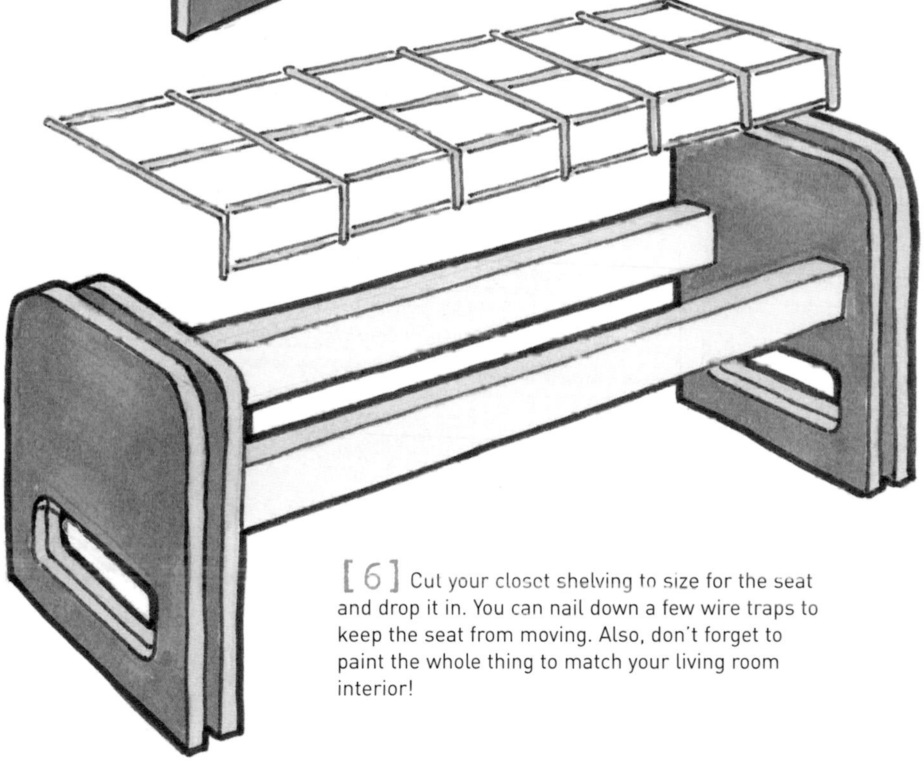

[6] Cut your closet shelving to size for the seat and drop it in. You can nail down a few wire traps to keep the seat from moving. Also, don't forget to paint the whole thing to match your living room interior!

IT WORKS BEST TO PAINT THE PIECES ALL OVER BEFORE THEY ARE ASSEMBLED. A SIMPLE LATEX WALL PAINT WORKS WELL ON THE WOOD AND MDF PIECES AND YIELDS A NICE, FULL COVERAGE. A LACQUER SPRAY PAINT WILL GET INTO ALL THE LITTLE GROOVES OF THE SEAT QUICKLY AND PROVIDE A DURABLE FINISH, TOO. THE BENCH THAT YOU PUT TOGETHER CAN BE A LITTLE SHORTER OR EVEN A LITTLE LONGER! JUST REMEMBER TO BE CONSCIOUS OF THE SPACE YOU HAVE.

[huggy] TV STAND

If you haven't quite saved up enough dough for that huge flat-panel, high-def plasma-screen TV, then you're going to need somewhere to put that old faithful 12-incher. **This little guy is superhip and will get the telly off the box it came in!** Plus, it's got ample room to "hug" your game system, DVD player and film collection.

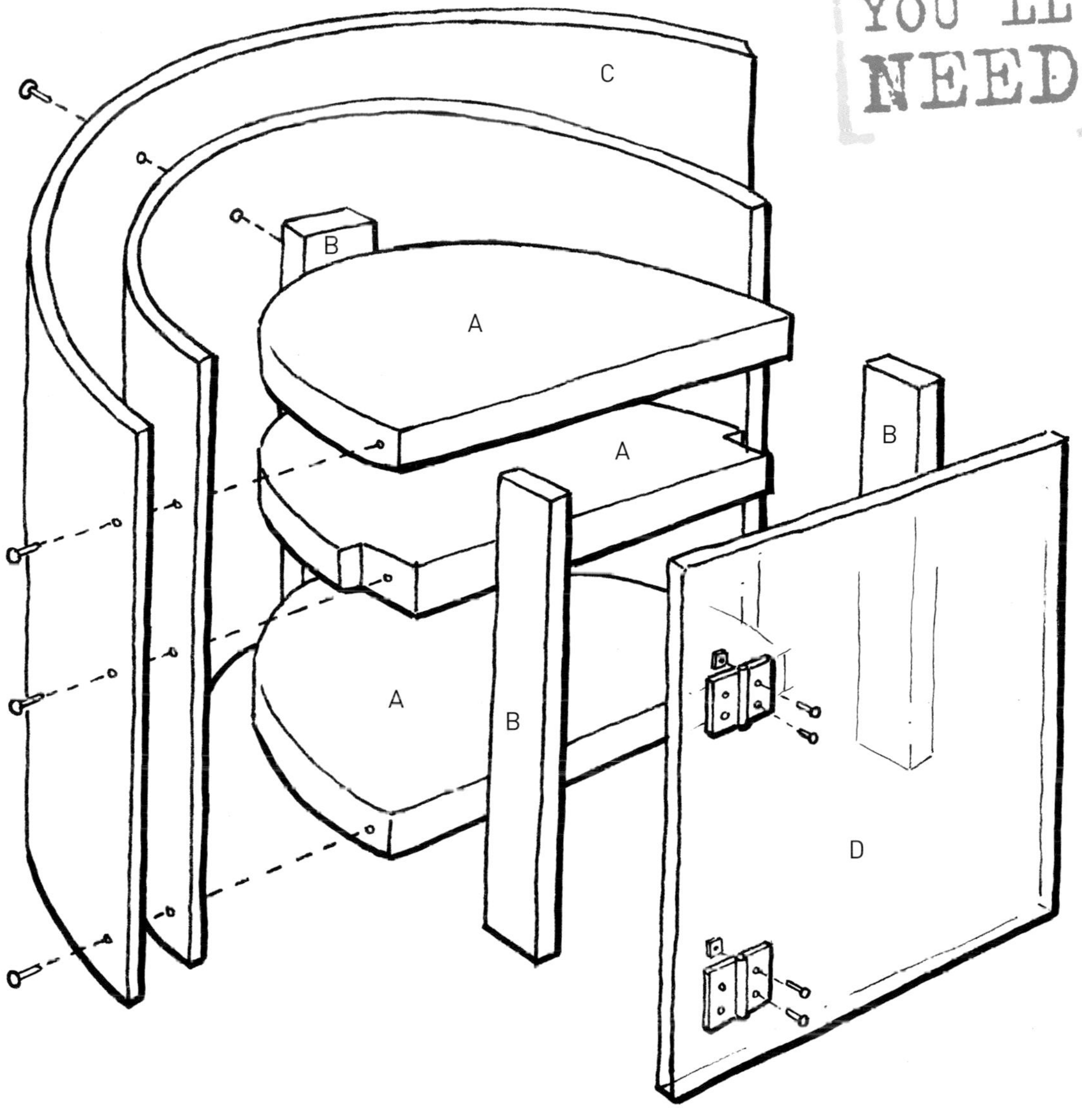

YOU'LL NEED

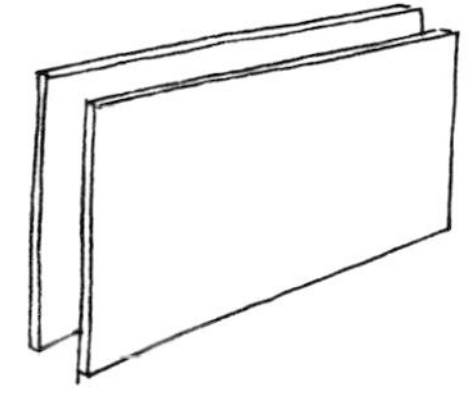

2 1/8" x 4' x 8'
(3mm x 1.2m x 2.4m)
fiberboard sheets

3 3/4" x 24" x 24"
(19mm x 610mm x 610mm)
MDF boards

1 24" x 30"
(610mm x 762mm)
acrylic sheet

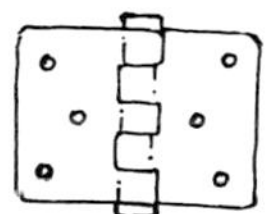

2 pair 1 1/4" x 1 1/2"
(32mm x 38mm)
butt hinges

4 No.10-1/2" (13mm) flathead
machine screws

2 rare earth magnets

4 No.10 hex nuts

18 1 1/2" (40mm) wood screws

50 to 60 3/4" (20mm) flathead sheet
metal screws

4 3/4" (20mm) wood screws

wood glue

cutting list

				THICKNESS X WIDTH X LENGTH	
REF.	NO.	PART	STOCK	INCHES	MILLIMETERS
A	3	shelves	MDF	3/4 x 18 x 23 1/2	19 x 457 x 597
B	3	braces	MDF	3/4 x 3 x 24 1/2	19 x 76 x 622
C	2	shells	fiberboard	1/8 x 32 x 52	3 x 813 x 1321
D	1	door	acrylic	1/4 x 24 x 26	6 x 610 x 660

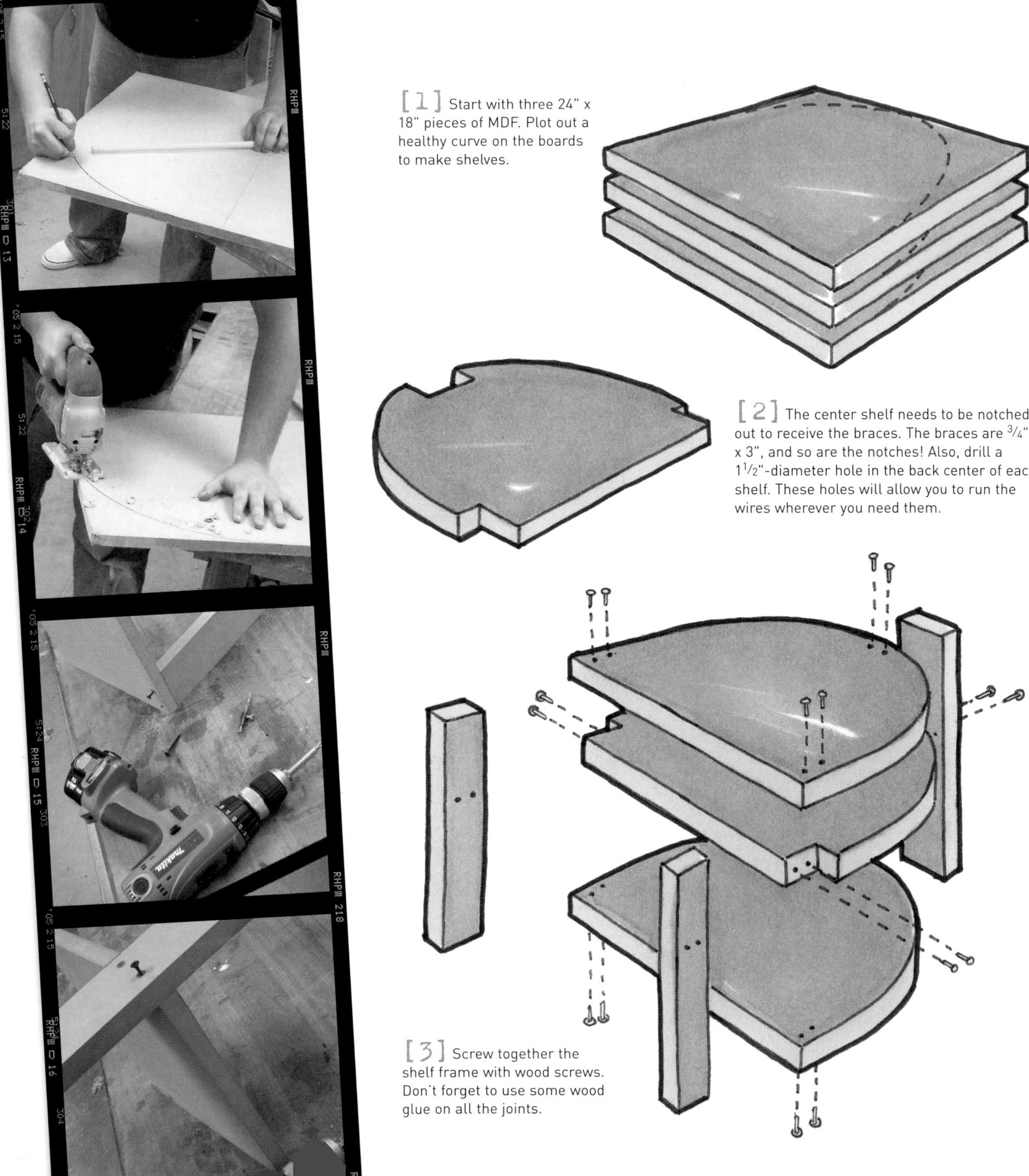

[1] Start with three 24" x 18" pieces of MDF. Plot out a healthy curve on the boards to make shelves.

[2] The center shelf needs to be notched out to receive the braces. The braces are $\frac{3}{4}$" x 3", and so are the notches! Also, drill a $1\frac{1}{2}$"-diameter hole in the back center of each shelf. These holes will allow you to run the wires wherever you need them.

[3] Screw together the shelf frame with wood screws. Don't forget to use some wood glue on all the joints.

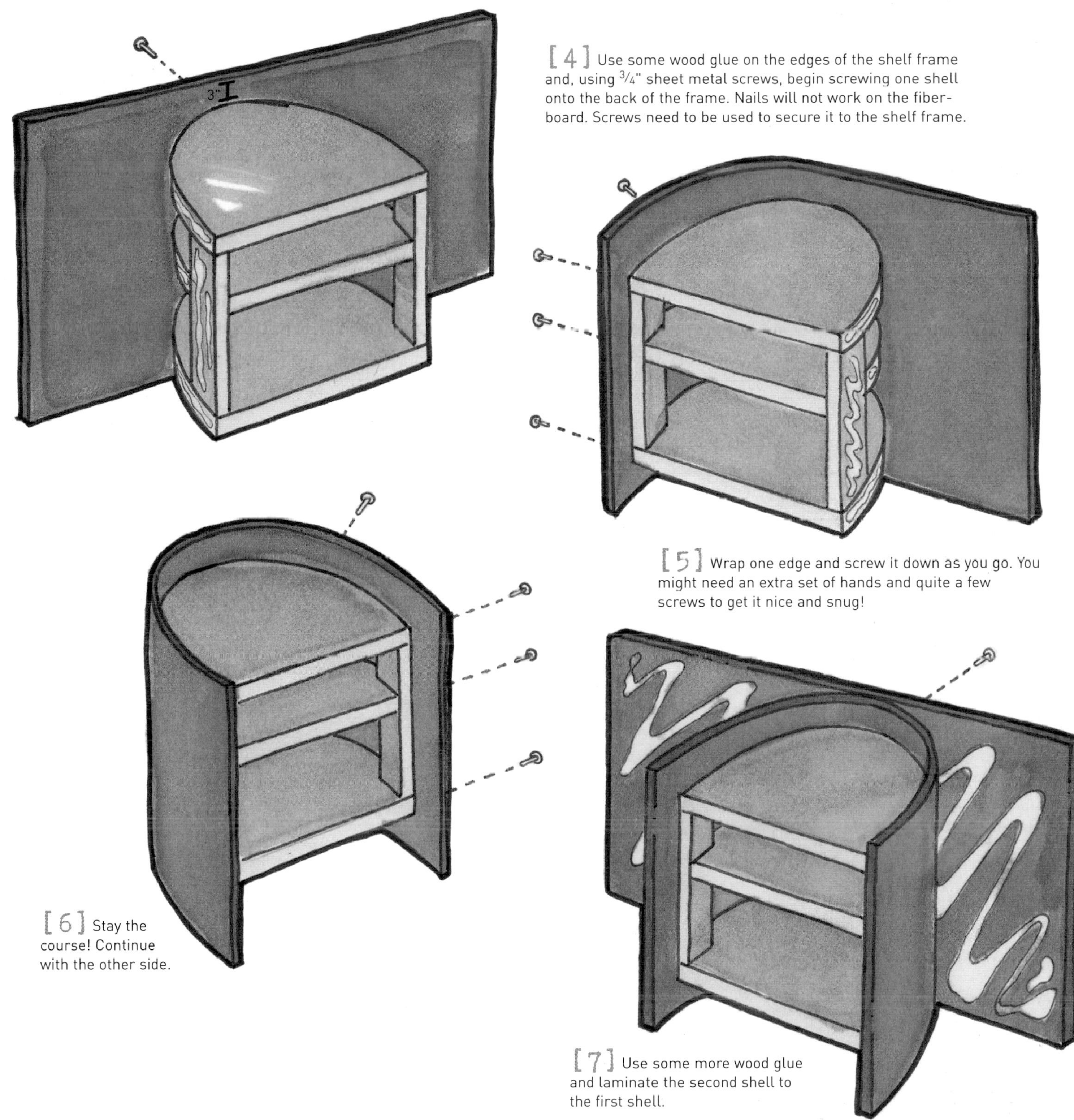

[4] Use some wood glue on the edges of the shelf frame and, using 3/4" sheet metal screws, begin screwing one shell onto the back of the frame. Nails will not work on the fiberboard. Screws need to be used to secure it to the shelf frame.

[5] Wrap one edge and screw it down as you go. You might need an extra set of hands and quite a few screws to get it nice and snug!

[6] Stay the course! Continue with the other side.

[7] Use some more wood glue and laminate the second shell to the first shell.

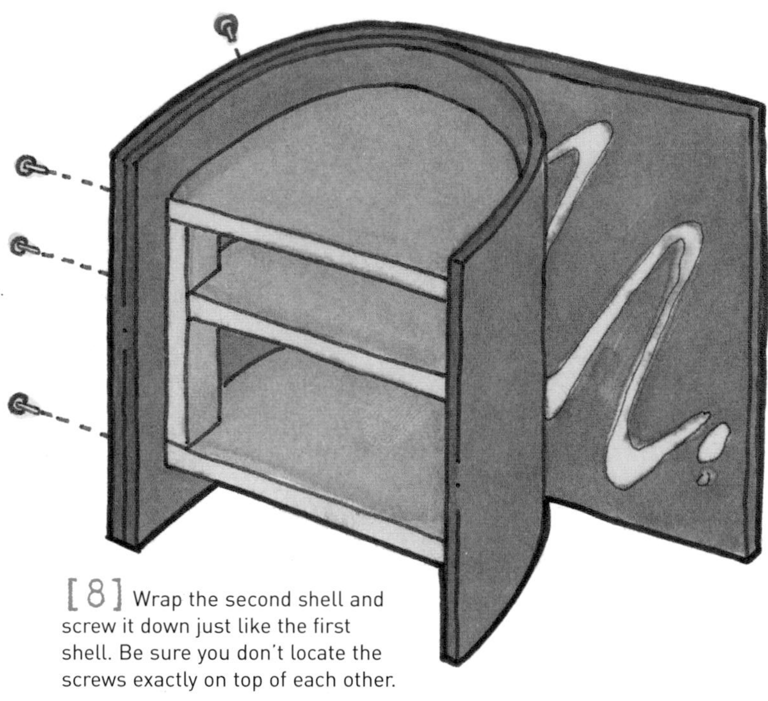

[8] Wrap the second shell and screw it down just like the first shell. Be sure you don't locate the screws exactly on top of each other.

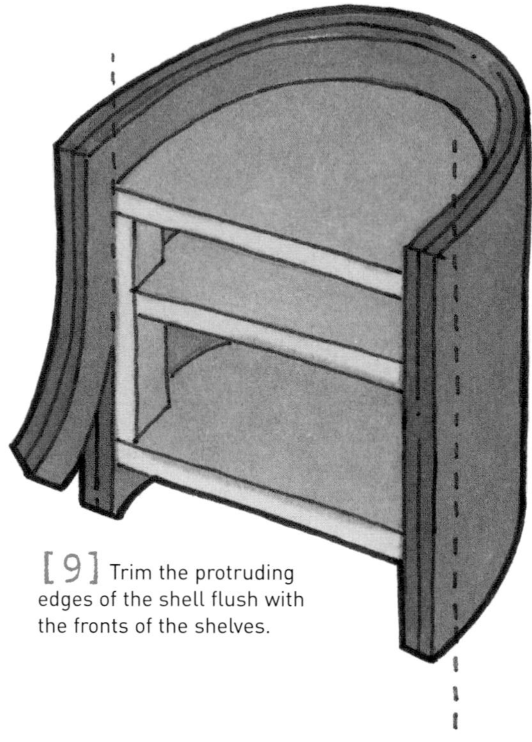

[9] Trim the protruding edges of the shell flush with the fronts of the shelves.

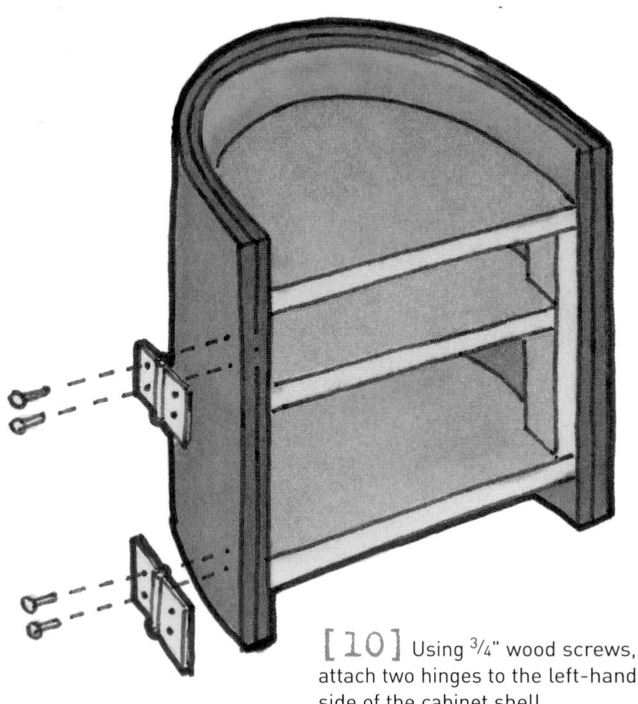

[10] Using 3/4" wood screws, attach two hinges to the left-hand side of the cabinet shell.

[THE FIBERBOARD SHELL CREATES THE FEET OF THE UNIT. YOU CAN NOTCH OUT MORE LITERAL FOOTSIES IF YOU WANT OR LOP OFF THAT BOTTOM STRIP AND PUT CASTERS INTO PLACE FOR A TV ON THE GO. THE MDF BOARDS AND THE FIBERBOARD LOOK GOOD TOGETHER RAW, **BUT YOU COULD PAINT THEM BLACK FOR A SLEEKER LOOK.**]

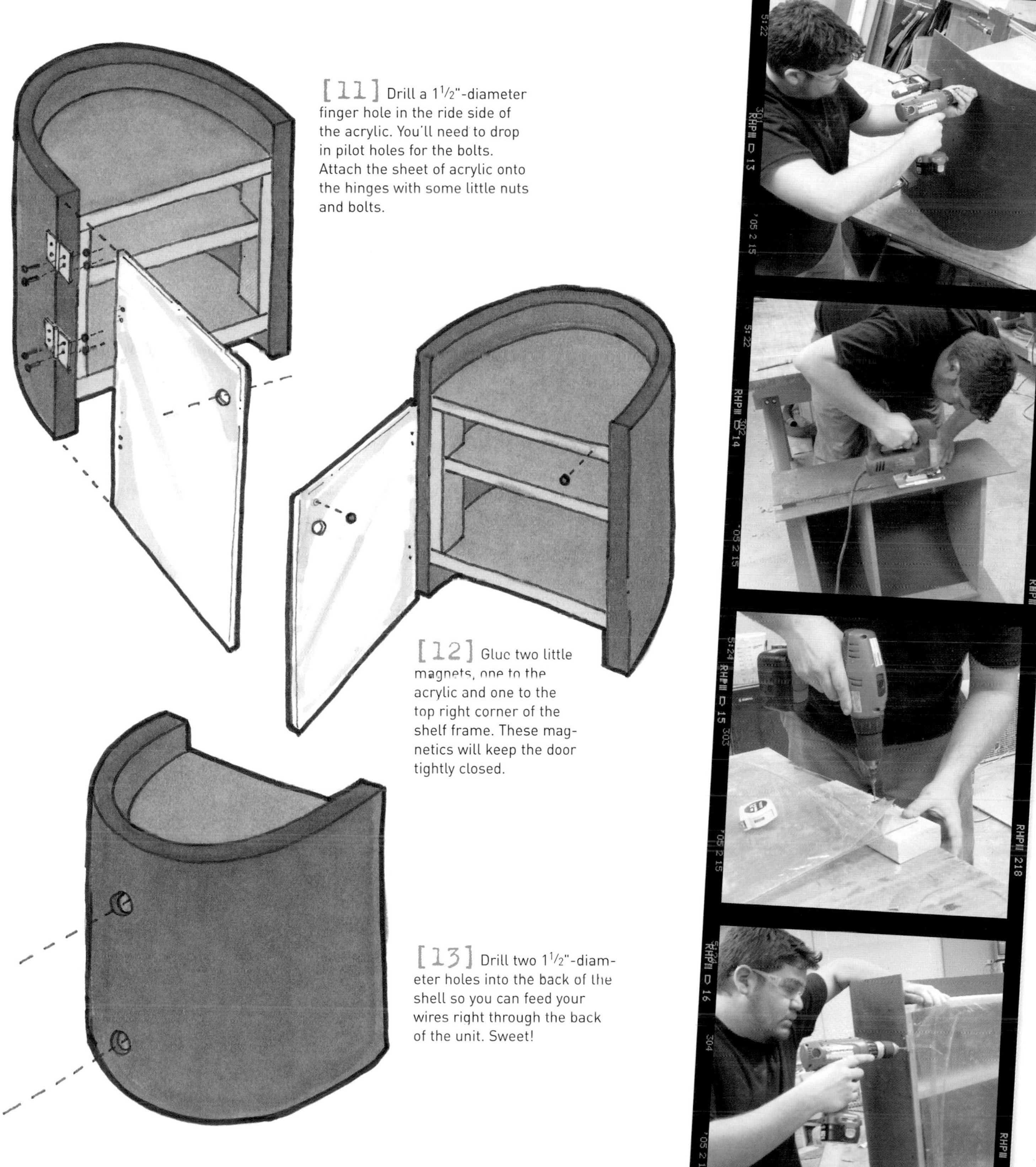

[11] Drill a $1^1/_2$"-diameter finger hole in the ride side of the acrylic. You'll need to drop in pilot holes for the bolts. Attach the sheet of acrylic onto the hinges with some little nuts and bolts.

[12] Gluc two little magnets, one to the acrylic and one to the top right corner of the shelf frame. These magnetics will keep the door tightly closed.

[13] Drill two $1^1/_2$"-diameter holes into the back of the shell so you can feed your wires right through the back of the unit. Sweet!

[BEDROOM]

THEY SAY YOU SPEND ALMOST HALF YOUR LIFE IN YOUR BEDROOM. THAT TIME INCLUDES SLEEPING, READING BOOKS, WATCHING TV, AND ANY OTHER EXTRACURRICULARS! IF THAT'S TRUE, THEN I FEEL REALLY SAD FOR THOSE OF YOU WITH A MATTRESS ON THE FLOOR AND A PILE OF CLOTHES FOR A CLOSET. **YOU DESERVE TO HAVE NICER THINGS IN THE ROOM THAT YOU'RE GOING TO SPEND SOME OF YOUR BEST HOURS.** THINK HOW MUCH HAPPIER YOU'D BE WITH A NICE PLATFORM BED AND MATCHING NIGHTSTAND, A CONTEMPORARY ARMOIRE TO HANG YOUR CLEAN SHIRTS AND A PLACE TO PUT THEM AFTER WEARING THEM 17 TIMES, AND SOME SLEEK DECORATIVE ACCESSORIES OR ARTWORK!

[ripple] HEADBOARD

A modern designer bed is another furniture piece that's great but definitely doesn't fit into anybody's budget — at least not anybody that I know! **The "Ripple" headboard is super classy and so simple to build and will put you out only a few bucks.** Trust me, it'll impress those overnight guests!

YOU'LL NEED

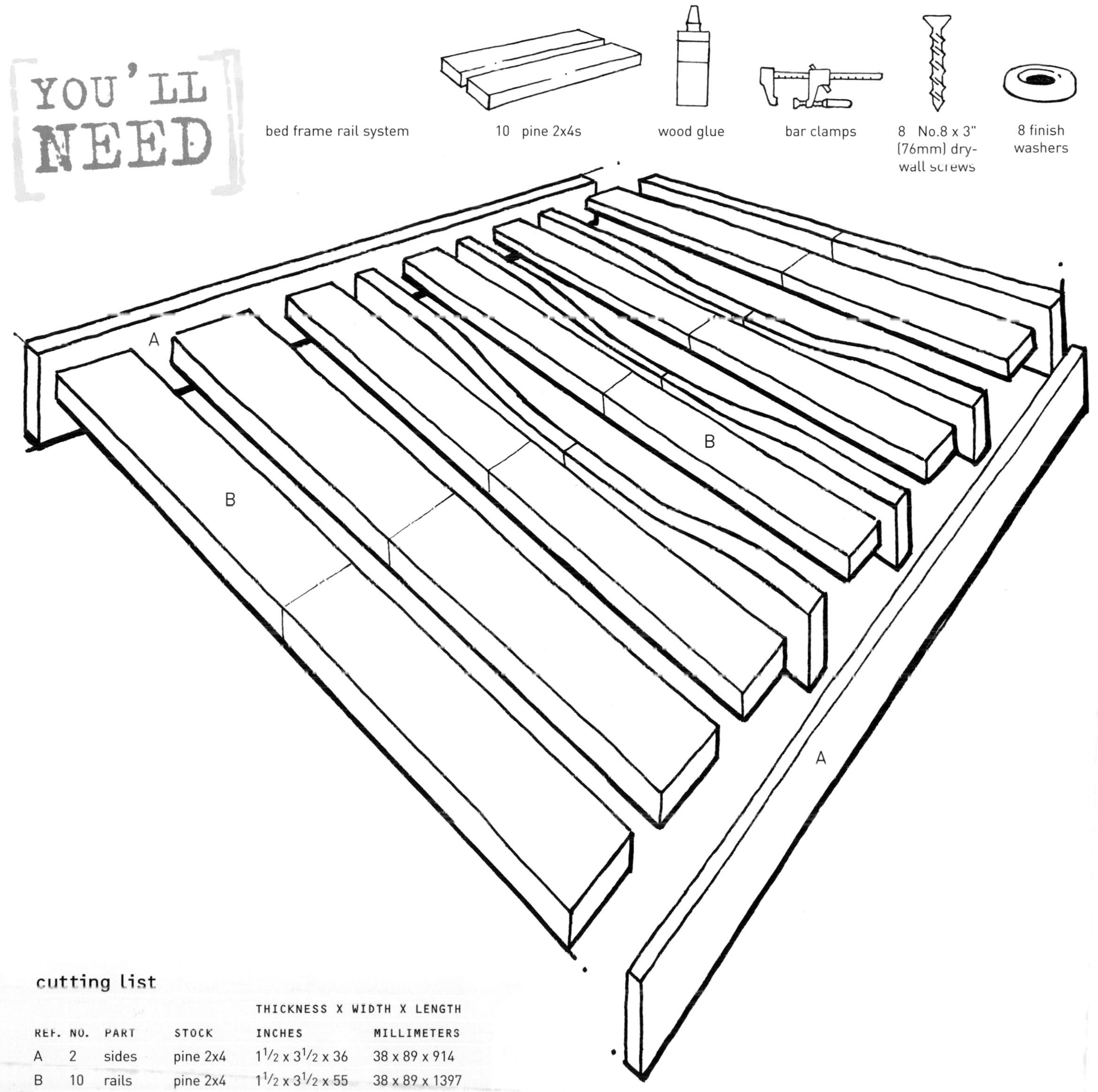

cutting list

REF.	NO.	PART	STOCK	THICKNESS X WIDTH X LENGTH INCHES	MILLIMETERS
A	2	sides	pine 2x4	$1^1/_2$ x $3^1/_2$ x 36	38 x 89 x 914
B	10	rails	pine 2x4	$1^1/_2$ x $3^1/_2$ x 55	38 x 89 x 1397

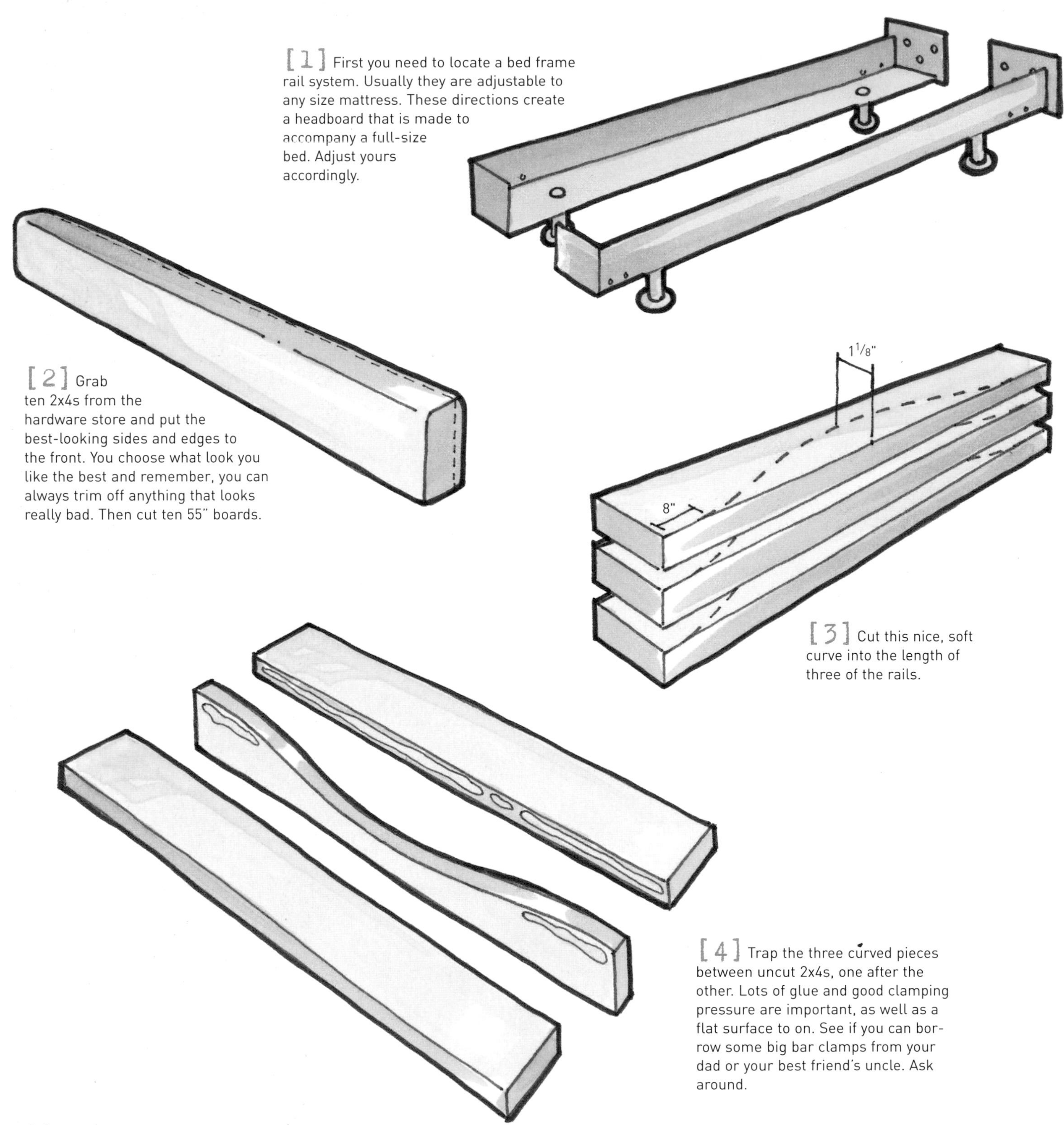

[1] First you need to locate a bed frame rail system. Usually they are adjustable to any size mattress. These directions create a headboard that is made to accompany a full-size bed. Adjust yours accordingly.

[2] Grab ten 2x4s from the hardware store and put the best-looking sides and edges to the front. You choose what look you like the best and remember, you can always trim off anything that looks really bad. Then cut ten 55" boards.

[3] Cut this nice, soft curve into the length of three of the rails.

[4] Trap the three curved pieces between uncut 2x4s, one after the other. Lots of glue and good clamping pressure are important, as well as a flat surface to on. See if you can borrow some big bar clamps from your dad or your best friend's uncle. Ask around.

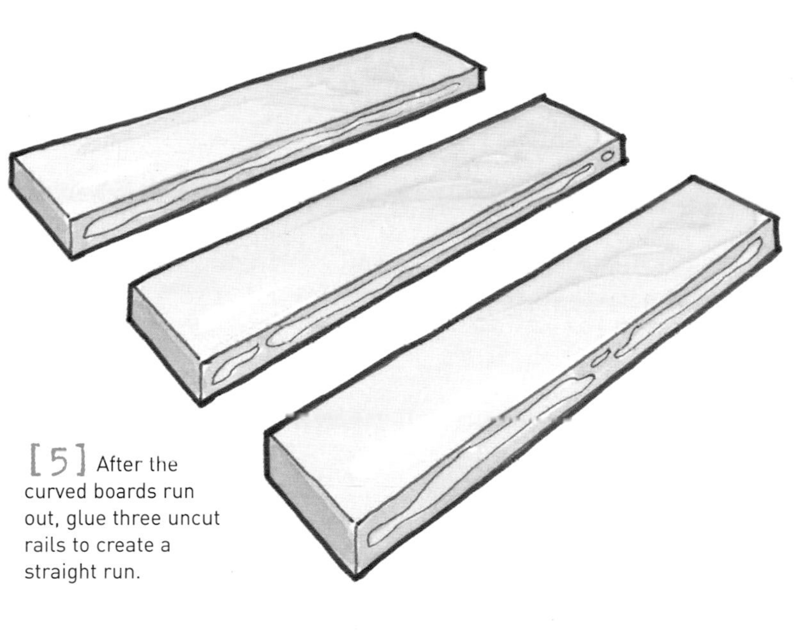

[5] After the curved boards run out, glue three uncut rails to create a straight run.

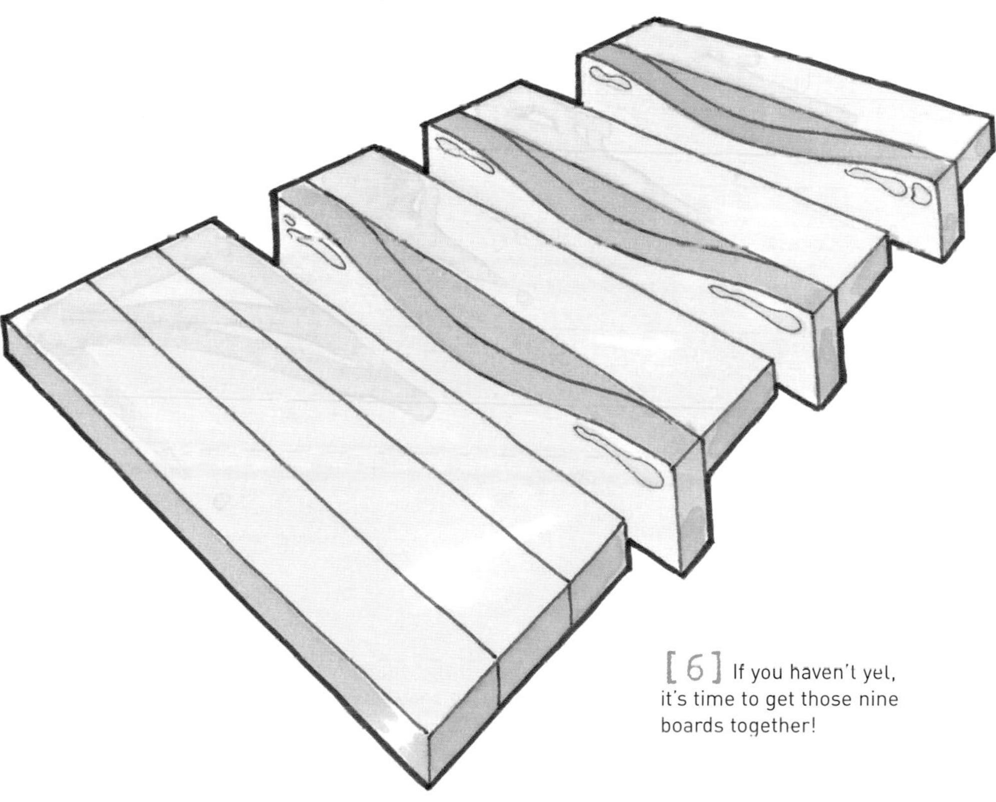

[6] If you haven't yet, it's time to get those nine boards together!

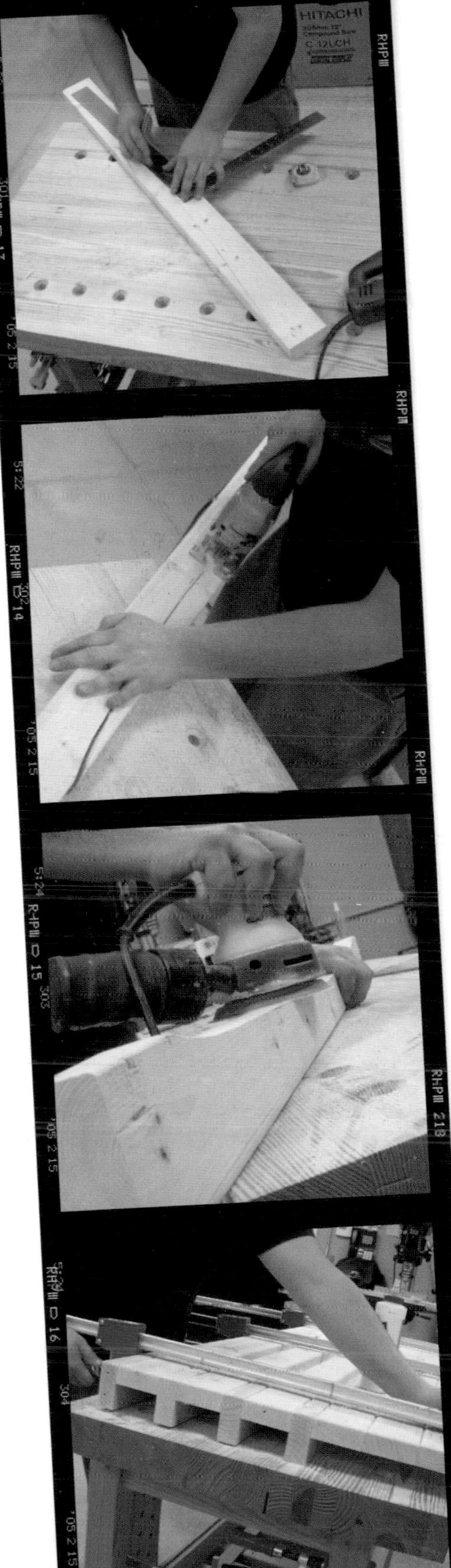

[7] Screw or glue down the last rail to the top of the stack.

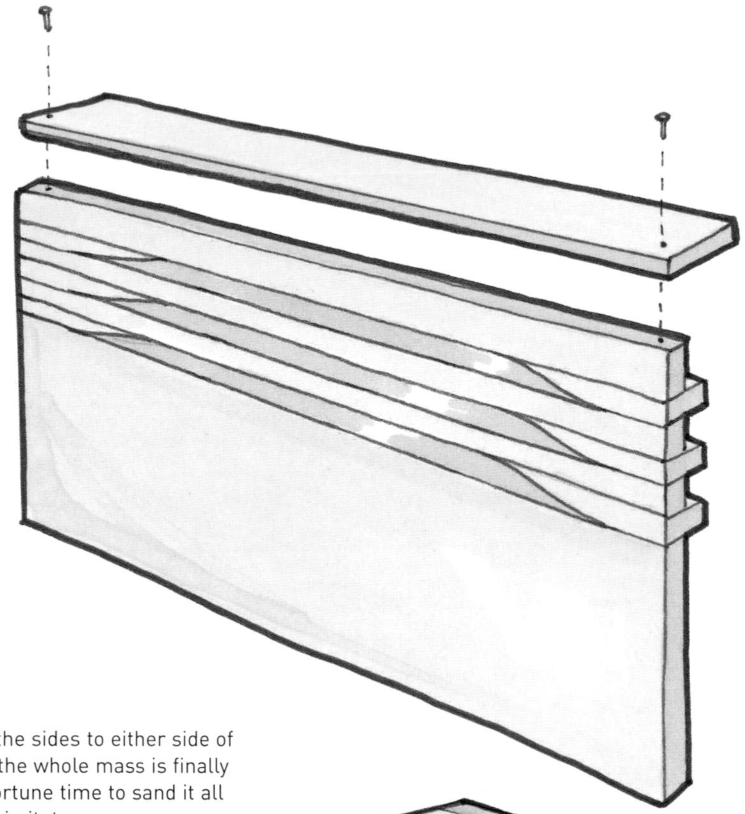

[8] Screw down the sides to either side of the assembly. When the whole mass is finally together, it's an opportune time to sand it all flush and paint or stain it, too.

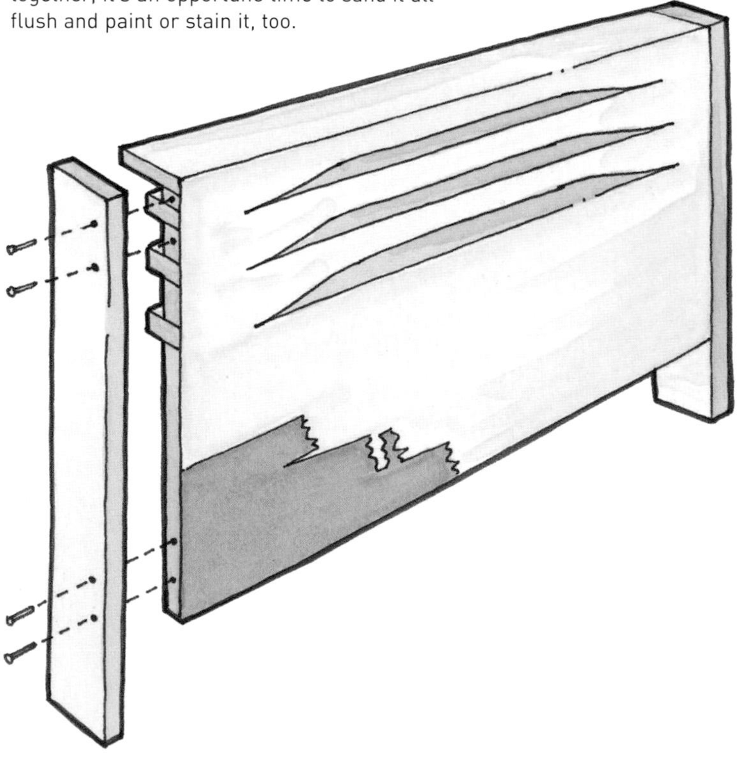

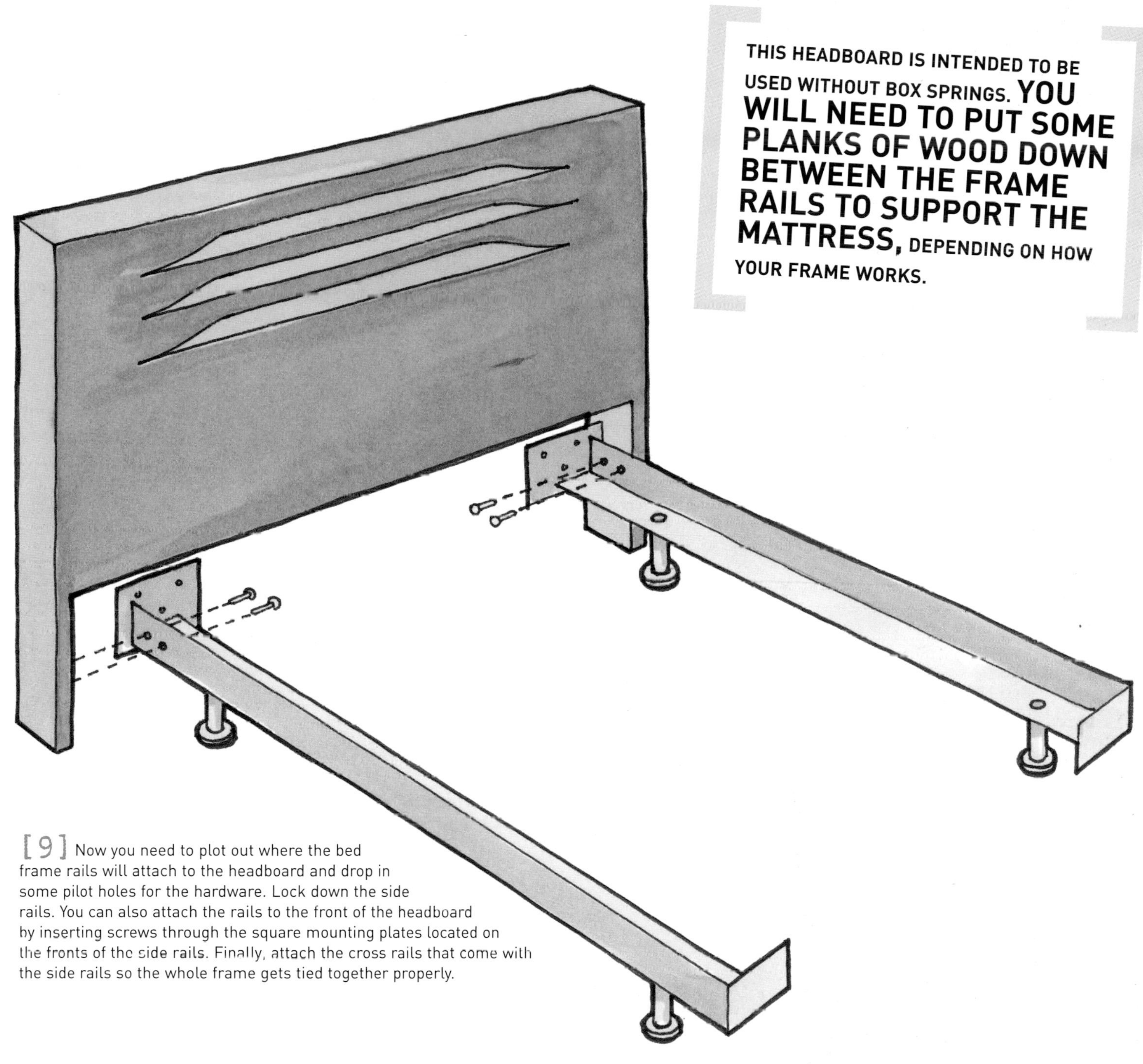

THIS HEADBOARD IS INTENDED TO BE USED WITHOUT BOX SPRINGS. YOU WILL NEED TO PUT SOME PLANKS OF WOOD DOWN BETWEEN THE FRAME RAILS TO SUPPORT THE MATTRESS, DEPENDING ON HOW YOUR FRAME WORKS.

[9] Now you need to plot out where the bed frame rails will attach to the headboard and drop in some pilot holes for the hardware. Lock down the side rails. You can also attach the rails to the front of the headboard by inserting screws through the square mounting plates located on the fronts of the side rails. Finally, attach the cross rails that come with the side rails so the whole frame gets tied together properly.

[splash]

NIGHTSTAND

This little unit is the perfect complement to the ripple headboard. Wait, a matching bedroom set? You? Yes! **Any way you stack it, this little nightstand is extremely versatile and very cool.**

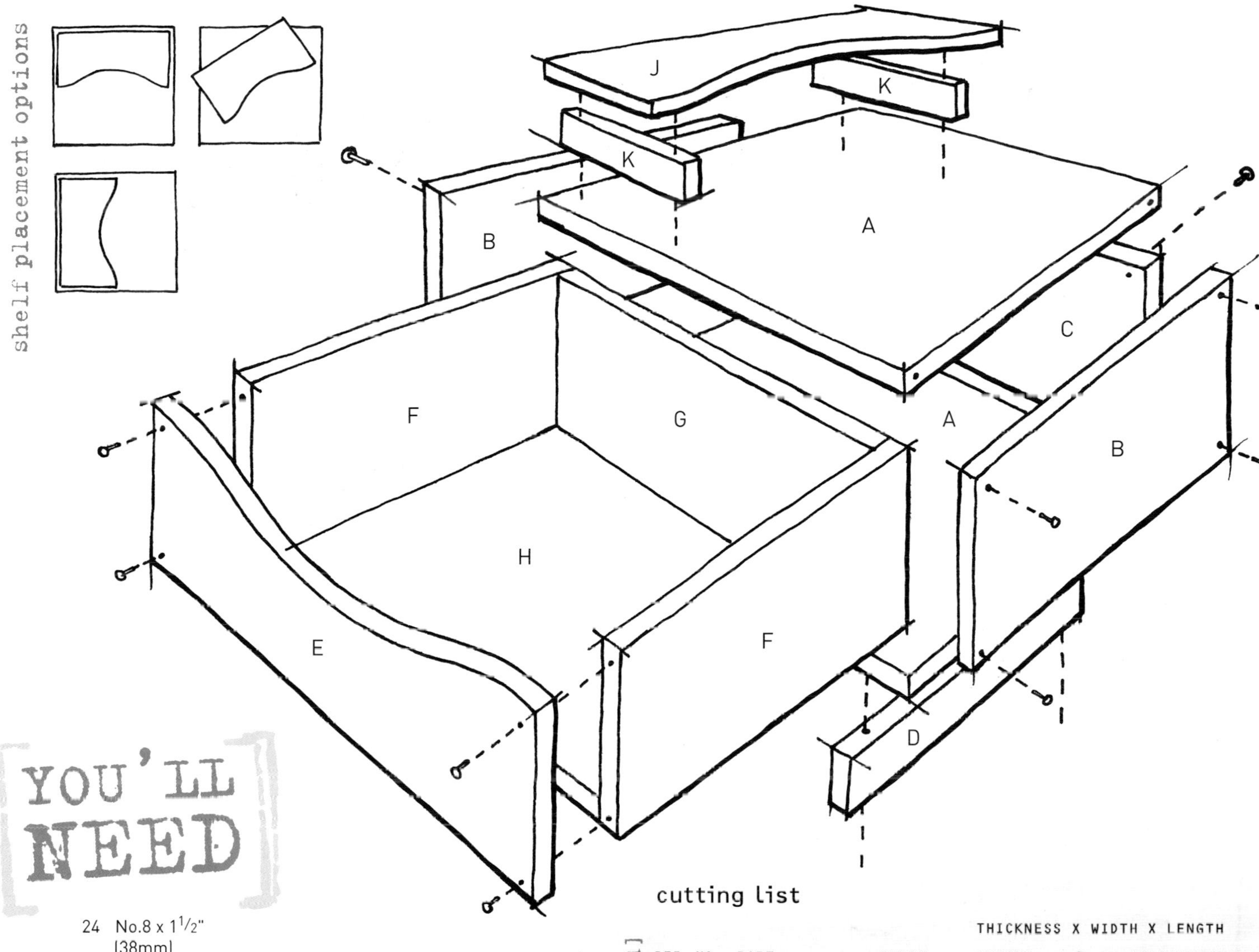

YOU'LL NEED

24 No.8 x $1\frac{1}{2}$" (38mm) wood screws

1 $\frac{3}{4}$" x 4' x 8' (19mm x 1.2m x 2.4m) plywood sheet

1 2" x 4' x 8' (51mm x 1.2m x 2.4m) pine 2x4

8 rubber feet

wood glue

12 bevel washers

cutting list

	REF.	NO.	PART	STOCK	THICKNESS X WIDTH X LENGTH INCHES	MILLIMETERS
[nightstand]	A	2	top & bottom	plywood	$\frac{3}{4}$ x 24 x 24	19 x 610 x 610
	B	2	sides	plywood	$\frac{3}{4}$ x $10\frac{1}{2}$ x 24	19 x 267 x 610
	C	1	back	plywood	$\frac{3}{4}$ x $10\frac{1}{2}$ x $22\frac{1}{2}$	19 x 267 x 572
	D	2	feet	pine 2x4	$1\frac{1}{2}$ x $3\frac{1}{2}$ x 20	38 x 89 x 508
[box]	E	1	drawer front	plywood	$\frac{3}{4}$ x 12 x 24	19 x 305 x 610
	F	2	drawer sides	plywood	$\frac{3}{4}$ x $10\frac{3}{8}$ x $22\frac{1}{2}$	19 x 264 x 572
	G	1	drawer back	plywood	$\frac{3}{4}$ x $10\frac{3}{8}$ x $20\frac{7}{8}$	19 x 264 x 530
	H	1	drawer bottom	plywood	$\frac{3}{4}$ x $20\frac{7}{8}$ x $21\frac{3}{4}$	19 x 530 x 553
[shelf]	J	1	shelf	plywood	$\frac{3}{4}$ x 12 x 24	19 x 305 x 610
	K	2	feet	pine 2x4	$1\frac{1}{2}$ x $3\frac{1}{2}$ x 9	38 x 89 x 229

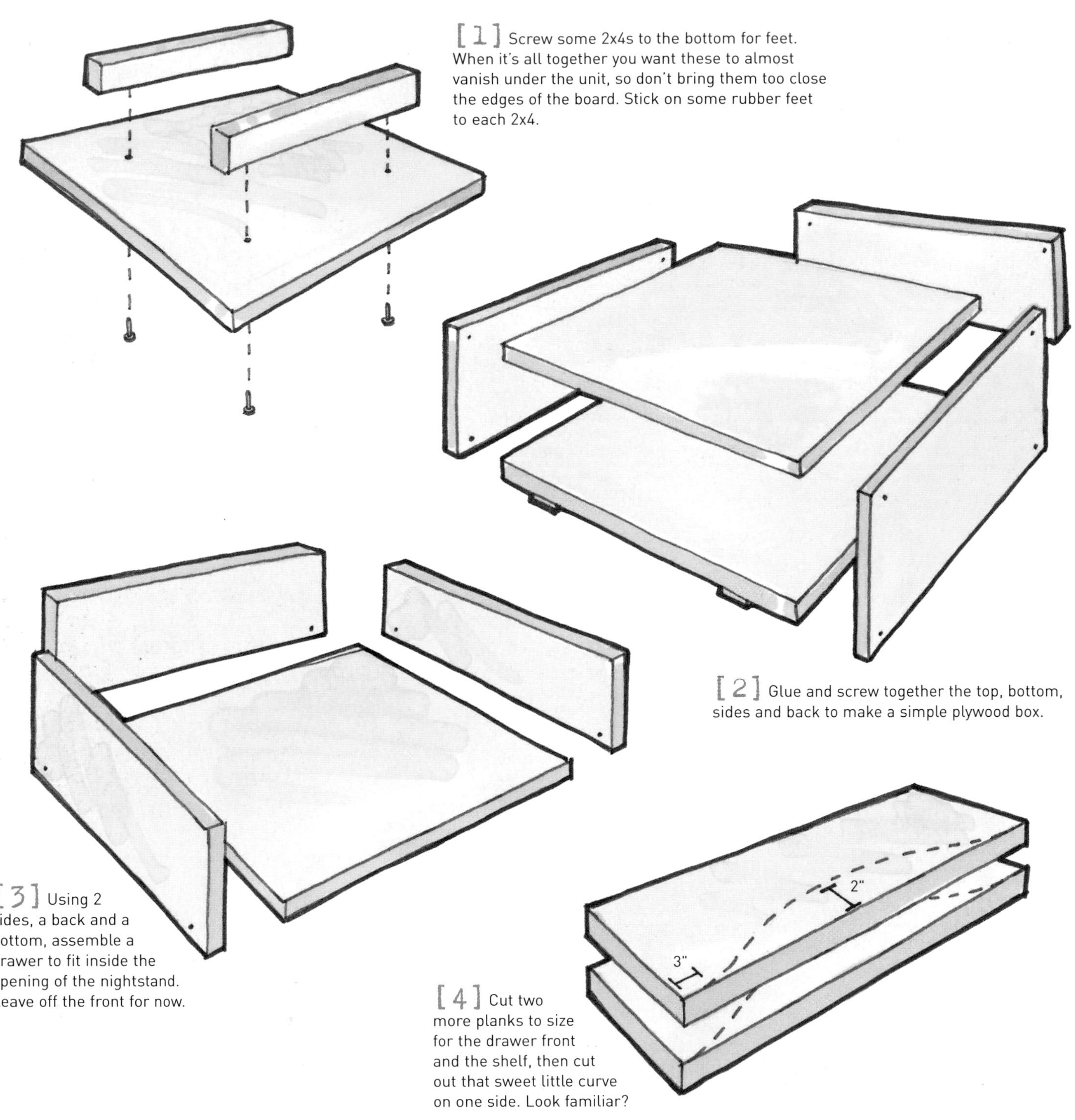

[1] Screw some 2x4s to the bottom for feet. When it's all together you want these to almost vanish under the unit, so don't bring them too close the edges of the board. Stick on some rubber feet to each 2x4.

[2] Glue and screw together the top, bottom, sides and back to make a simple plywood box.

[3] Using 2 sides, a back and a bottom, assemble a drawer to fit inside the opening of the nightstand. Leave off the front for now.

[4] Cut two more planks to size for the drawer front and the shelf, then cut out that sweet little curve on one side. Look familiar?

[5] Screw the front on the drawer.

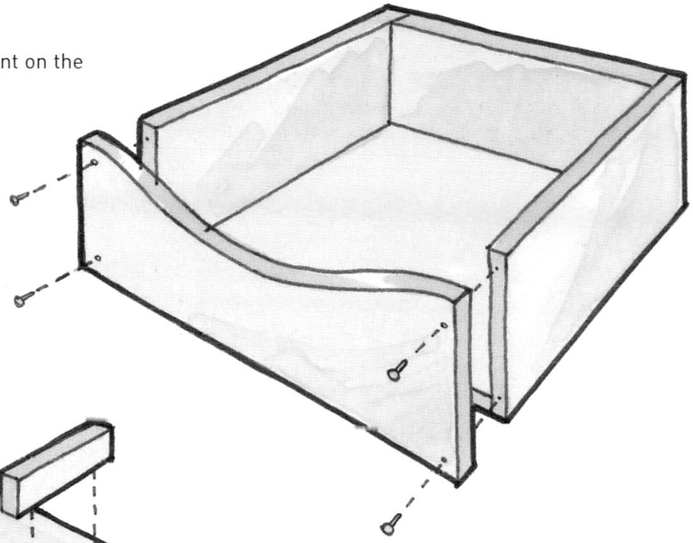

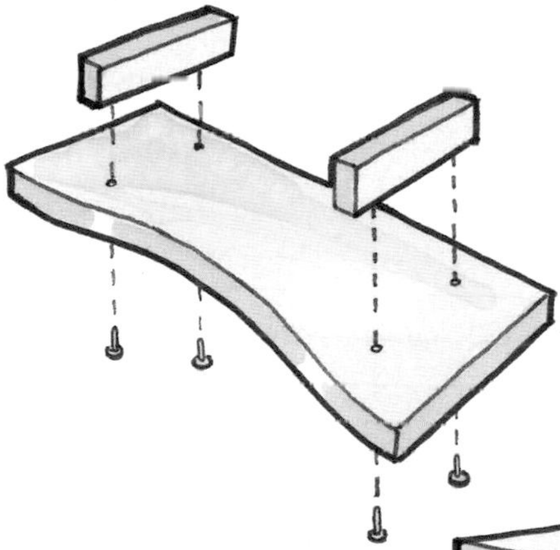

[6] Rubber feet might be nice on the feet here, too, so you can move this shelf around and not have to worry about scratching up the top.

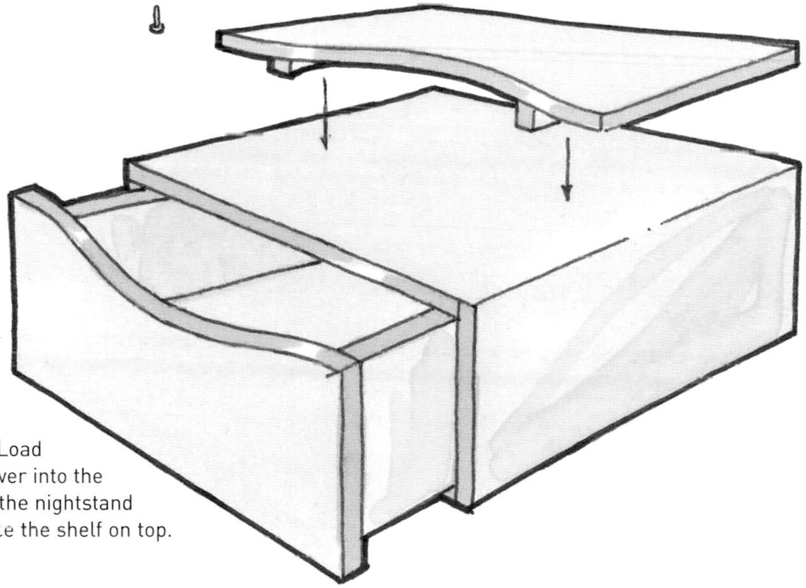

[7] Load the drawer into the front of the nightstand and place the shelf on top.

YOU CAN ORIENT THE TOP SHELF ANY WAY YOU DESIRE ON THE NIGHTSTAND. DEPENDING ON WHERE YOU PUT THE UNIT (IN THE CORNER, BY THE BED, ETC.), YOU MIGHT WANT TO CHANGE IT AROUND.

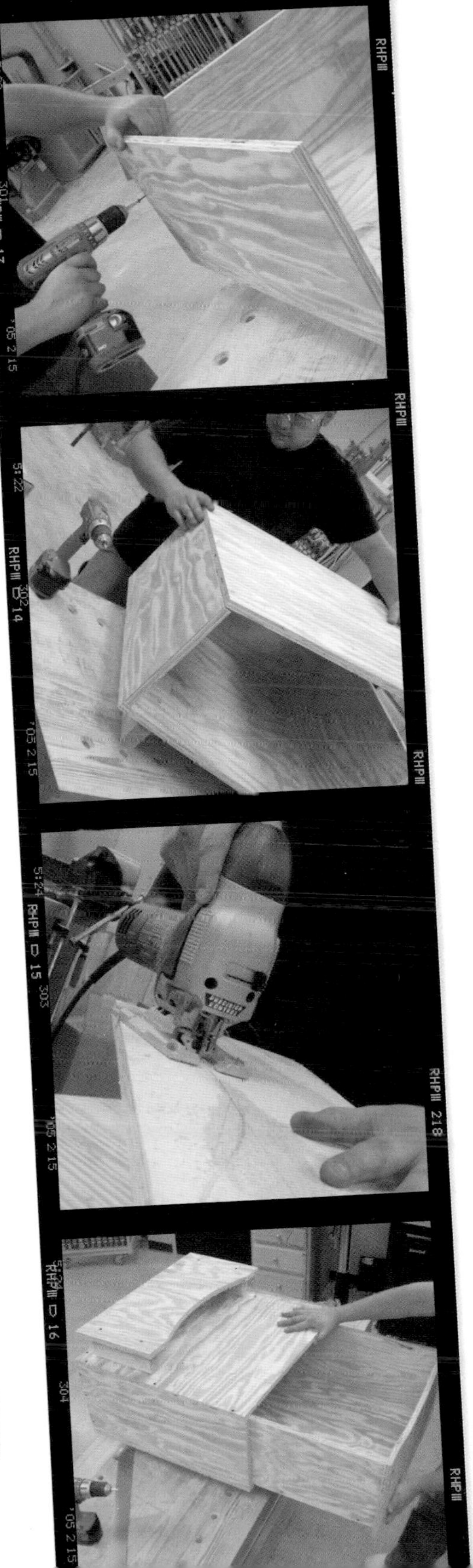

ARMOIRE [hungover]

Your apartment doesn't quite have the walk-in closet that you've always dreamed of, right? **This simple and sleek armoire will give you a place to hang all your professional clothes and store your dress shoes.** You do have some of those, don't you?

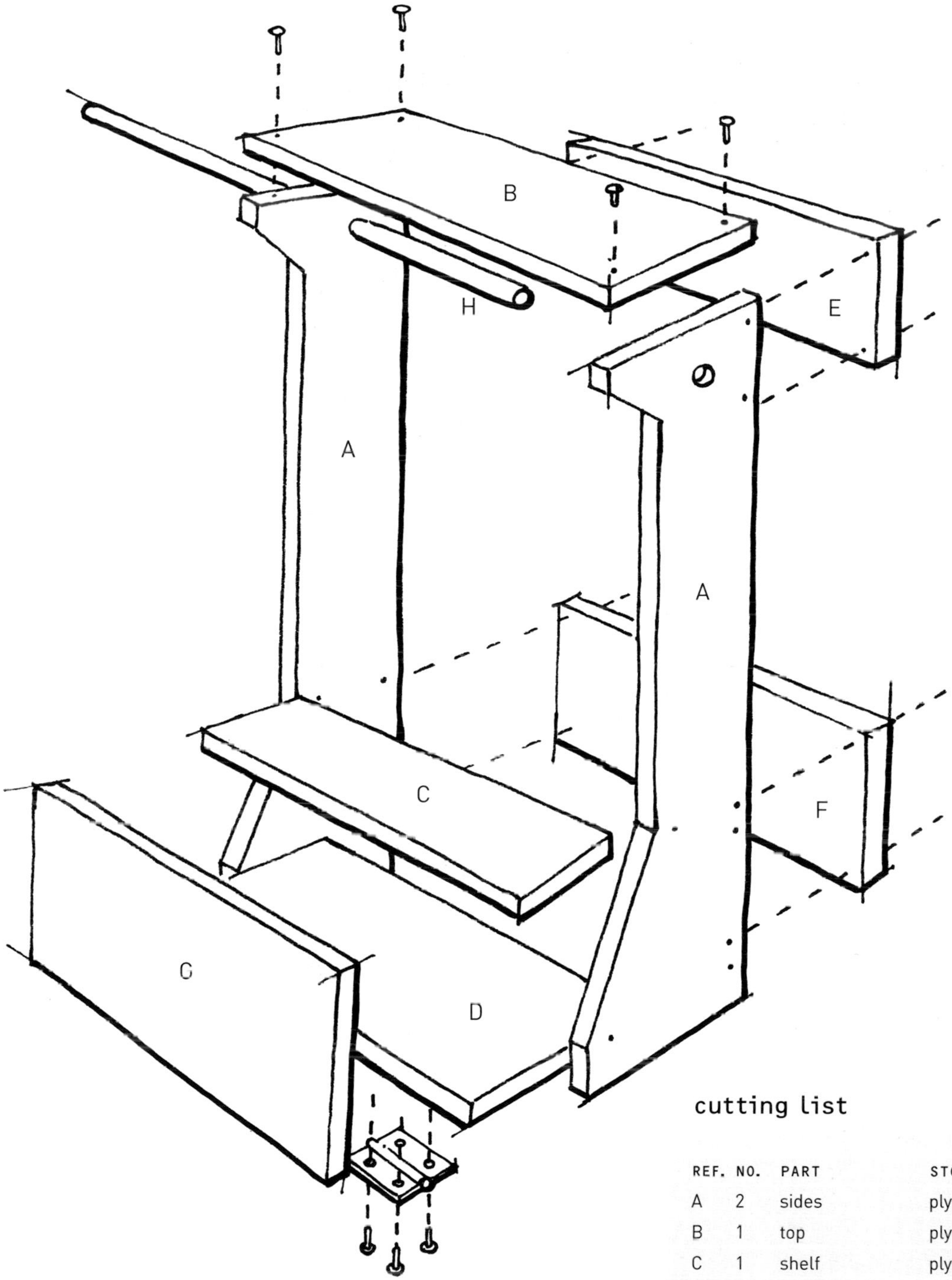

YOU'LL NEED

1 $^3/_4$" x 4' x 8'
(19mm x 1.2m x 2.4m)
plywood sheet

1 pair 1$^1/_4$" x 1$^1/_2$"
(32mm x 38mm)
butt hinges

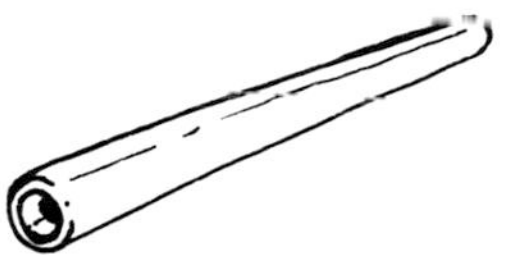

1 1"-diameter (25mm) steel rod

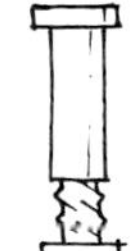

2 $^1/_4$" x 1$^1/_2$" (6mm x 38mm)
binding barrel bolts

20 No.8 x 3" (76mm) drywall screws

20 finish washers

8 $^3/_4$" (19mm) wood screws

20 3" (76mm) wood screws

cutting list

				THICKNESS X WIDTH X LENGTH	
REF.	NO.	PART	STOCK	INCHES	MILLIMETERS
A	2	sides	plywood	$^3/_4$ x 24 x 64	19 x 610 x 1626
B	1	top	plywood	$^3/_4$ x 20 x 26	19 x 508 x 622
C	1	shelf	plywood	$^3/_4$ x 18 x 24$^1/_2$	19 x 457 x 622
D	1	bottom	plywood	$^3/_4$ x 24 x 24$^1/_2$	19 x 610 x 622
E	1	top rail	plywood	$^3/_4$ x 6 x 24$^1/_2$	19 x 152 x 622
F	1	bottom rail	plywood	$^3/_4$ x 10$^1/_2$ x 24$^1/_2$	19 x 267 x 622
G	1	door	plywood	$^3/_4$ x 18$^1/_2$ x 26	19 x 470 x 660
H	1	hanging rod	steel	1 dia. x 32	25 x 813

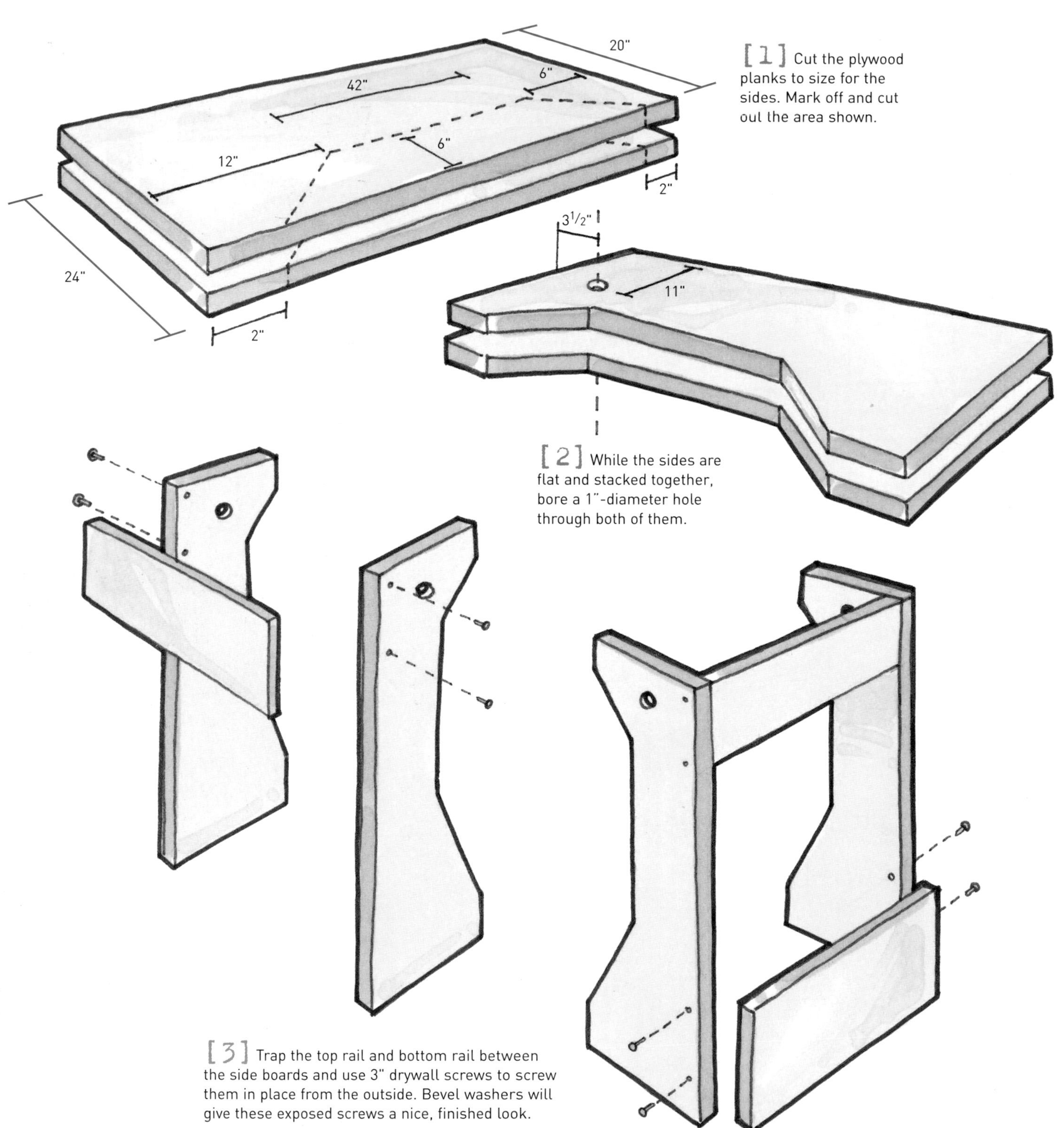

[1] Cut the plywood planks to size for the sides. Mark off and cut out the area shown.

[2] While the sides are flat and stacked together, bore a 1"-diameter hole through both of them.

[3] Trap the top rail and bottom rail between the side boards and use 3" drywall screws to screw them in place from the outside. Bevel washers will give these exposed screws a nice, finished look.

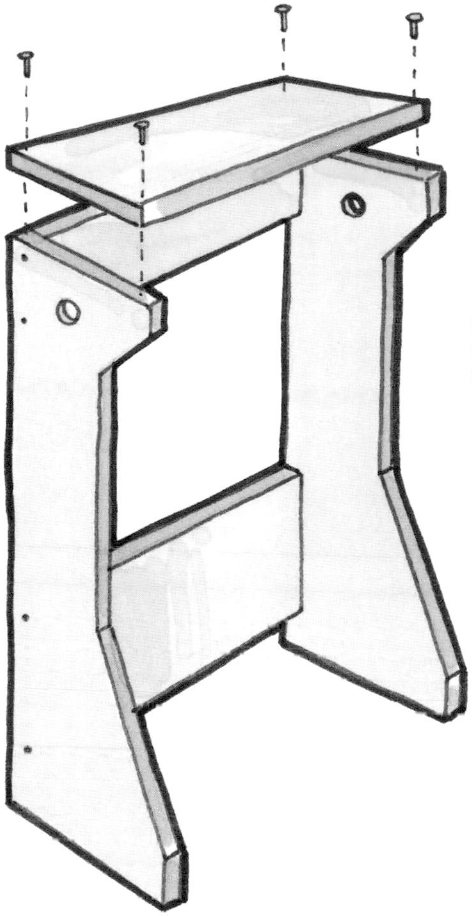

[4] Drop on the top and lock it down with some more wood screws and washers.

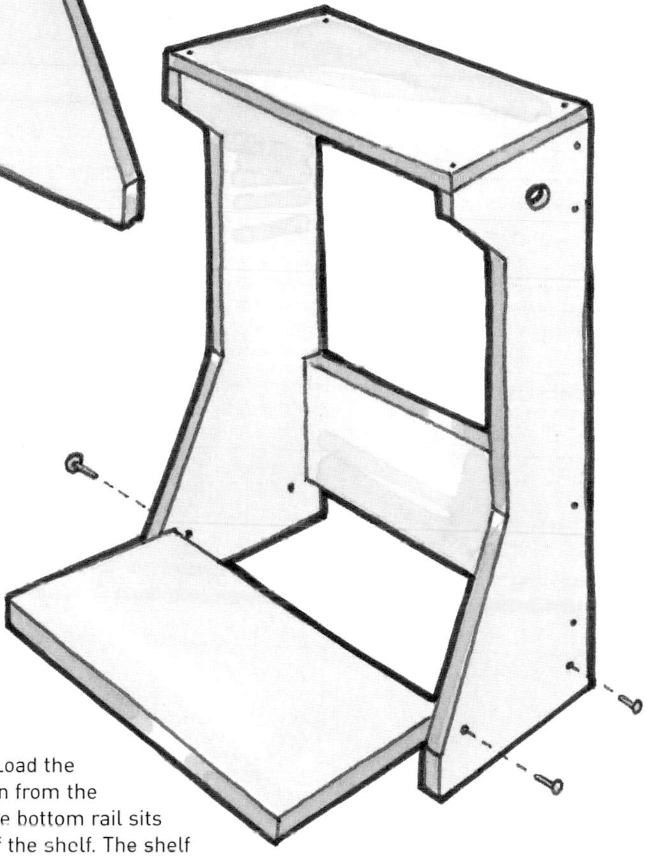

[5] Load the bottom in from the front. The bottom rail sits on top of the shelf. The shelf gets screwed in from the outside.

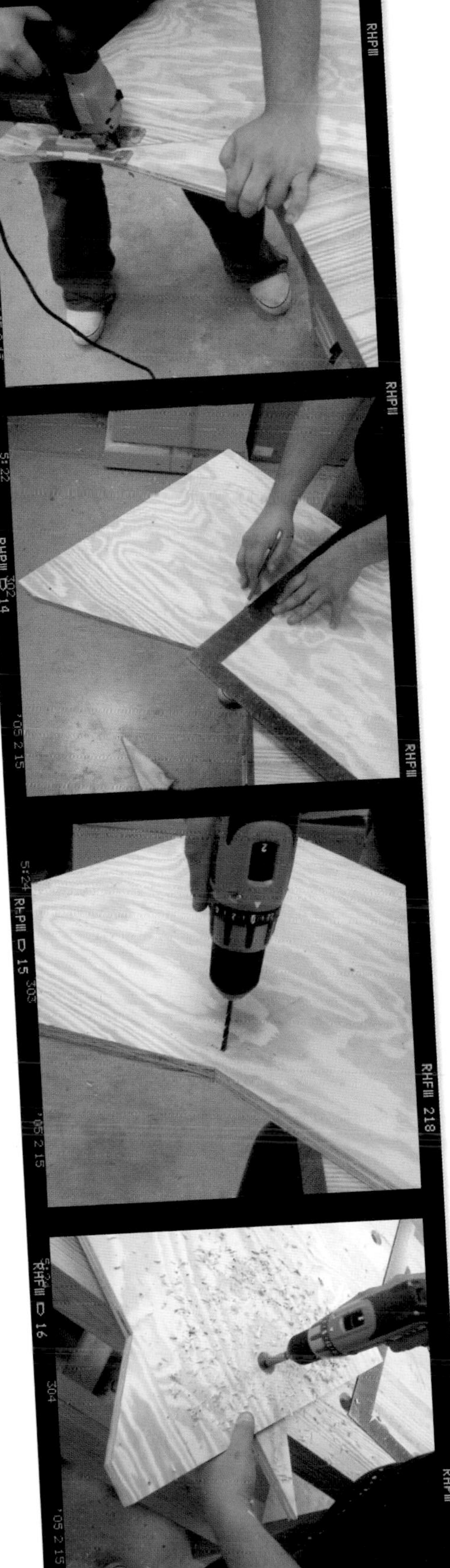

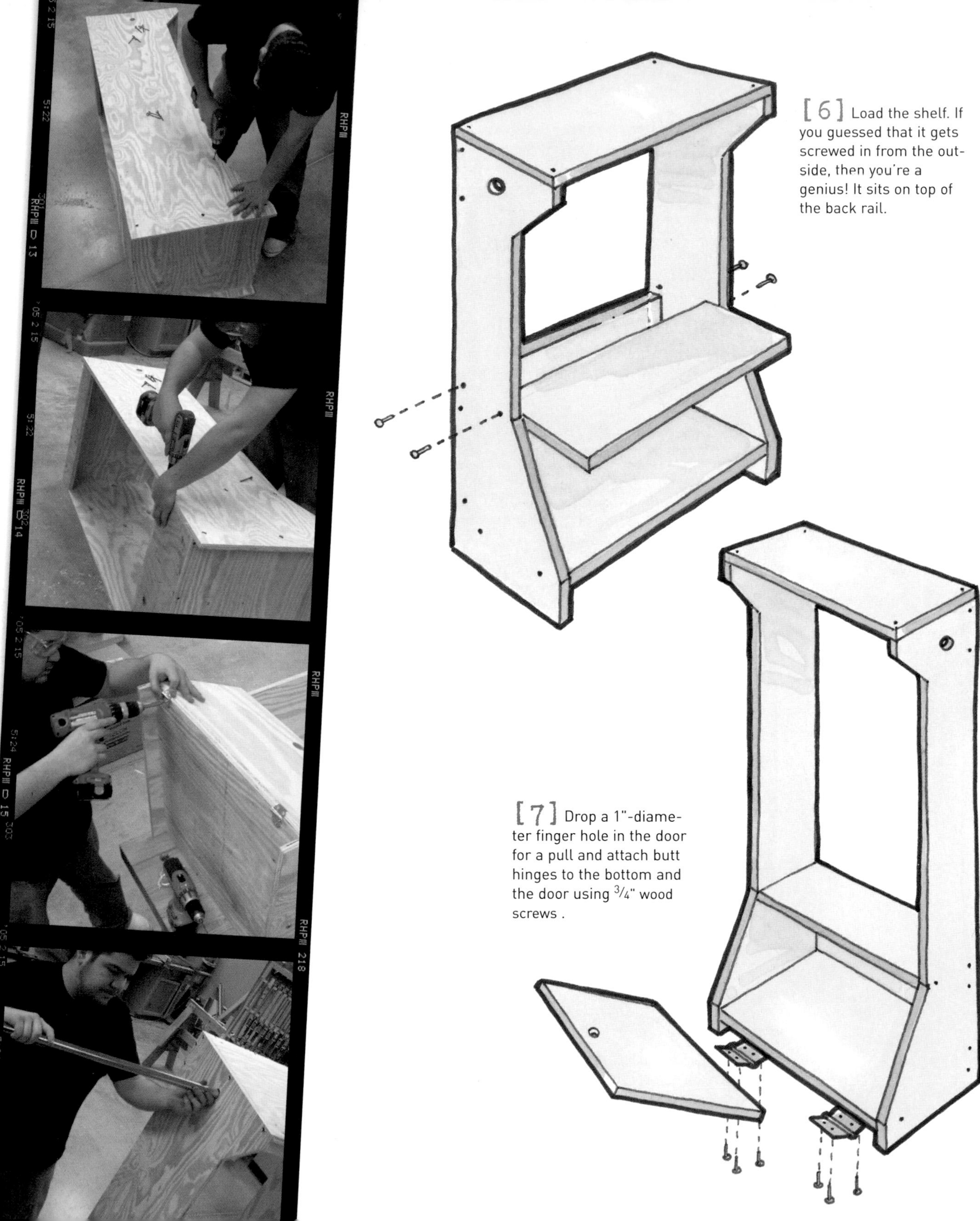

[6] Load the shelf. If you guessed that it gets screwed in from the outside, then you're a genius! It sits on top of the back rail.

[7] Drop a 1"-diameter finger hole in the door for a pull and attach butt hinges to the bottom and the door using 3/4" wood screws .

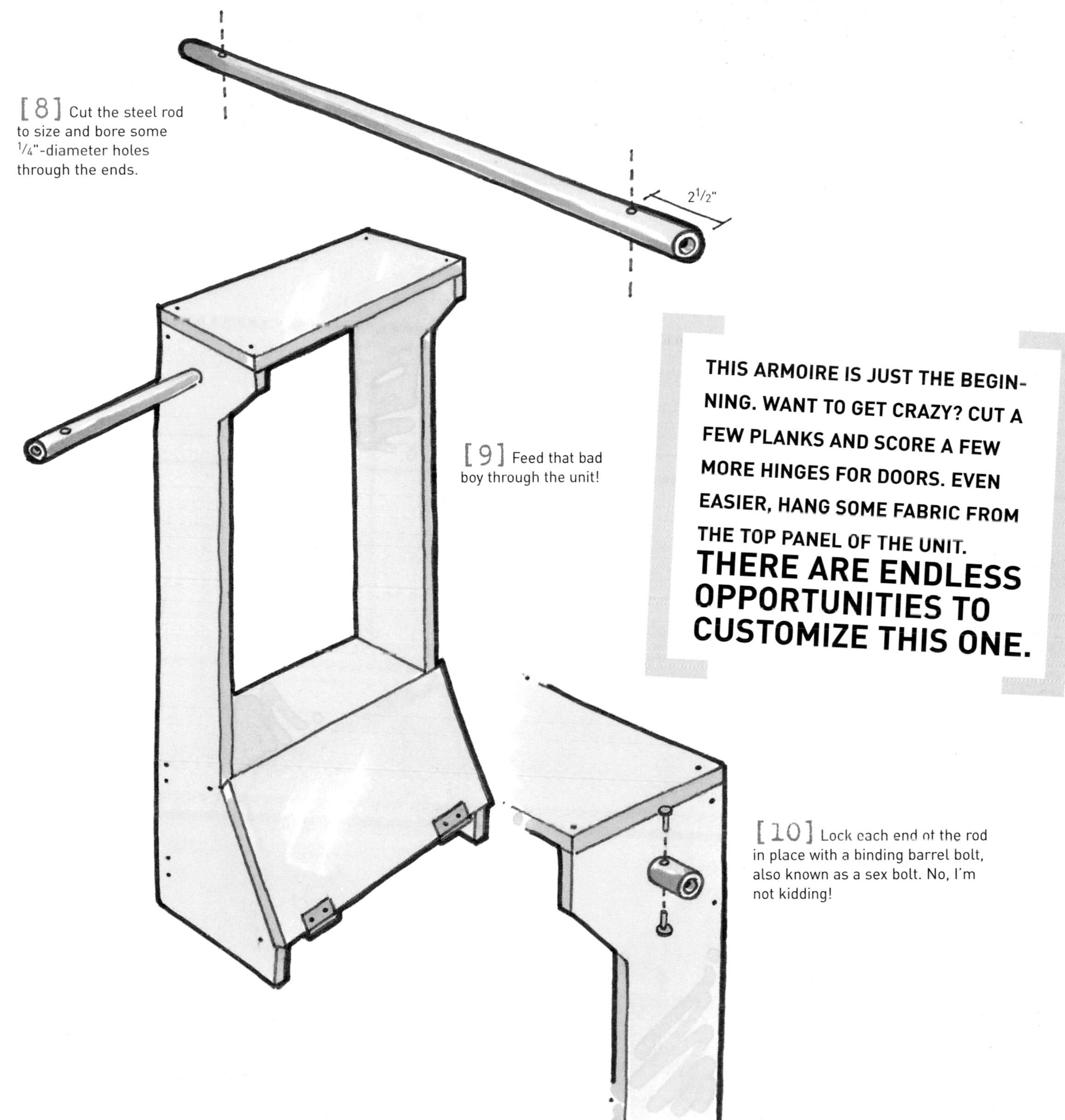

[8] Cut the steel rod to size and bore some $^1/_4$"-diameter holes through the ends.

[9] Feed that bad boy through the unit!

[10] Lock each end of the rod in place with a binding barrel bolt, also known as a sex bolt. No, I'm not kidding!

THIS ARMOIRE IS JUST THE BEGINNING. WANT TO GET CRAZY? CUT A FEW PLANKS AND SCORE A FEW MORE HINGES FOR DOORS. EVEN EASIER, HANG SOME FABRIC FROM THE TOP PANEL OF THE UNIT.

THERE ARE ENDLESS OPPORTUNITIES TO CUSTOMIZE THIS ONE.

HAMPER

[cased clothes]

No matter what size my bedrooms have been throughout the years, the floor has never been safe from the dirty clothes pile or piles, to be more truthful. **This simple and handy little clothes hamper is super neat,** and it will help you keep your room that way, too!

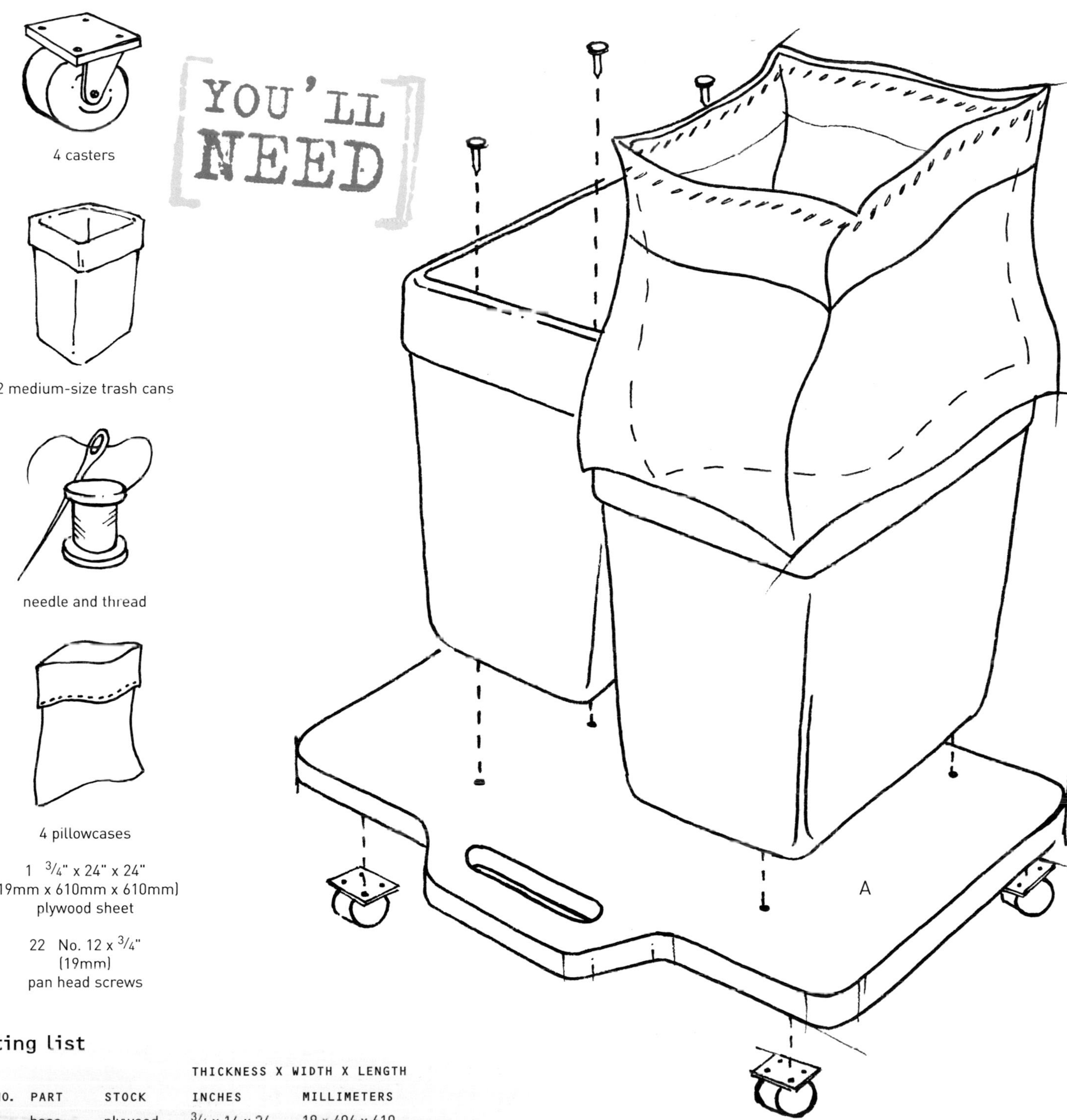

4 casters

2 medium-size trash cans

needle and thread

4 pillowcases

1 3/4" x 24" x 24"
(19mm x 610mm x 610mm)
plywood sheet

22 No. 12 x 3/4"
(19mm)
pan head screws

cutting list

				THICKNESS X WIDTH X LENGTH	
REF.	NO.	PART	STOCK	INCHES	MILLIMETERS
A	1	base	plywood	3/4 x 16 x 24	19 x 406 x 610

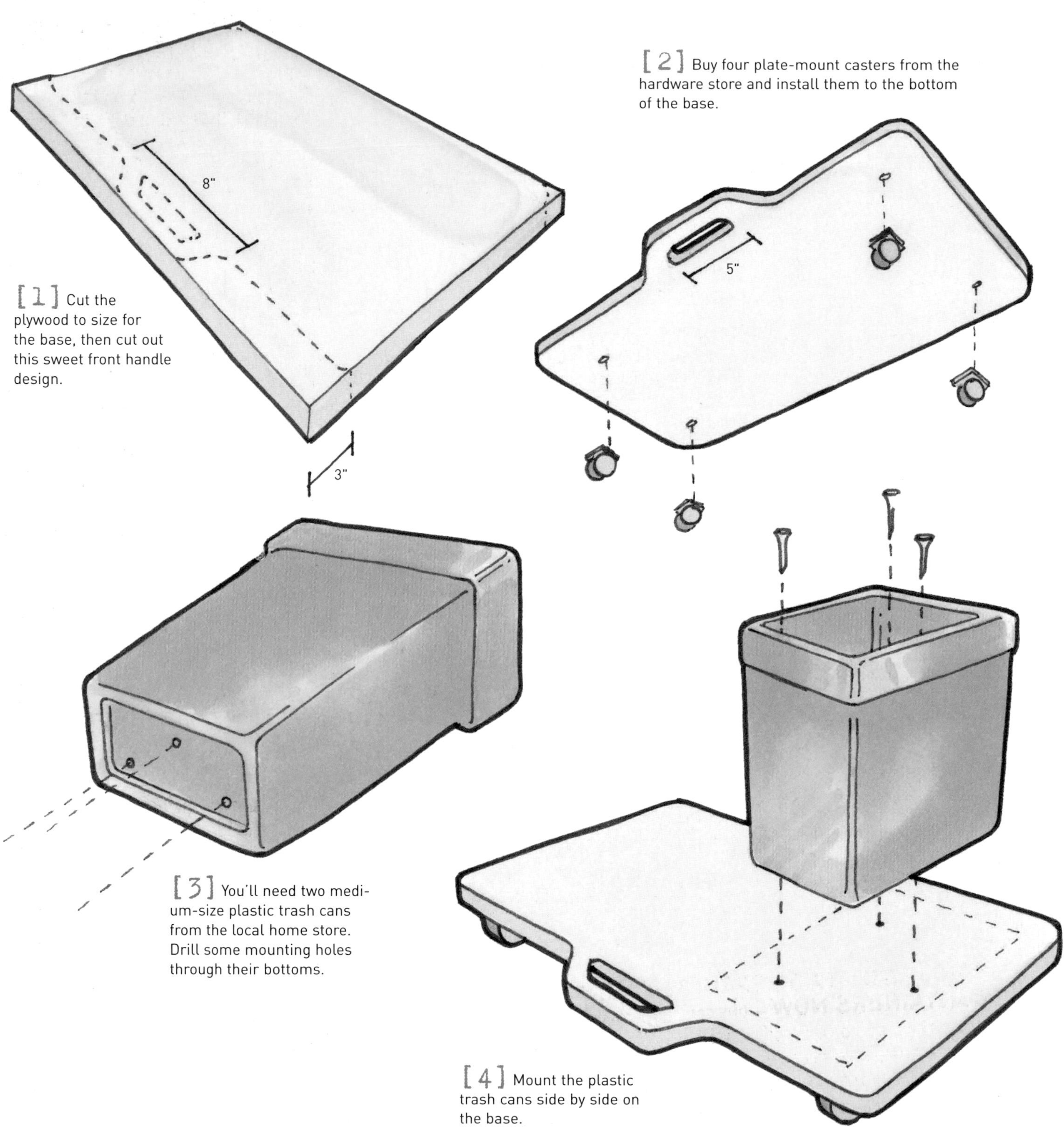

[1] Cut the plywood to size for the base, then cut out this sweet front handle design.

[2] Buy four plate-mount casters from the hardware store and install them to the bottom of the base.

[3] You'll need two medium-size plastic trash cans from the local home store. Drill some mounting holes through their bottoms.

[4] Mount the plastic trash cans side by side on the base.

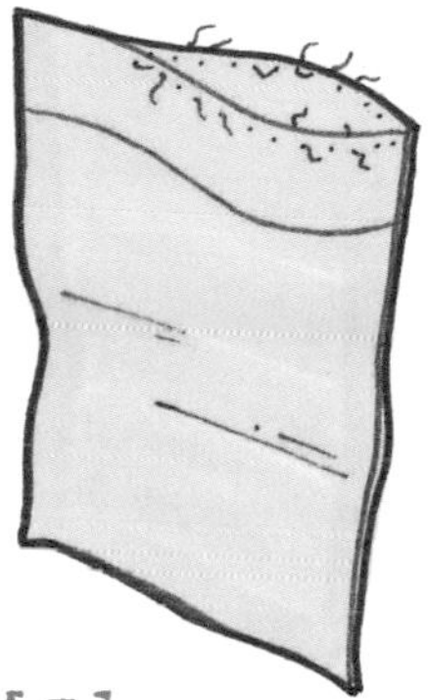

[6] Sleeve this newly opened end over another pillowcase and stitch the two open-end edges together.

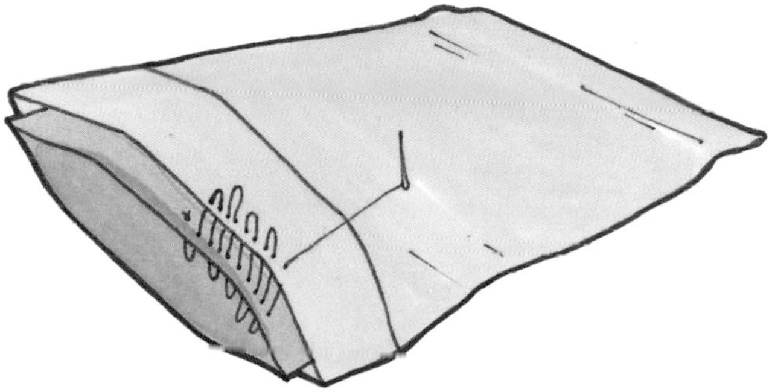

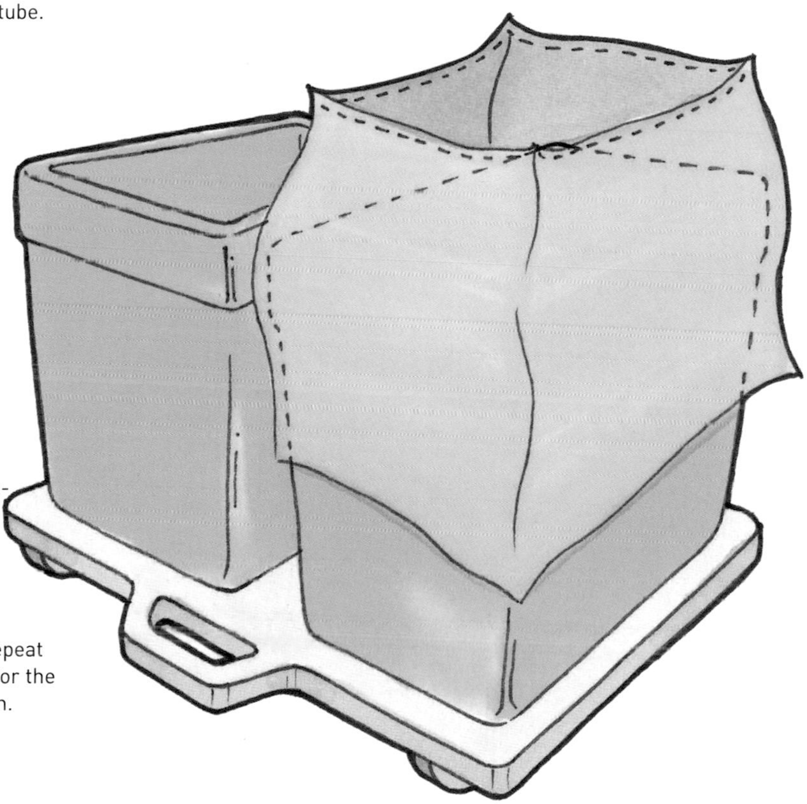

[5] Take a pillowcase and open the seam on the stitched end to make a fabric tube.

[7] Sleeve the outer case around the outside of one trash can and allow the inner case to become the inside liner. Repeat steps 5 and 6 for the other trash can.

YOU'VE GOT TWO SEPARATE DIRTY-CLOTHES CONTAINERS NOW — ONE FOR CLOTHES AND ONE FOR UNMENTIONABLES OR ONE FOR LIGHTS AND ONE FOR DARKS. WHEN IT'S LAUNDRY TIME, SIMPLY PULL UP ON THE OUTSIDE CASE AND LIFT ALL THE CLOTHES OUT OF THE HAMPER. YOU'LL EVEN HAVE ENOUGH ROOM IN THE BAG TO TIE A KNOT IN THE TOP! YOUR ROOMMATES WILL BE SO JEALOUS!

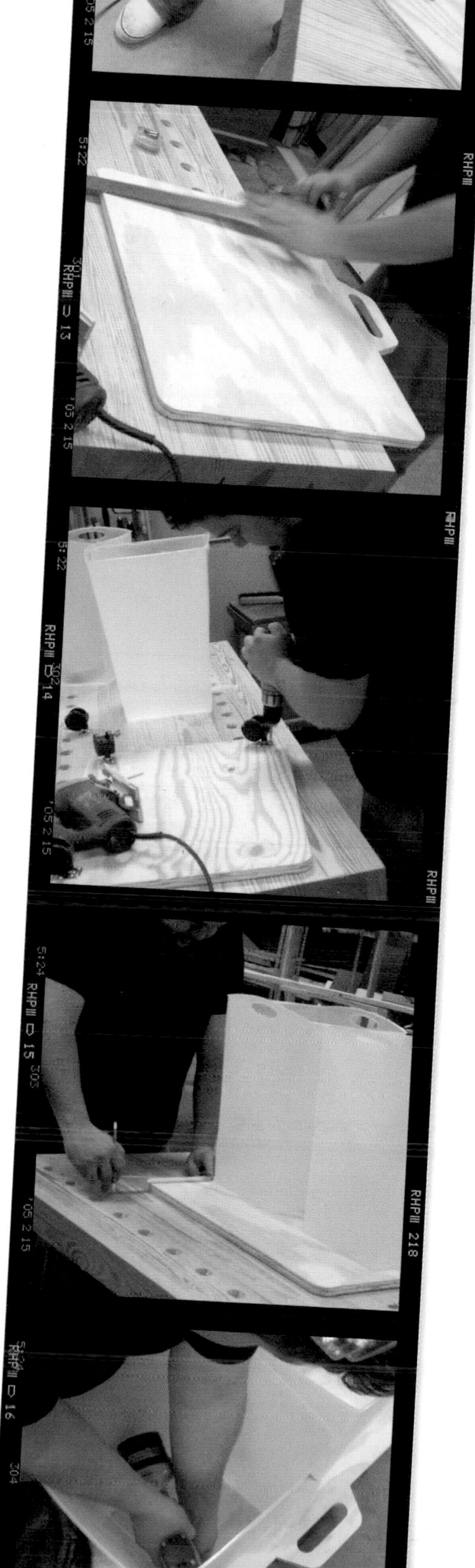

[wallflower]

SHOJI SCREEN

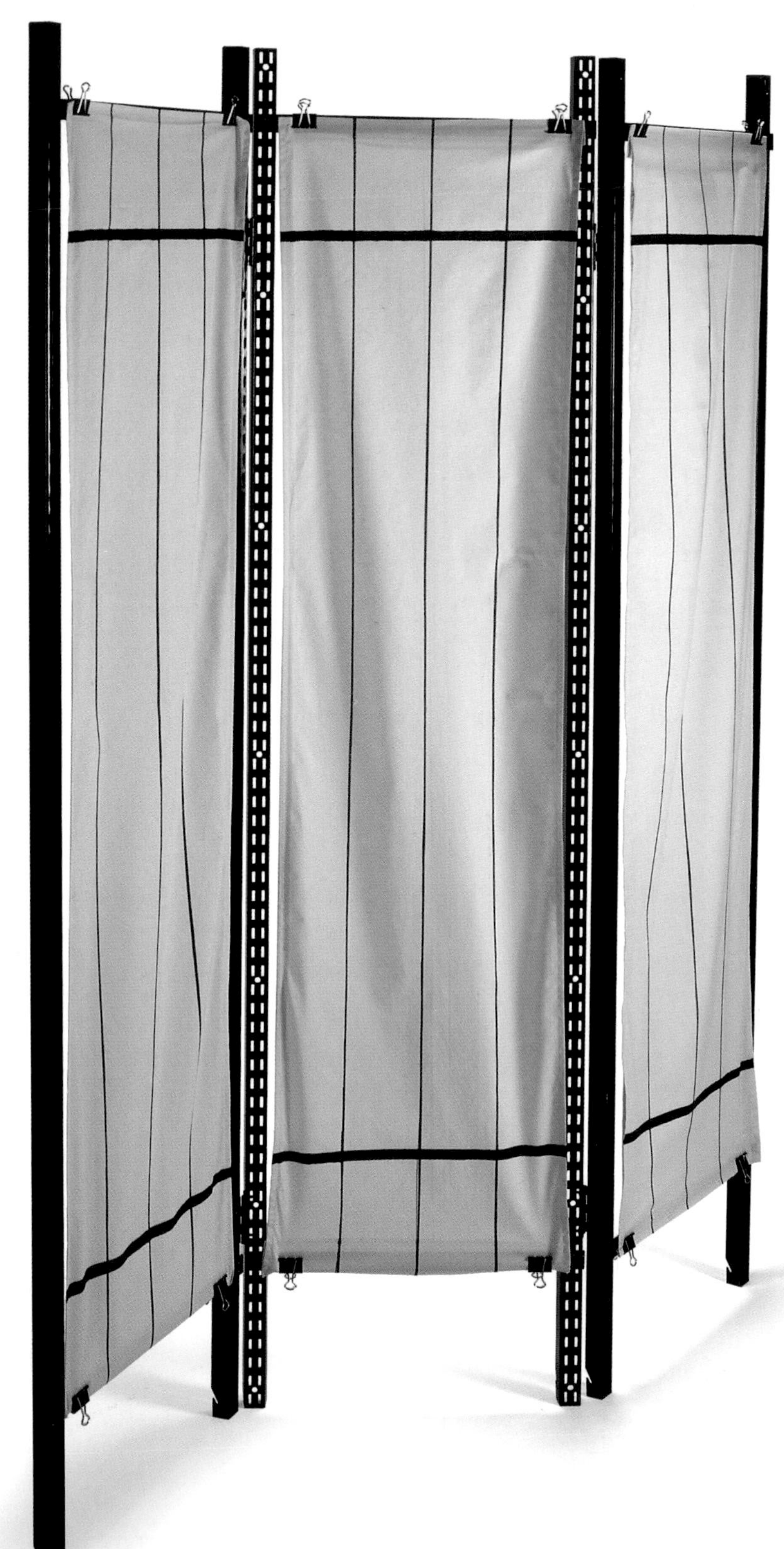

The shoji screen is such a cool thing — rich in culture and history. Beautiful fine wood and paper screens could cost you thousands of dollars, but this interpretation is just as attractive and definitely easier on the billfold. And who else do you know with a shoji in their crib?

YOU'LL NEED

12 medium $1\frac{1}{4}$" (32mm) binder clips

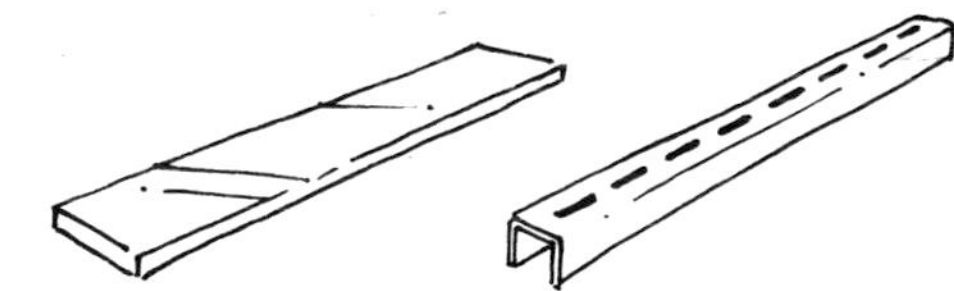

3 $\frac{1}{8}$" x 1" x 36" (914mm) steel bar

6 6' (1.8m) utility shelving track

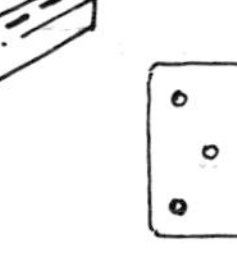

2 pairs $1\frac{1}{2}$" x 2" (38mm x 51mm) butt hinges

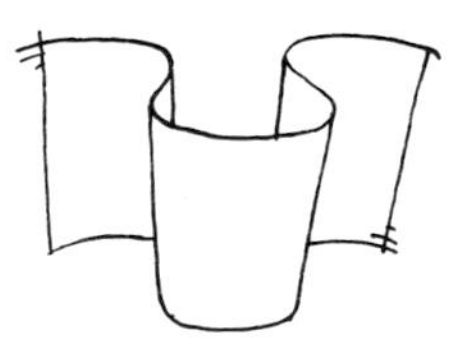

2 yards of muslin

spray paint

40 No.4 x $\frac{5}{8}$" (16mm) machine screws

40 No.4 flat washers

40 No. 4 hex nuts

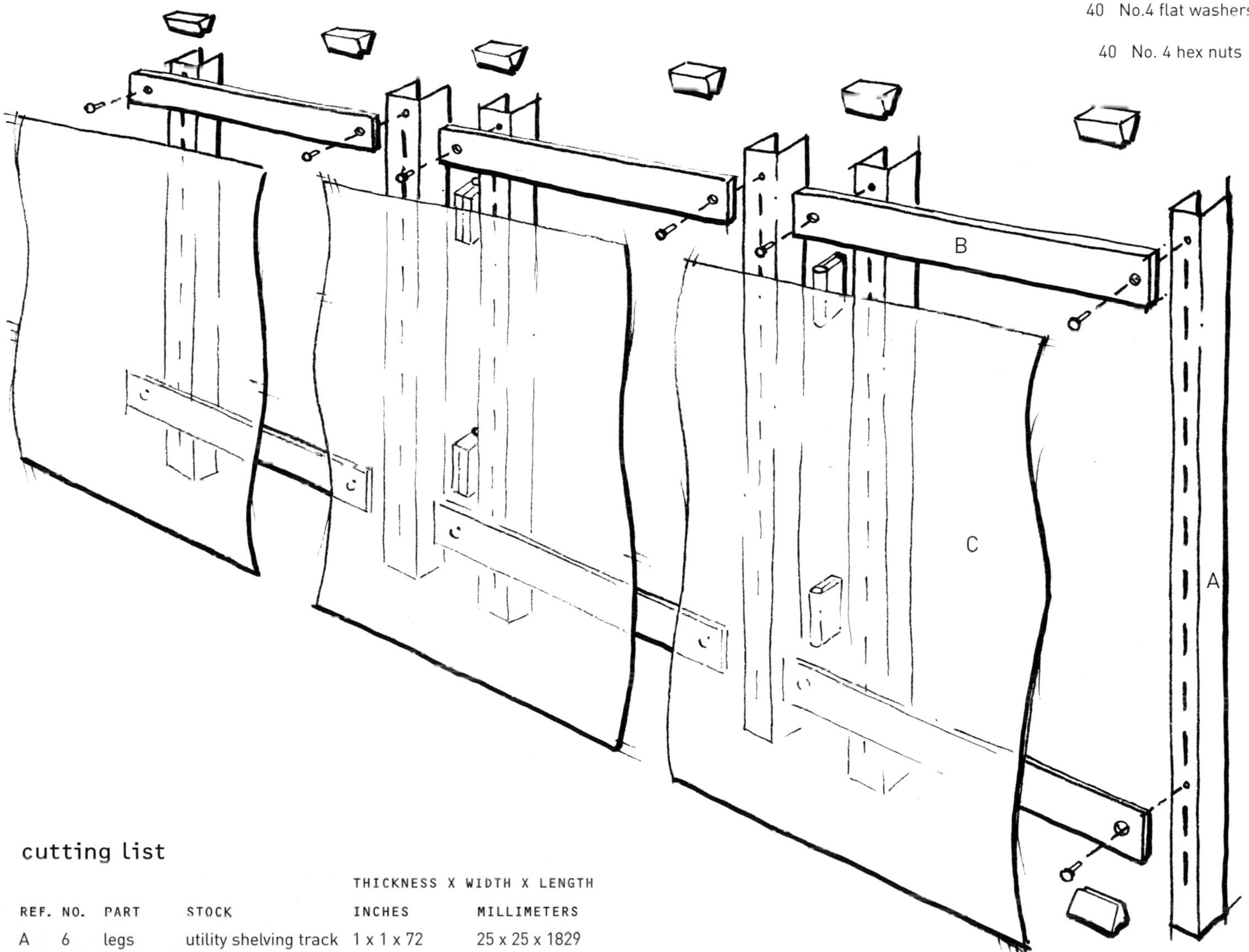

cutting list

REF.	NO.	PART	STOCK	THICKNESS X WIDTH X LENGTH INCHES	MILLIMETERS
A	6	legs	utility shelving track	1 x 1 x 72	25 x 25 x 1829
B	6	rails	steel strap	$\frac{1}{8}$ x 1 x 18	3 x 25 x 457
C	3	panels	muslin	16 x 63	406 x 1600

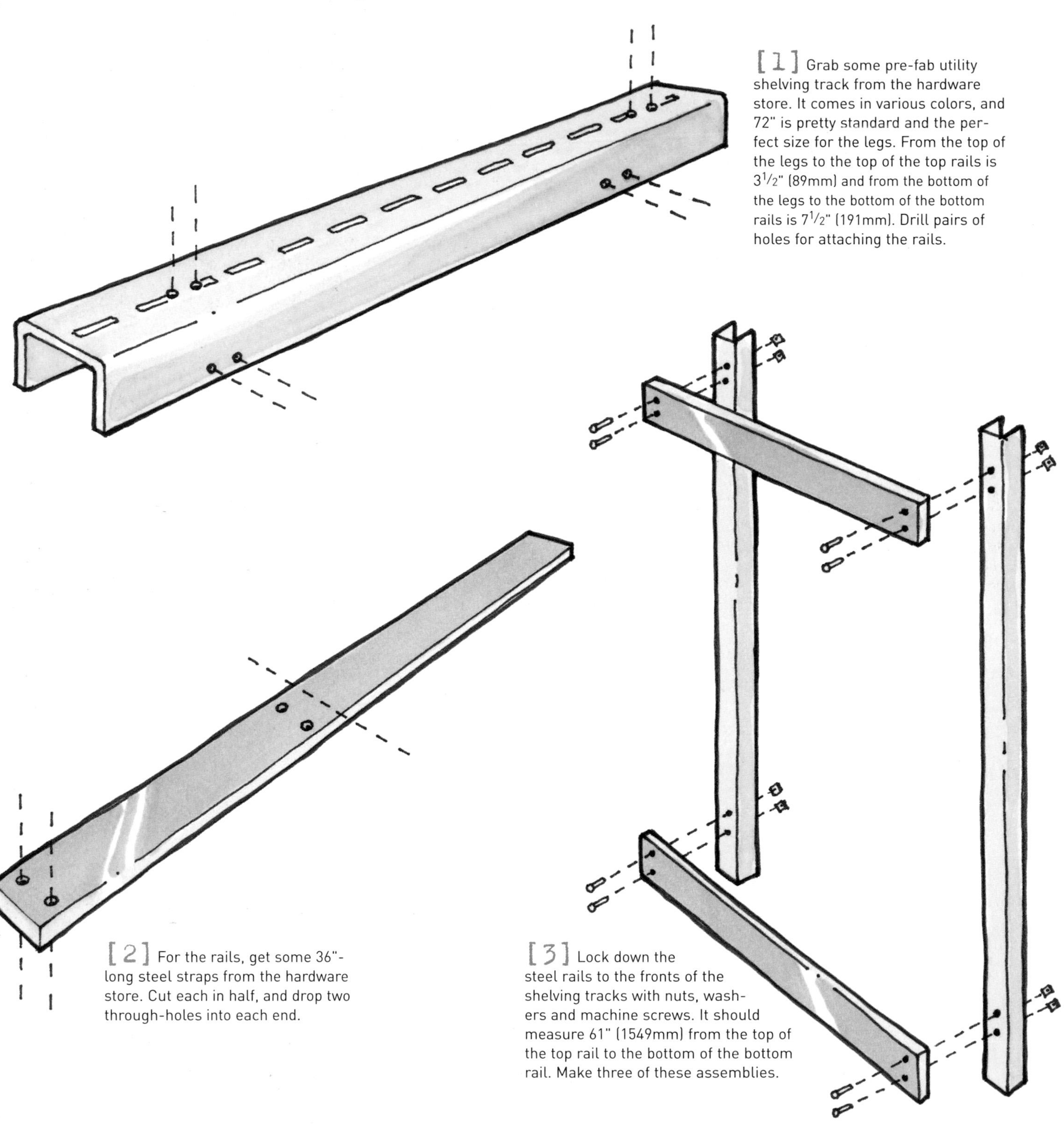

[1] Grab some pre-fab utility shelving track from the hardware store. It comes in various colors, and 72" is pretty standard and the perfect size for the legs. From the top of the legs to the top of the top rails is $3^1/_2$" (89mm) and from the bottom of the legs to the bottom of the bottom rails is $7^1/_2$" (191mm). Drill pairs of holes for attaching the rails.

[2] For the rails, get some 36"-long steel straps from the hardware store. Cut each in half, and drop two through-holes into each end.

[3] Lock down the steel rails to the fronts of the shelving tracks with nuts, washers and machine screws. It should measure 61" (1549mm) from the top of the top rail to the bottom of the bottom rail. Make three of these assemblies.

[4] Now is a good time to apply some spray paint. Black or brown would be the more traditional colors, but this is your screen, not mine!

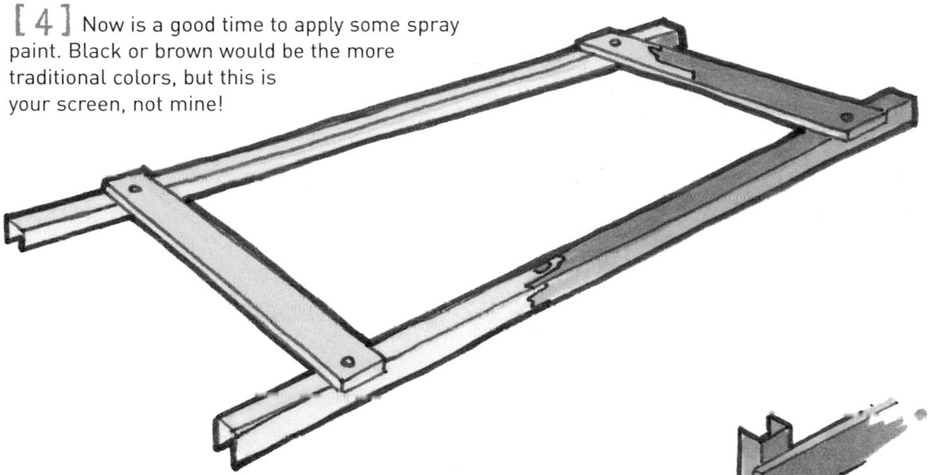

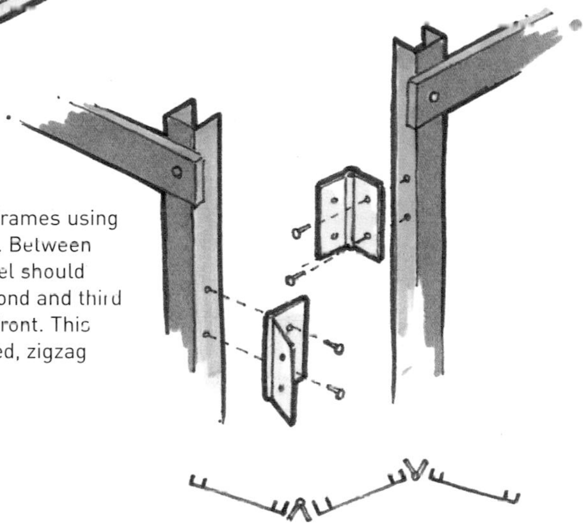

[5] Mount hinges between the frames using nuts, washers and machine screws. Between the first two frames, the hinge barrel should face the back, and between the second and third frames, the barrel should face the front. This will give the assembly that staggered, zigzag appeal.

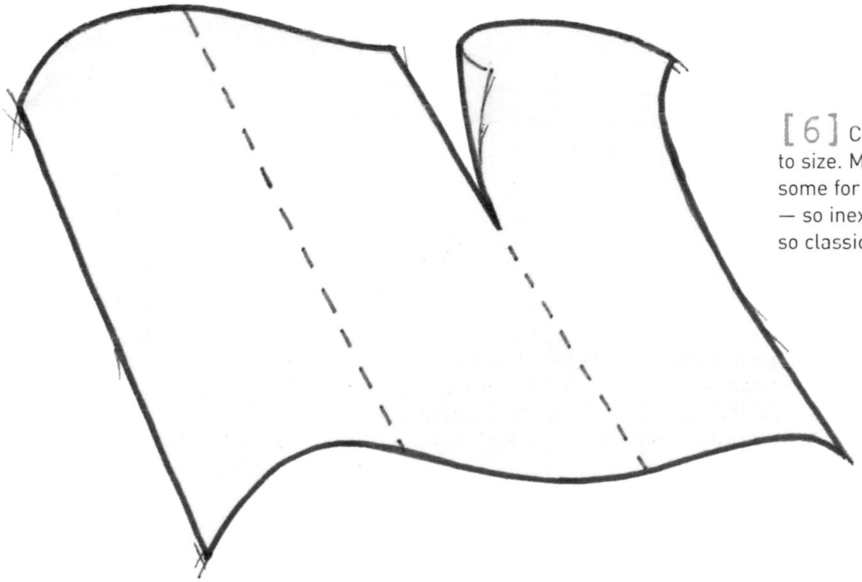

[6] Cut the muslin to size. Muslin is awesome for this project — so inexpensive, yet so classic looking.

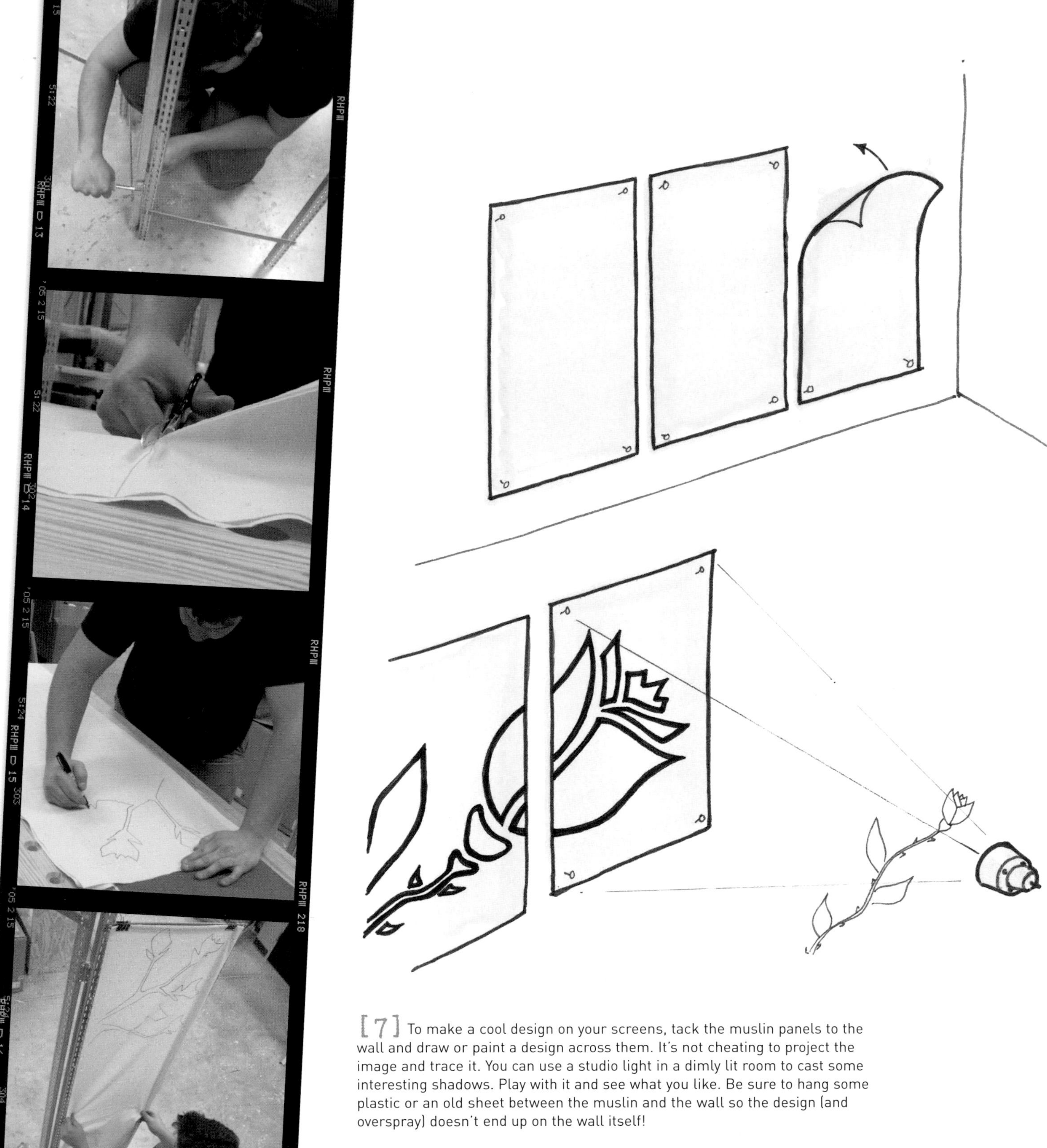

[7] To make a cool design on your screens, tack the muslin panels to the wall and draw or paint a design across them. It's not cheating to project the image and trace it. You can use a studio light in a dimly lit room to cast some interesting shadows. Play with it and see what you like. Be sure to hang some plastic or an old sheet between the muslin and the wall so the design (and overspray) doesn't end up on the wall itself!

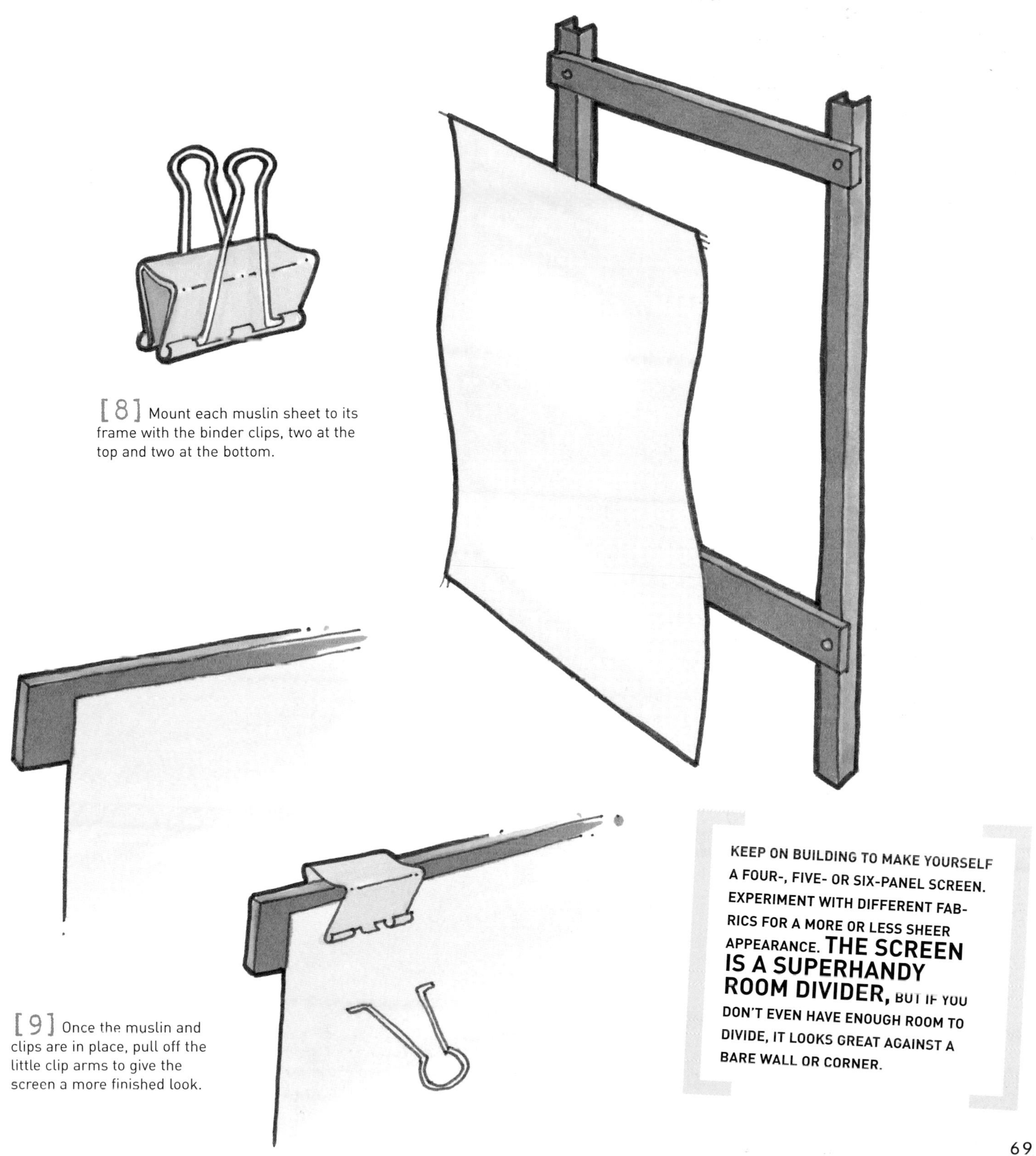

[8] Mount each muslin sheet to its frame with the binder clips, two at the top and two at the bottom.

[9] Once the muslin and clips are in place, pull off the little clip arms to give the screen a more finished look.

[KEEP ON BUILDING TO MAKE YOURSELF A FOUR-, FIVE- OR SIX-PANEL SCREEN. EXPERIMENT WITH DIFFERENT FABRICS FOR A MORE OR LESS SHEER APPEARANCE. **THE SCREEN IS A SUPERHANDY ROOM DIVIDER,** BUT IF YOU DON'T EVEN HAVE ENOUGH ROOM TO DIVIDE, IT LOOKS GREAT AGAINST A BARE WALL OR CORNER.]

[shady] LAMP

A hip little lamp on your bedside table or on a bookshelf is always a great indicator of good taste and a keen design eye. The only thing that could be cooler is designing and building the lamp yourself and not just getting the same one everyone else bought!

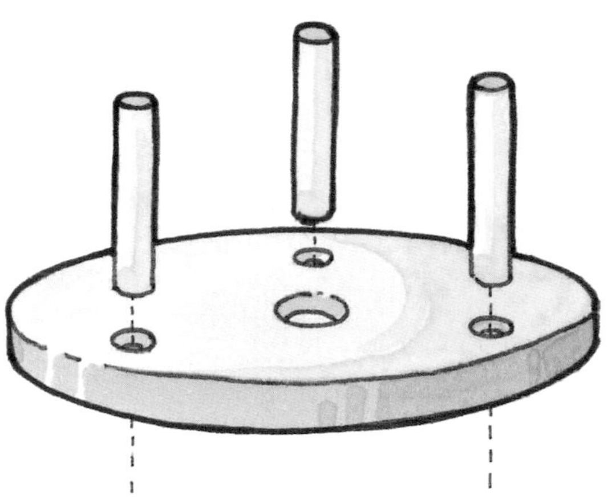

[1] Start with a circle of at least 1/2"-thick MDF or plywood at a diameter of 5". Drill some holes and drop three 1/4"-diameter dowels through the disk and stick them in place with some epoxy or wood glue.

[2] Wire up a lightbulb into the middle of the disk. I find cool fluorescent bulbs a little more versatile in custom-design projects like these. Be sure to grab a cord with one of those handy in-line cord thumb switches on it. Get some help from a friendly helper person at your local lighting shop.

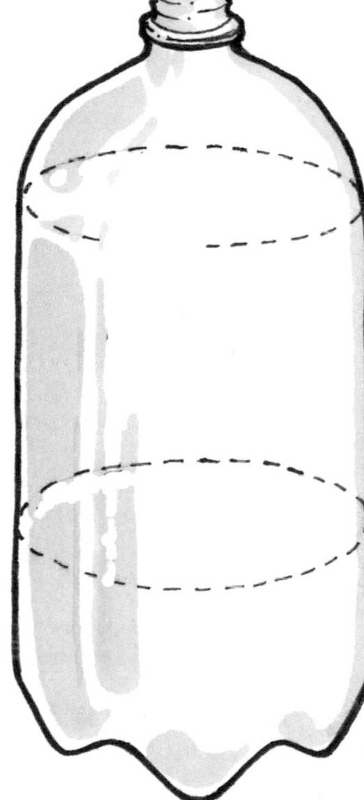

[3] This part is cool! Take an empty 2-liter bottle and dust it with a lacquer spray paint — just enough to frost the plastic a little. Then cut out the cylinder body of the bottle.

[THIS PROJECT IS SO CUSTOMIZABLE THAT **YOU CAN MAKE YOUR OWN COOL, UNIQUE LAMP.** MESS WITH THE COLORS YOU PAINT IT AND THE SHAPE THAT YOU CUT IT OUT IN. TRY USING THE WHOLE BODY OF THE BOTTLE AND PAINTING IT MANY COLORS, OR CUTTING CIRCLES OR TRIANGLES OUT OF THE BOTTLE!]

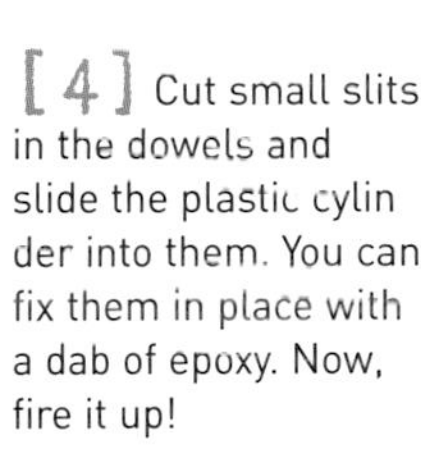

[4] Cut small slits in the dowels and slide the plastic cylinder into them. You can fix them in place with a dab of epoxy. Now, fire it up!

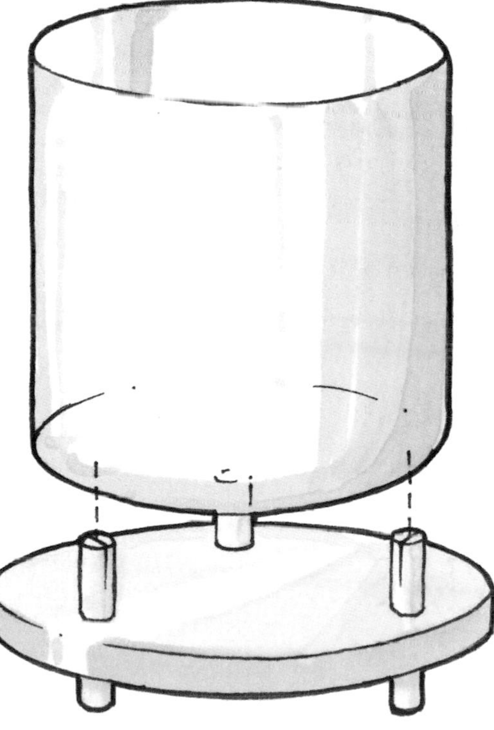

you'll need

1/2"-thick x 5"-diameter (13mm x 127mm) MDF or plywood

3 1/4"-diameter x 2" (6mm x 51mm) dowels

epoxy or wood glue

fluorescent lightbulb

electric cord with toggle switch

lacquer spray paint

2-liter plastic bottle (with label removed)

[oklahoma] CANDLEHOLDER

Don't have candles? You should! **Maybe you haven't gotten the memo, but candles are cool for anyone and everyone.** Add this simple candleholder to any room to change it from a crappy college apartment to a room with at least a little sophistication. Light some candles when a friend comes over for dinner, when you're chillin' out on the couch with a book or when you host the chess club's evening meeting.

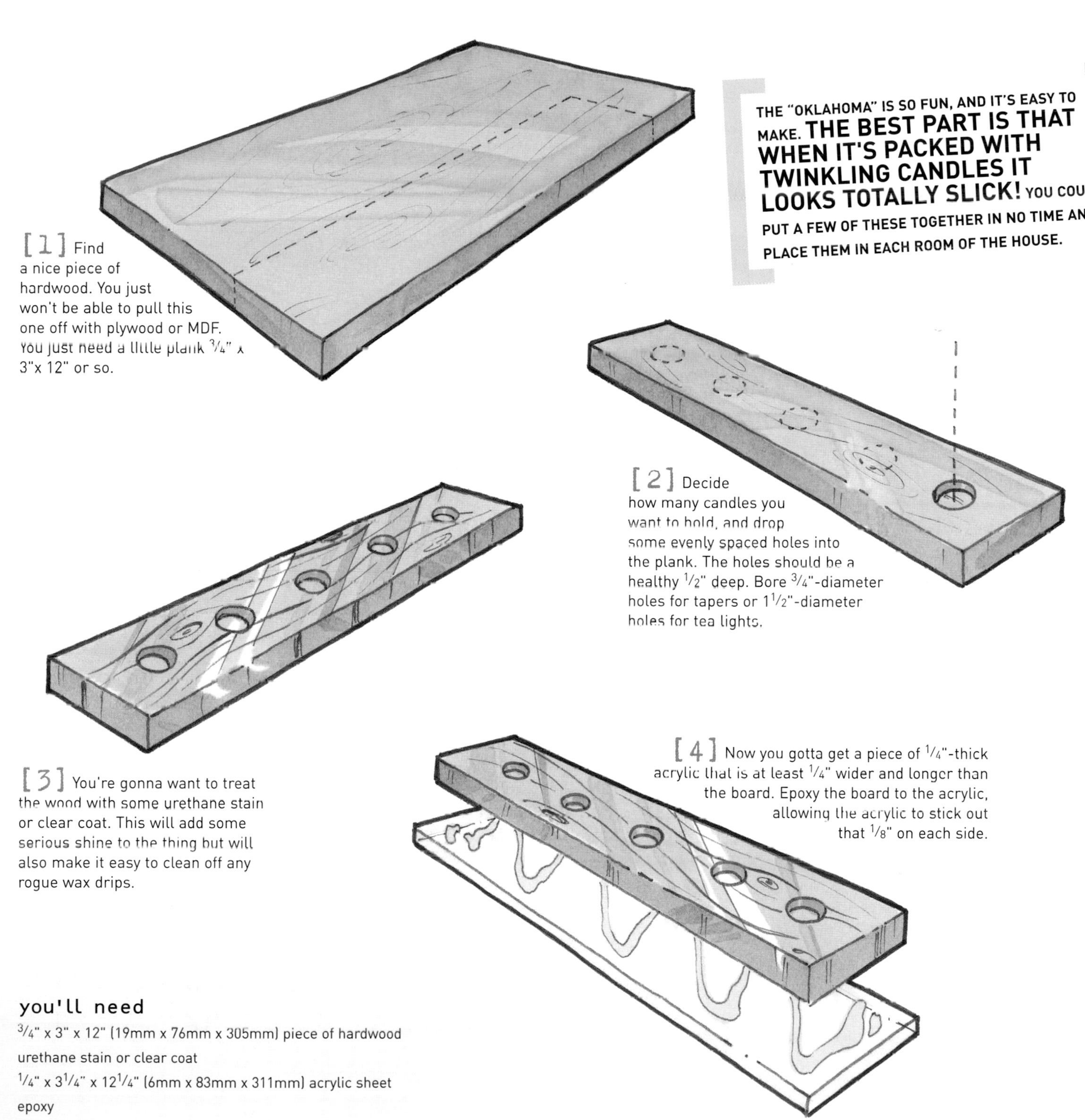

THE "OKLAHOMA" IS SO FUN, AND IT'S EASY TO MAKE. **THE BEST PART IS THAT WHEN IT'S PACKED WITH TWINKLING CANDLES IT LOOKS TOTALLY SLICK!** YOU COULD PUT A FEW OF THESE TOGETHER IN NO TIME AND PLACE THEM IN EACH ROOM OF THE HOUSE.

[1] Find a nice piece of hardwood. You just won't be able to pull this one off with plywood or MDF. You just need a little plank 3/4" x 3"x 12" or so.

[2] Decide how many candles you want to hold, and drop some evenly spaced holes into the plank. The holes should be a healthy 1/2" deep. Bore 3/4"-diameter holes for tapers or 1 1/2"-diameter holes for tea lights.

[3] You're gonna want to treat the wood with some urethane stain or clear coat. This will add some serious shine to the thing but will also make it easy to clean off any rogue wax drips.

[4] Now you gotta get a piece of 1/4"-thick acrylic that is at least 1/4" wider and longer than the board. Epoxy the board to the acrylic, allowing the acrylic to stick out that 1/8" on each side.

you'll need

3/4" x 3" x 12" (19mm x 76mm x 305mm) piece of hardwood

urethane stain or clear coat

1/4" x 3 1/4" x 12 1/4" (6mm x 83mm x 311mm) acrylic sheet

epoxy

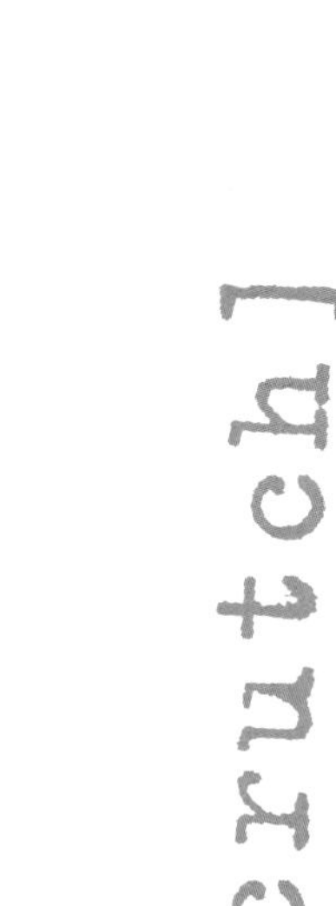

COATRACK

If you live at all like I live — coats and parkas occupying different nooks of the living room, dress shirts and pants strewn around the bedroom floor, plus towels and silk robes hanging from any odds and ends in the bathroom — then you're going to need a few of these handy clothes hangers.

Put a "Crutch" together for the front door, and when you see how handy it is, you'll be building one for every room!

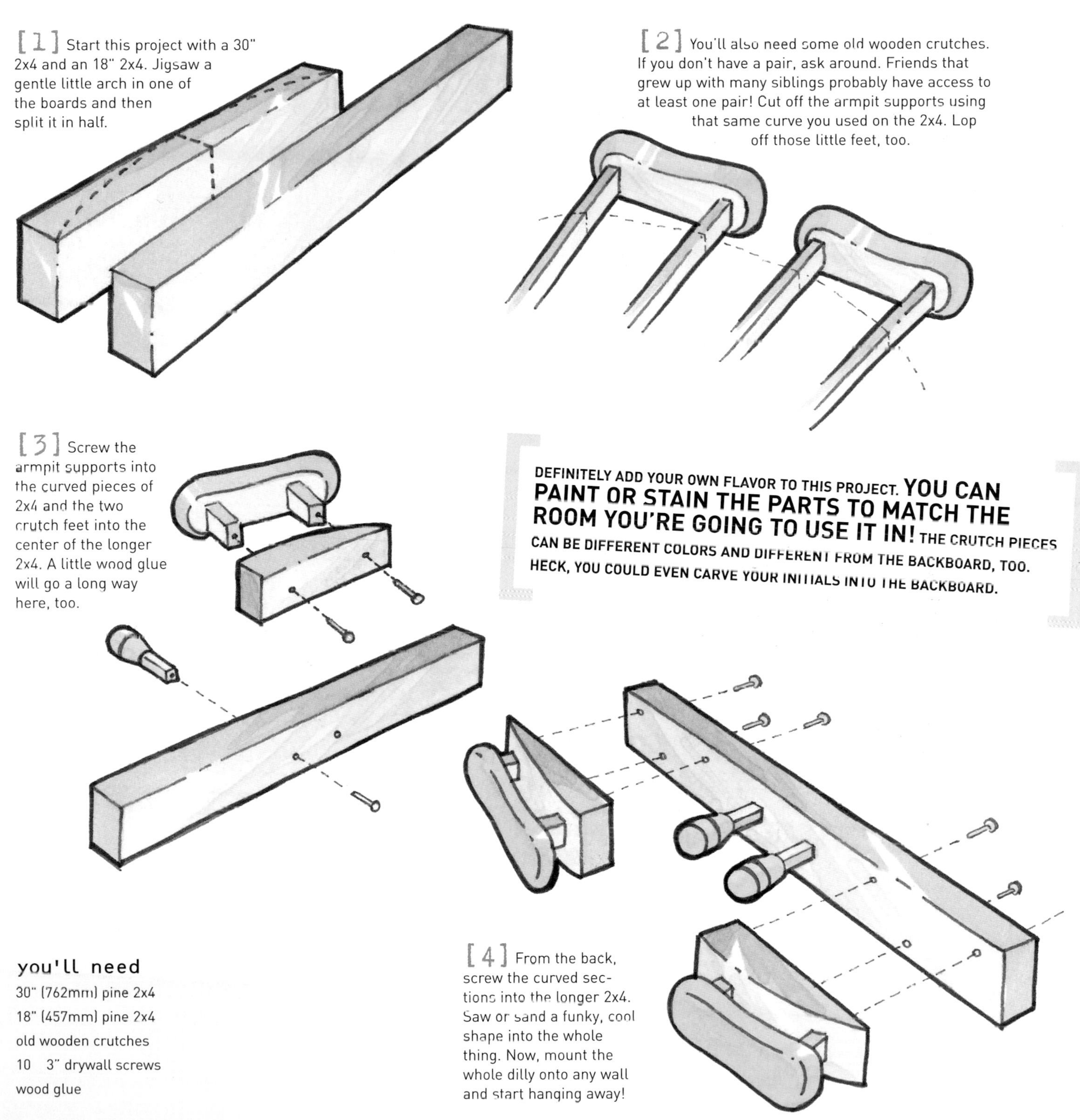

[1] Start this project with a 30" 2x4 and an 18" 2x4. Jigsaw a gentle little arch in one of the boards and then split it in half.

[2] You'll also need some old wooden crutches. If you don't have a pair, ask around. Friends that grew up with many siblings probably have access to at least one pair! Cut off the armpit supports using that same curve you used on the 2x4. Lop off those little feet, too.

[3] Screw the armpit supports into the curved pieces of 2x4 and the two crutch feet into the center of the longer 2x4. A little wood glue will go a long way here, too.

[DEFINITELY ADD YOUR OWN FLAVOR TO THIS PROJECT. **YOU CAN PAINT OR STAIN THE PARTS TO MATCH THE ROOM YOU'RE GOING TO USE IT IN!** THE CRUTCH PIECES CAN BE DIFFERENT COLORS AND DIFFERENT FROM THE BACKBOARD, TOO. HECK, YOU COULD EVEN CARVE YOUR INITIALS INTO THE BACKBOARD.]

[4] From the back, screw the curved sections into the longer 2x4. Saw or sand a funky, cool shape into the whole thing. Now, mount the whole dilly onto any wall and start hanging away!

you'll need

30" (762mm) pine 2x4

18" (457mm) pine 2x4

old wooden crutches

10 3" drywall screws

wood glue

[dumpster] JUNK BOWL

Have you ever been late for an important date and as you were about to race out the door, you realized you had no idea where you'd left your keys and wallet? The "Dumpster" is the ultra-mod solution to that problem. **Now, your wallet, keys and loose change have a home!**

YOU CAN MAKE LITTLE TEST SAMPLES TO SEE WHICH COLOR TAKES THE BEST WITH YOUR RUBBER. IT'S POSSIBLE EVEN TO POUR LAYERS OF DIFFERENT COLORS; JUST BE SURE THE PREVIOUS ONE IS COMPLETELY CURED. FEEL FREE TO MESS WITH THE MOLD. **GLUE THINGS INTO THE MOLD TO CREATE DIFFERENT TEXTURES AND DESIGNS!**

[1] You need two vastly different-size bowls. The small bowl should fit easily into the other one, and upside down at that! Dig around some thrift stores, yard sales or Mom's kitchen for some old, cheap kitchenware.

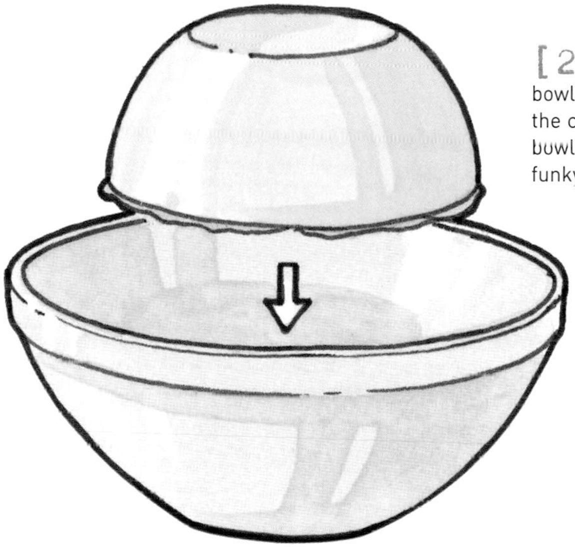

[2] Epoxy the smaller bowl upside down into the center of the larger bowl. This is now your funky mold.

[3] Now you need to pour some rubber into the mold. I used a two-part urethane mixture purchased off of the Internet. The density I chose is called shore 40A, and it feels kind of like a bouncy ball. Don't forget some kind of release agent! See the suppliers list at the back of the book.

[4] When you mix your rubber, feel free to add some food coloring so you don't get a really bland color. Pour the mixture into the mold and watch as it cures. When it's done, pop it out and voila!

you'll need

2 bowls of different sizes

epoxy

two-part urethane mixture

release agent

food coloring

[WORK SPACE]

EVERYONE NEEDS A PLACE TO PUT THE PEN TO THE PAD. **HOW PRODUCTIVE WE ARE, HOW CREATIVE OUR WORK IS AND HOW MUCH WE WORK IS AFFECTED BY OUR WORK SPACE SURROUNDINGS.** AFTER YOU PUT THE PIECES IN THIS CHAPTER TOGETHER, YOU'LL FIND THAT YOU STAY MORE ORGANIZED, WORK MORE EFFICIENTLY AND CREATE BETTER OUTPUT. PROBABLY MOST IMPORTANT, WITH A LUXURIOUS NEW DESK, TRICKED-OUT SIDE TABLE AND ULTRACOOL CHAIR, YOU'LL WANT TO SIT DOWN AND GET WORK DONE. ADD AN AMPLE BOOKCASE AND FUN FILE CABINET, AND YOU'LL BE HUNTING FOR THINGS TO CATALOG AND ALPHABETIZE. JUST DON'T FORGET WHO HELPED YOU GET THERE WHEN YOU MAKE YOUR FIRST MILLION!

DESIGNS
DUE
MONDAY!

[royalty] DESK

We all need a place in the crib to get some work done. Whether it's for home-work, business or just a lot of bidding on eBay, the "Royalty" is the sleekest, coolest desk around. **Build this desk and just try not to get more work done and look good doing it!**

cutting list

REF.	NO.	PART	STOCK	INCHES	MILLIMETERS
				THICKNESS X WIDTH X LENGTH	
A	1	top	oak-faced ply	3/4 x 30 x 60	19 x 762 x 1524
B	2	stretchers	pine 2x4	1 1/2 x 3 1/2 x 48	38 x 89 x 1219
C	4	legs	pine 2x4	1 1/2 x 3 1/2 x 28	38 x 89 x 711

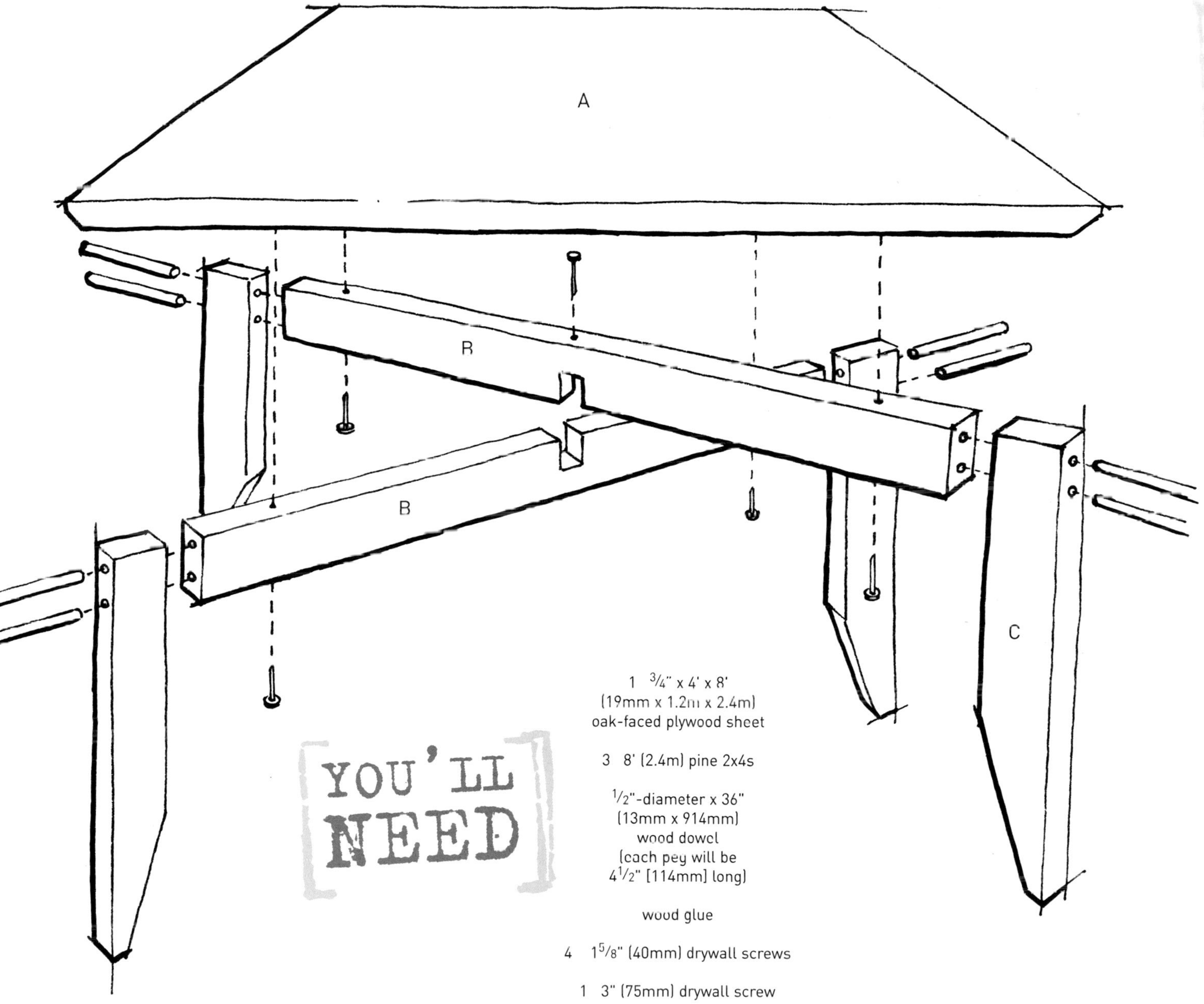

YOU'LL NEED

1 3/4" x 4' x 8' (19mm x 1.2m x 2.4m) oak-faced plywood sheet

3 8' (2.4m) pine 2x4s

1/2"-diameter x 36" (13mm x 914mm) wood dowel (each peg will be 4 1/2" [114mm] long)

wood glue

4 1 5/8" (40mm) drywall screws

1 3" (75mm) drywall screw

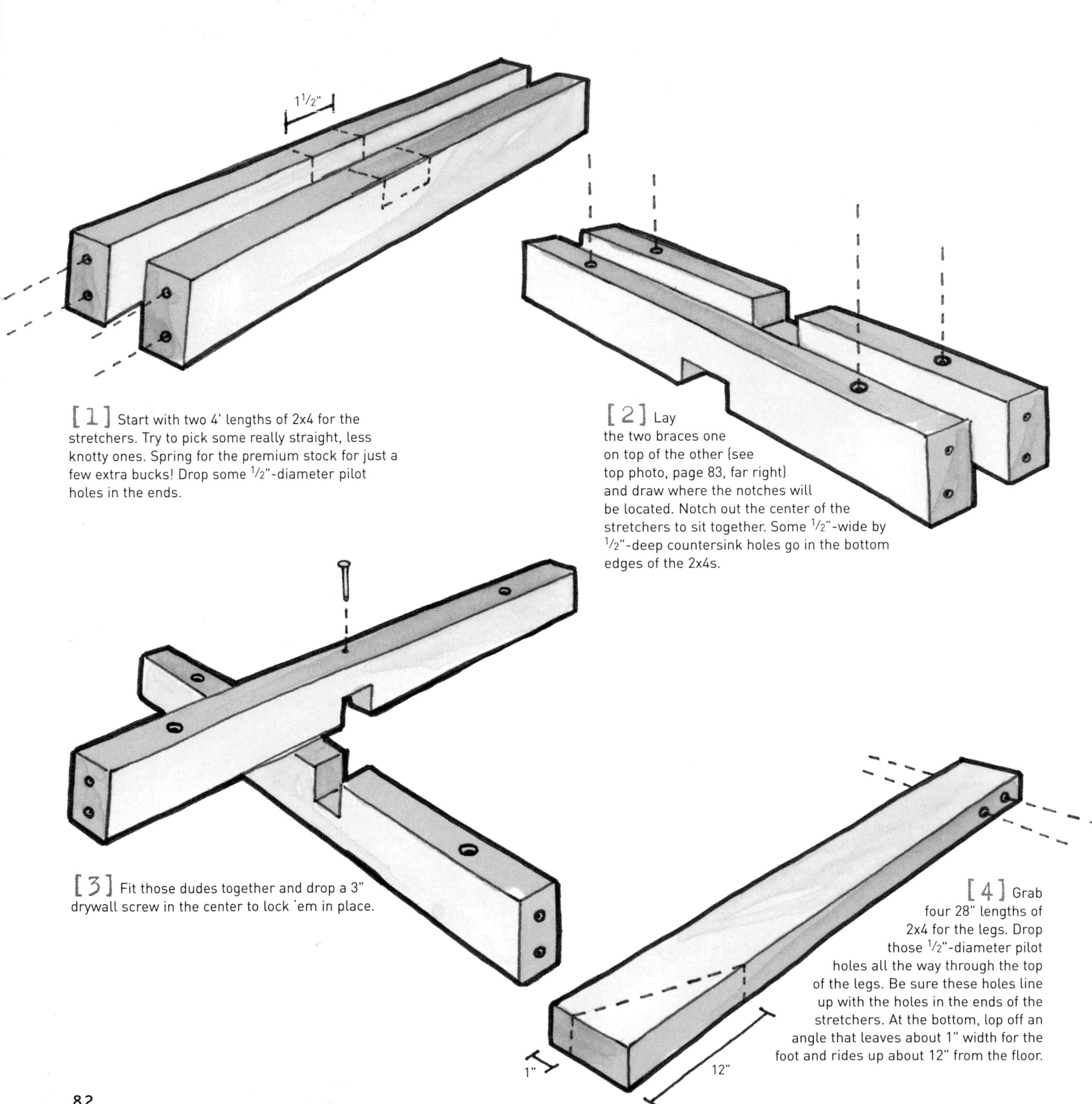

[1] Start with two 4' lengths of 2x4 for the stretchers. Try to pick some really straight, less knotty ones. Spring for the premium stock for just a few extra bucks! Drop some 1/2"-diameter pilot holes in the ends.

[2] Lay the two braces one on top of the other (see top photo, page 83, far right) and draw where the notches will be located. Notch out the center of the stretchers to sit together. Some 1/2"-wide by 1/2"-deep countersink holes go in the bottom edges of the 2x4s.

[3] Fit those dudes together and drop a 3" drywall screw in the center to lock 'em in place.

[4] Grab four 28" lengths of 2x4 for the legs. Drop those 1/2"-diameter pilot holes all the way through the top of the legs. Be sure these holes line up with the holes in the ends of the stretchers. At the bottom, lop off an angle that leaves about 1" width for the foot and rides up about 12" from the floor.

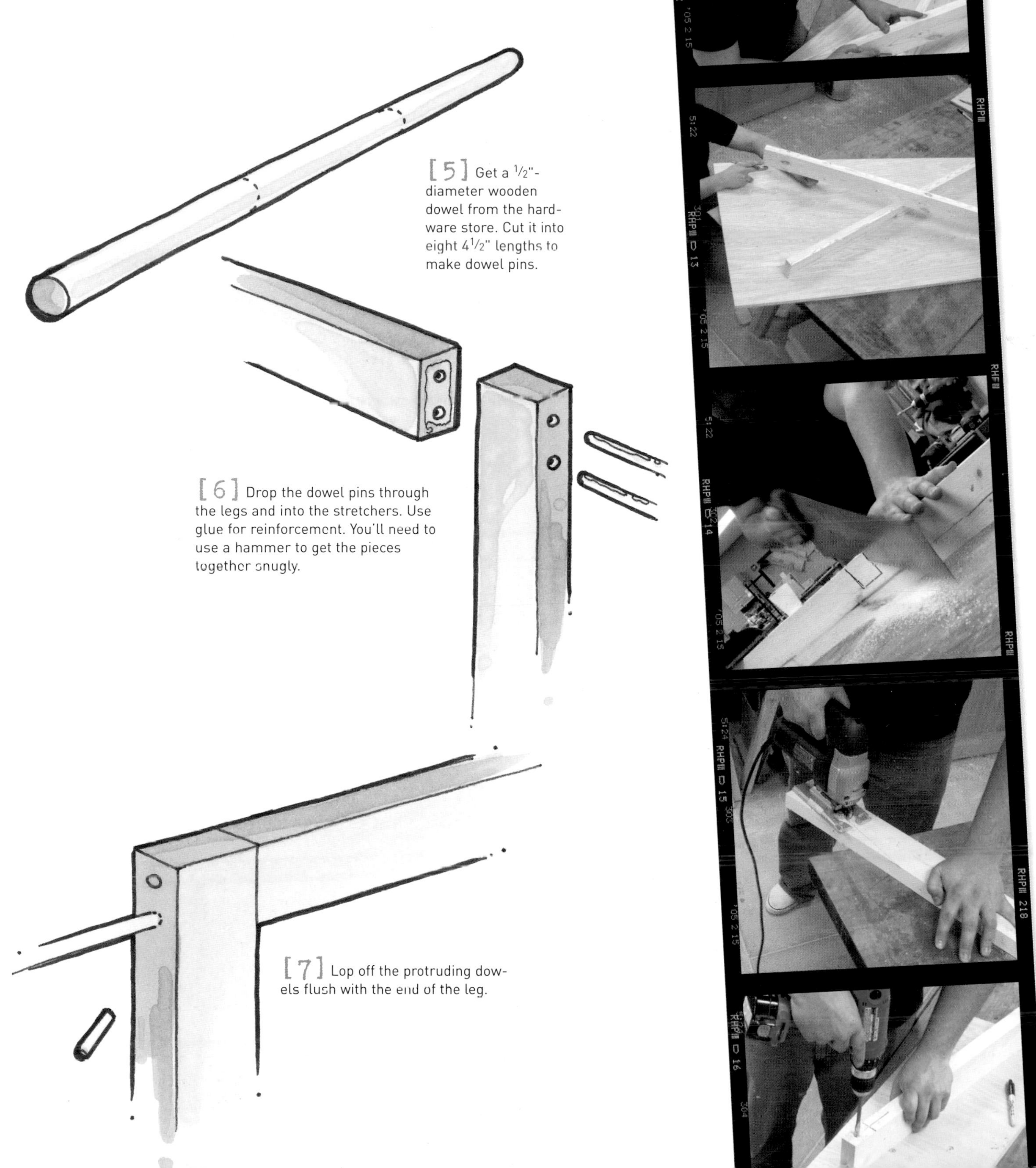

[5] Get a ½"-diameter wooden dowel from the hardware store. Cut it into eight 4½" lengths to make dowel pins.

[6] Drop the dowel pins through the legs and into the stretchers. Use glue for reinforcement. You'll need to use a hammer to get the pieces together snugly.

[7] Lop off the protruding dowels flush with the end of the leg.

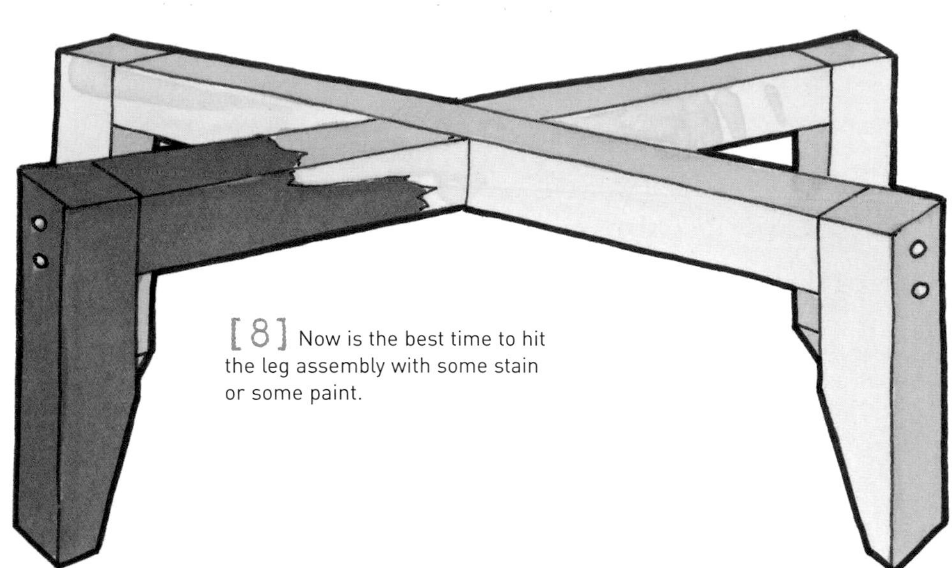

[8] Now is the best time to hit the leg assembly with some stain or some paint.

[9] Bevel the edge of a 3/4" x 30" x 60" sheet of plywood for the top. You should be able to find a nice veneered piece of plywood. It'll cost a bit more, but it'll look much better than the pine plywood. If you can't adjust the foot plate of your saw, you can rough-cut it freehand and then do a lot of sanding.

Side view of top's edge detail

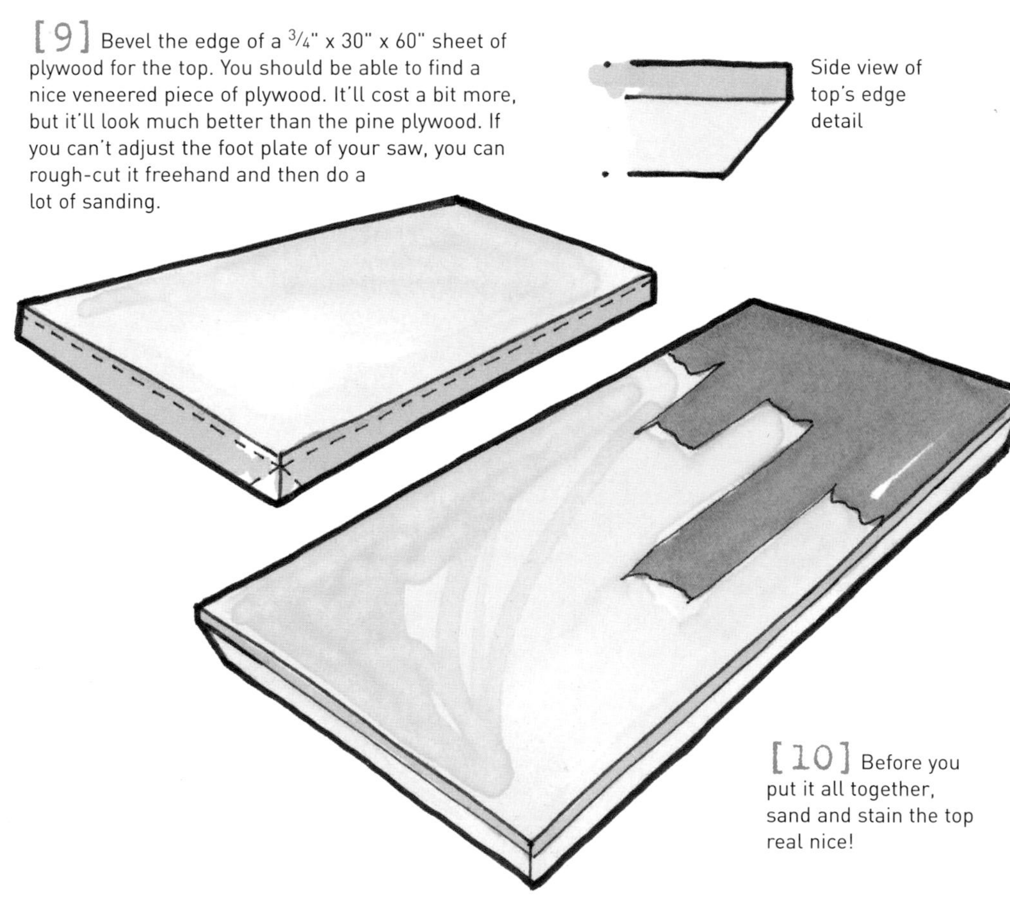

[10] Before you put it all together, sand and stain the top real nice!

[11] Drop the top onto the leg assembly now. Screw the top in place from the bottom up. Make sure the $1\frac{5}{8}$" drywall screws aren't too long so they don't penetrate the top face of the desk. Use a hand screwdriver to install these screws so you don't drive them too fast and things get out of control.

USE BLACK PAINT FOR THE LEGS AND A LIGHT STAIN ON THE TOP, OR YOU CAN PAINT YOURS PINK IF YOU WANT. IF YOU LIKE THAT SORT OF THING, I MEAN.

[little prince] SIDE TABLE

What's the perfect complement to that supernice desk you now have? How about an extremely handy matching side table?! **This *li'l thang* will add endless versatility to the desk or any office space,** and people will flip when they discover the handy slide-out second tabletop.

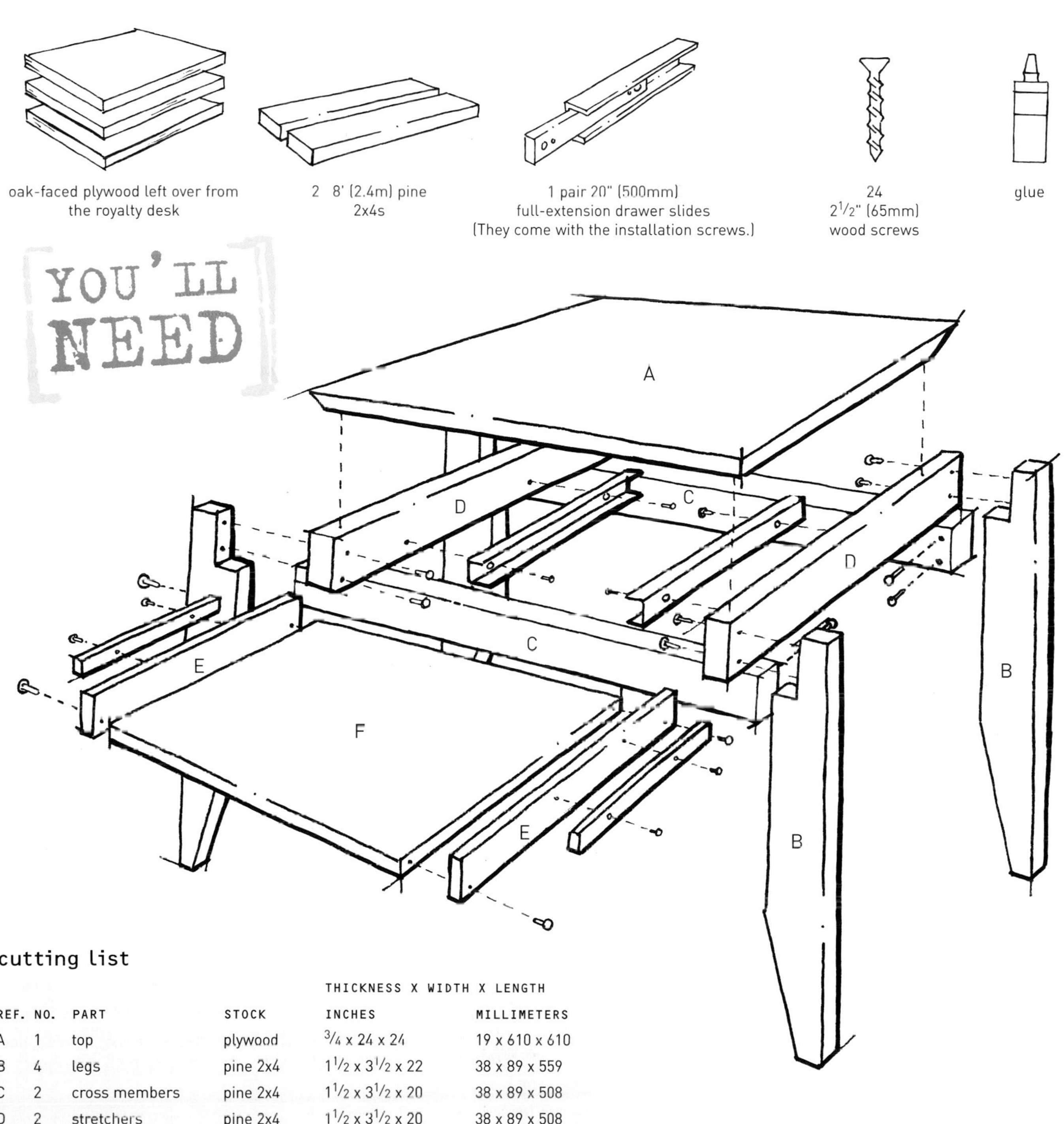

cutting list

REF.	NO.	PART	STOCK	THICKNESS X WIDTH X LENGTH INCHES	MILLIMETERS
A	1	top	plywood	3/4 x 24 x 24	19 x 610 x 610
B	4	legs	pine 2x4	1 1/2 x 3 1/2 x 22	38 x 89 x 559
C	2	cross members	pine 2x4	1 1/2 x 3 1/2 x 20	38 x 89 x 508
D	2	stretchers	pine 2x4	1 1/2 x 3 1/2 x 20	38 x 89 x 508
F	2	tray sides	plywood	3/4 x 2 x 20	19 x 51 x 508
F	1	tray bottom	plywood	3/4 x 10 x 20	19 x 254 x 508

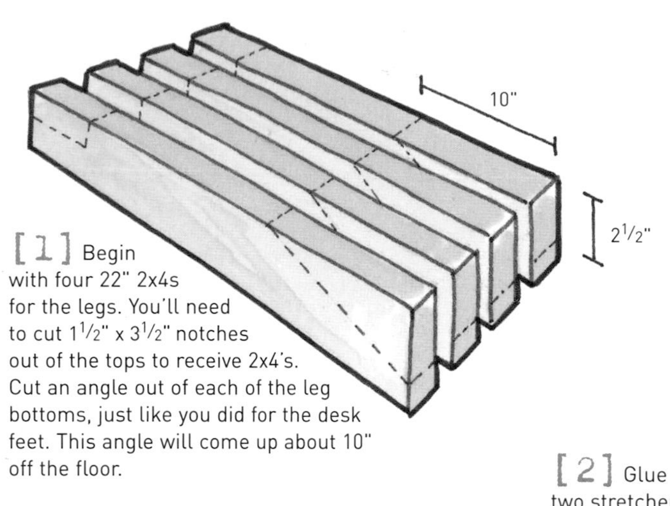

[1] Begin with four 22" 2x4s for the legs. You'll need to cut $1^1/_2$" x $3^1/_2$" notches out of the tops to receive 2x4's. Cut an angle out of each of the leg bottoms, just like you did for the desk feet. This angle will come up about 10" off the floor.

[2] Glue and screw two stretchers into the notches of the legs. Make two of these assemblies.

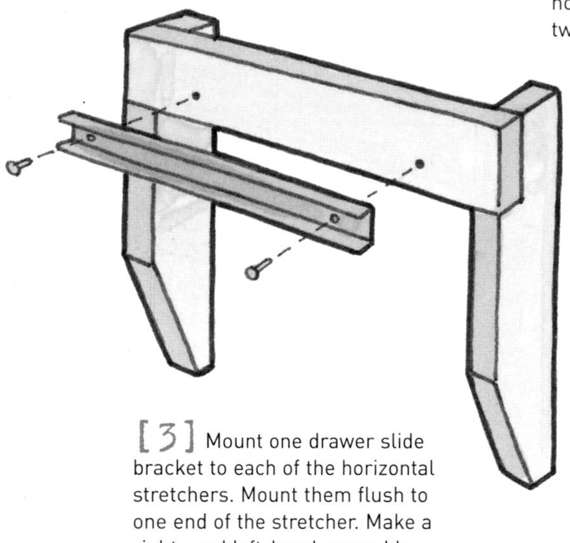

[3] Mount one drawer slide bracket to each of the horizontal stretchers. Mount them flush to one end of the stretcher. Make a right- and left-hand assembly.

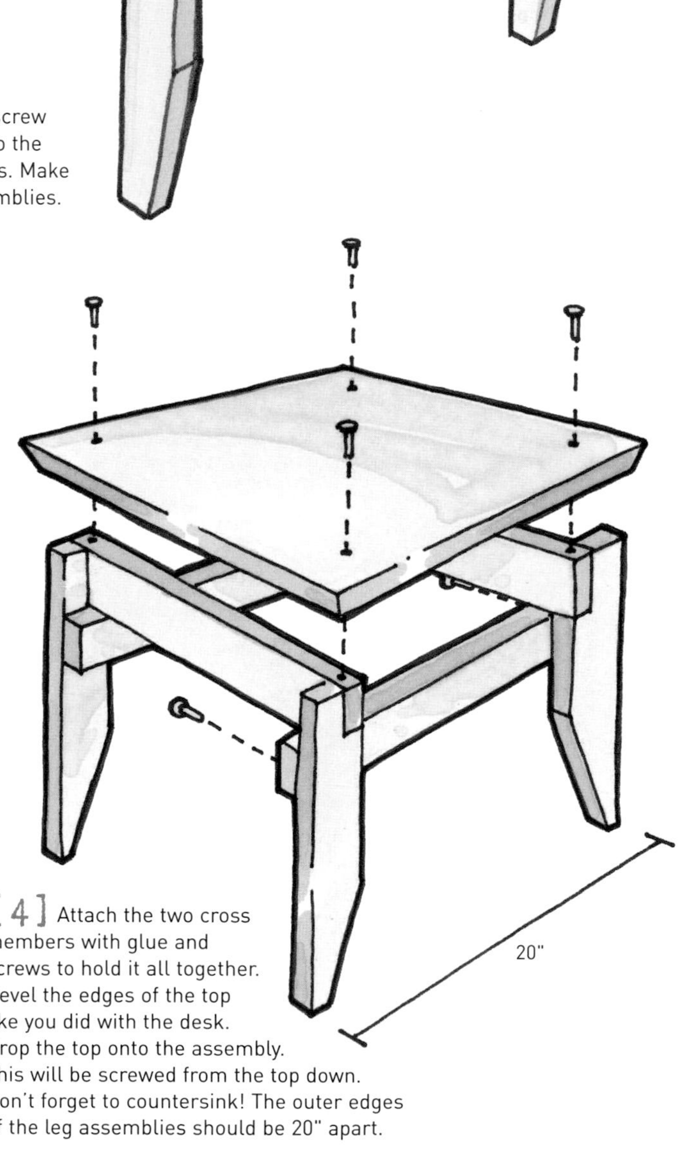

[4] Attach the two cross members with glue and screws to hold it all together. Bevel the edges of the top like you did with the desk. Drop the top onto the assembly. This will be screwed from the top down. Don't forget to countersink! The outer edges of the leg assemblies should be 20" apart.

YOU CAN MAKE YOUR SIDE TABLE ANY HEIGHT OR SIZE YOU WANT. THIS ONE WAS DESIGNED TO FIT UNDER THE DESK AND AWAY TO THE SIDE WHEN NOT IN USE. WANT TO GET EXTRA CRAZY? BEEF UP THE TABLETOP TO DESK HEIGHT AND USE THE SLIDE-OUT TRAY AS A KEYBOARD TRAY — AN AWESOME LITTLE COMPUTER DESK FOR THE PAD WITH A LITTLE LESS ROOM!

[5] Screw together the tray sides and bottom. This table is designed for use with 1/2"-thick drawer slides. Be sure your assembled tray is 1" smaller than the opening it goes into. Heads up!

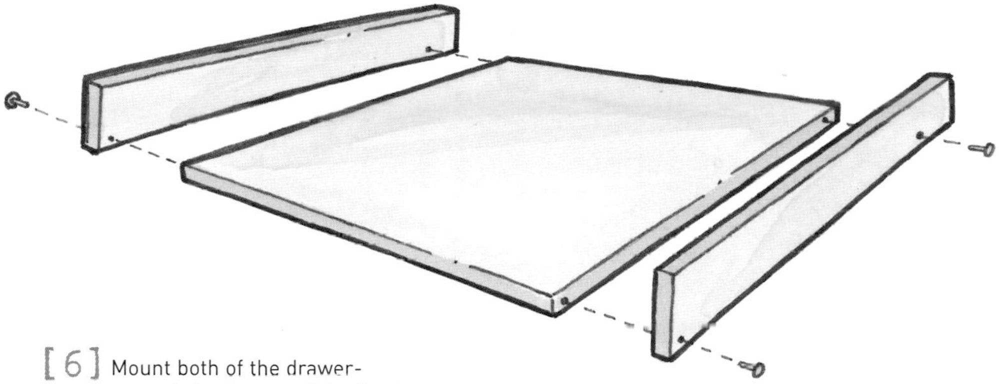

[6] Mount both of the drawer-mount parts of the drawer slides flush to the same edge of the tray sides.

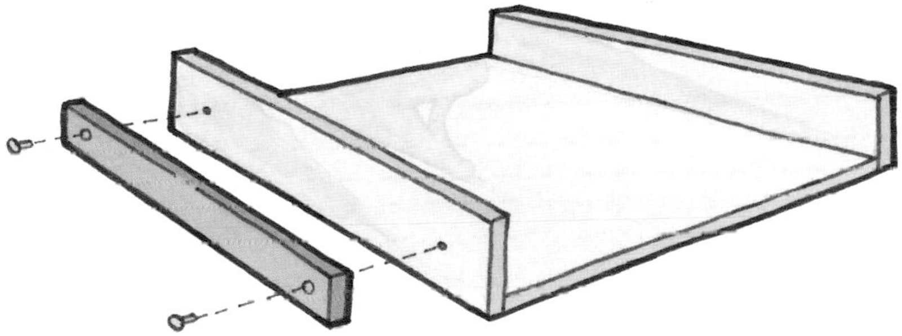

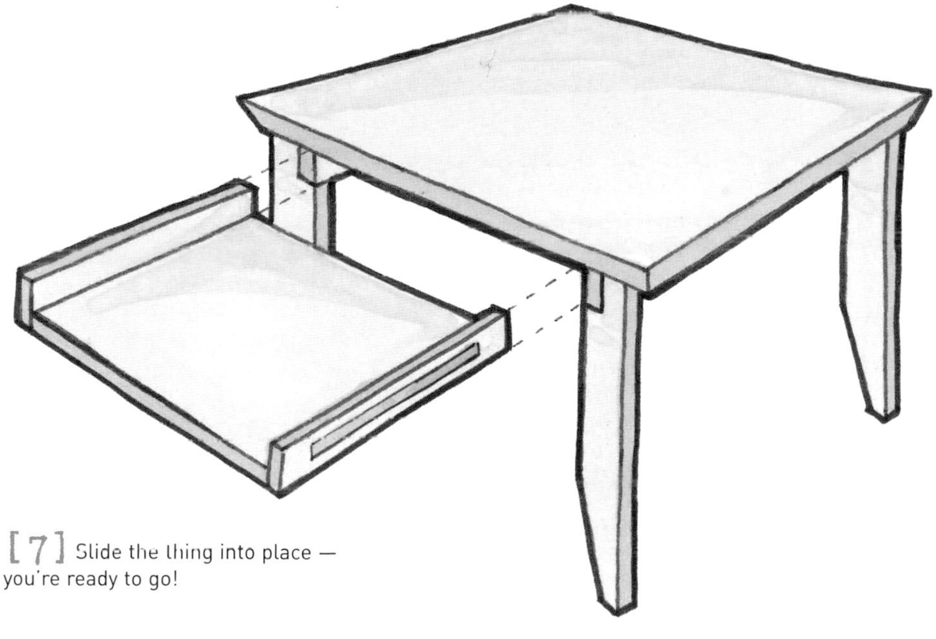

[7] Slide the thing into place — you're ready to go!

[five stack] BOOKCASE

Milk crates? Cinder blocks and wood boards? Puh-leez! **This bookcase isn't any harder to assemble than it is to stack wood and brick, so take a few minutes and put this project together.** Trust me, it'll be a much more elegant stack of wood than anything your buddies have.

YOU'LL NEED

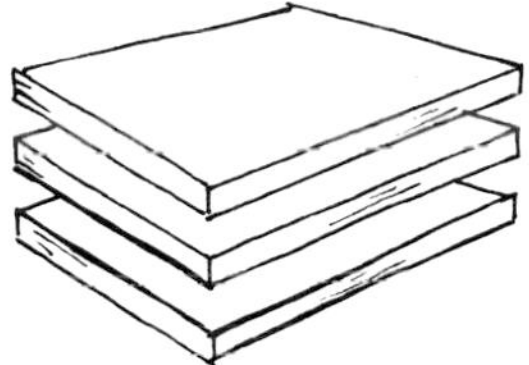

5 plywood or ready-made shelves

4 $1^{5}/_{8}$"-diameter x 6' (40mm x 1.8m) steel pipes

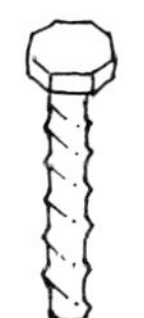

20 $^{1}/_{4}$" - 20 x $1^{3}/_{4}$" (6mm x 45mm hex bolts

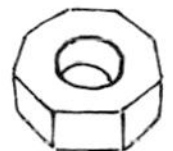

20 $^{1}/_{4}$" - 20 (6mm) hex nuts

20 2" (50mm) drywall screws

cutting list

				THICKNESS X WIDTH X LENGTH	
REF.	NO.	PART	STOCK	INCHES	MILLIMETERS
A	5	shelves	plywood	$^{3}/_{4}$ x 12 x 36	19 x 305 x 914
B	2	back supports	plywood	$^{3}/_{4}$ x 14 x $64^{3}/_{4}$	19 x 356 x 1645

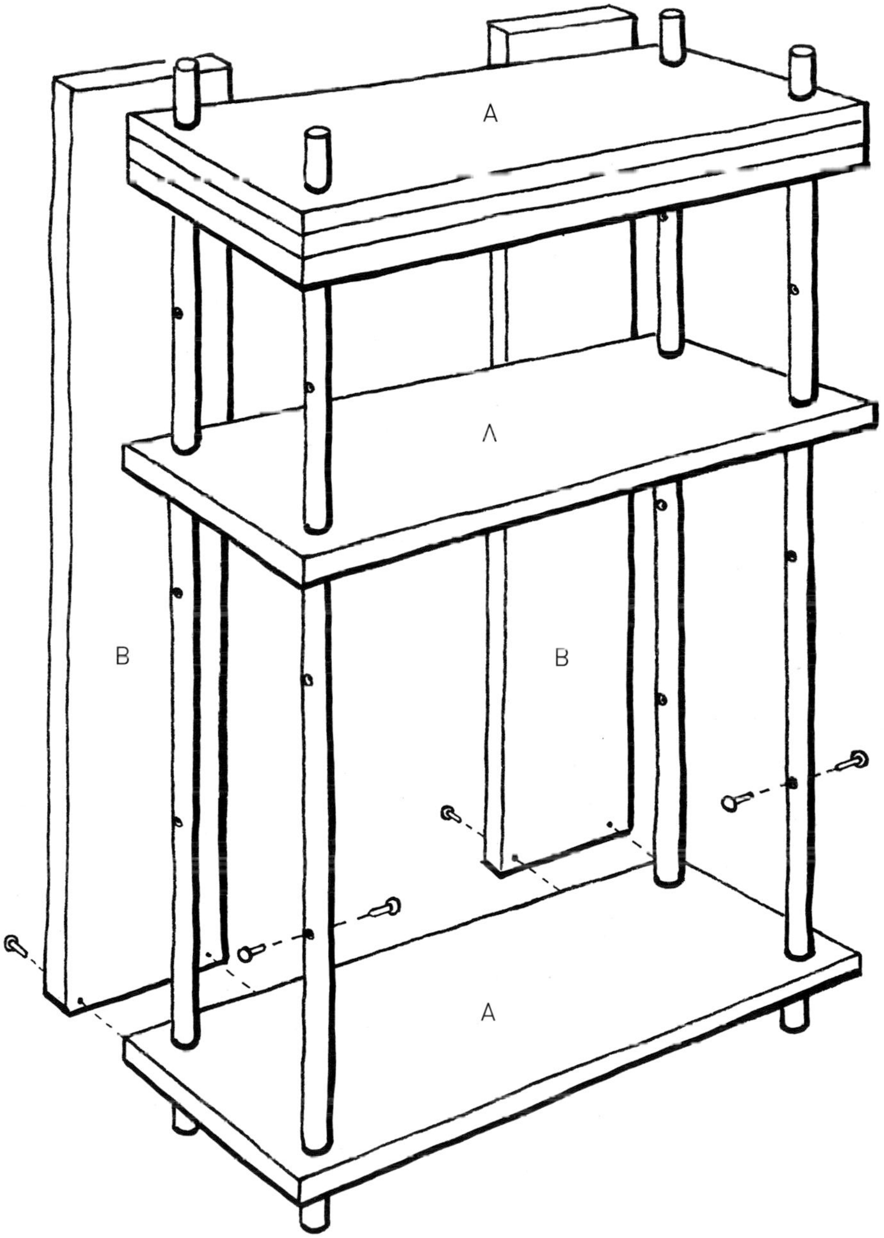

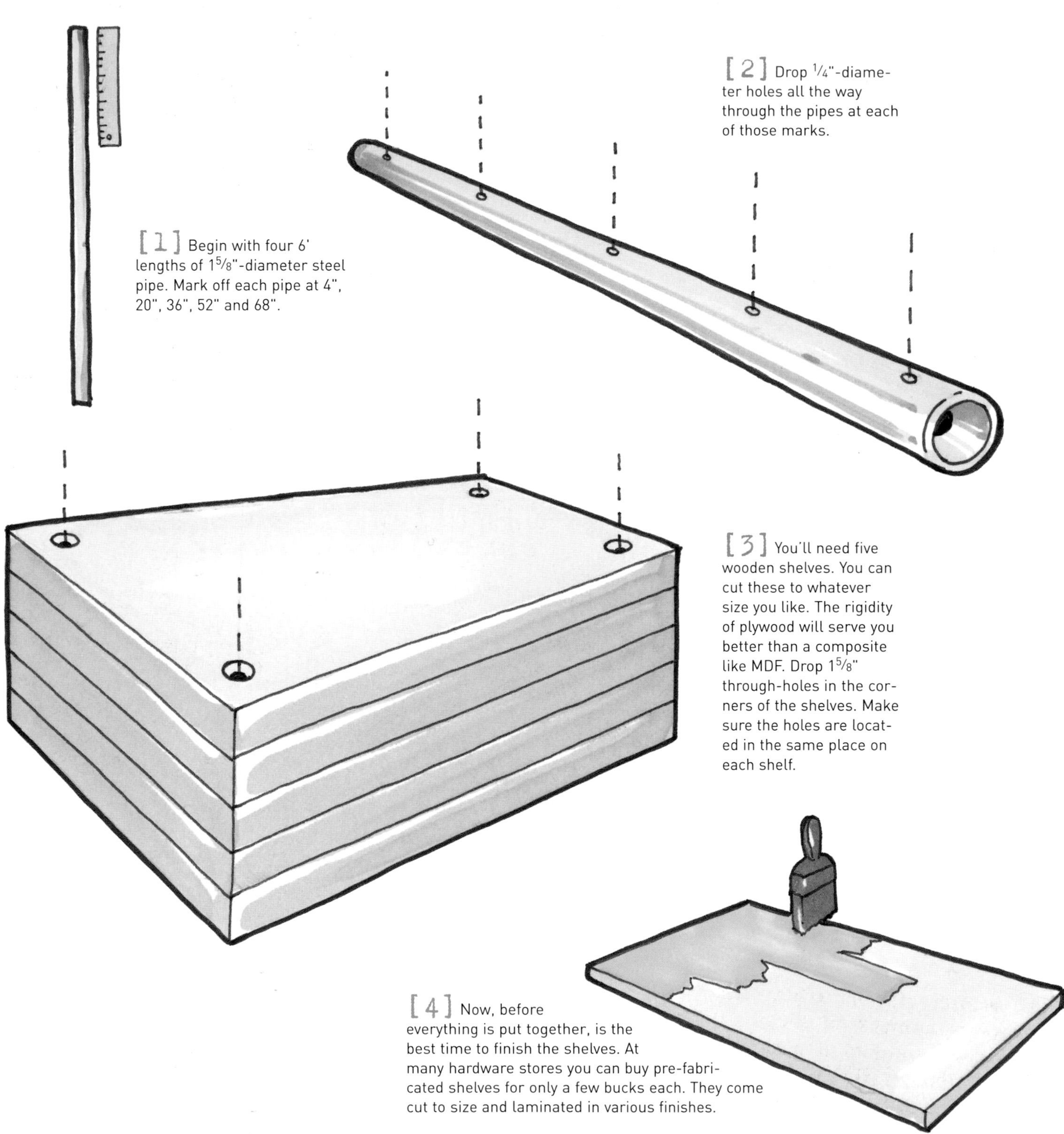

[1] Begin with four 6' lengths of $1\frac{5}{8}$"-diameter steel pipe. Mark off each pipe at 4", 20", 36", 52" and 68".

[2] Drop $\frac{1}{4}$"-diameter holes all the way through the pipes at each of those marks.

[3] You'll need five wooden shelves. You can cut these to whatever size you like. The rigidity of plywood will serve you better than a composite like MDF. Drop $1\frac{5}{8}$" through-holes in the corners of the shelves. Make sure the holes are located in the same place on each shelf.

[4] Now, before everything is put together, is the best time to finish the shelves. At many hardware stores you can buy pre-fabricated shelves for only a few bucks each. They come cut to size and laminated in various finishes.

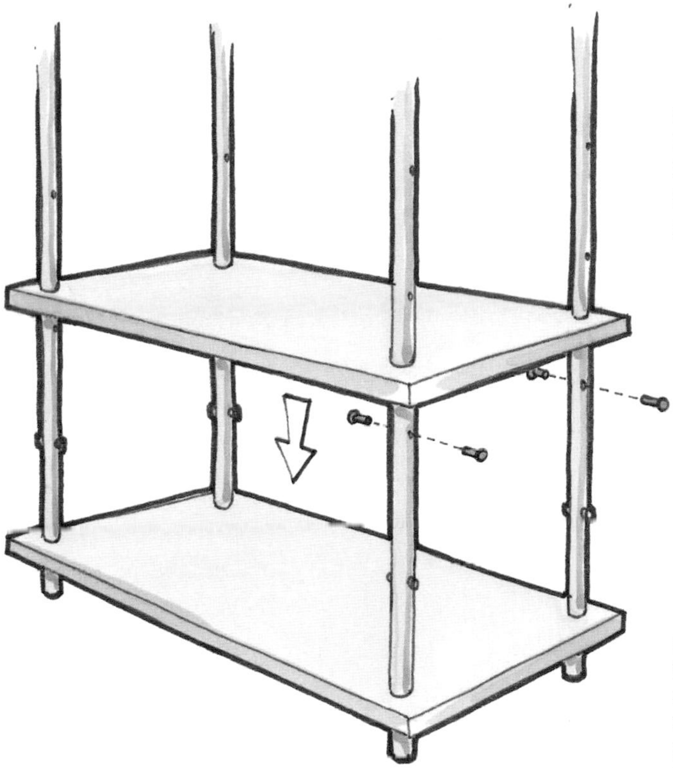

[5] Start by installing the hex bolts and nuts in the bottom hole of each pipe. Drop a shelf in place and repeat.

[6] Screw two supports onto the back of the bookcase. If you are using prelaminated shelves for these supports, join them behind the middle shelf.

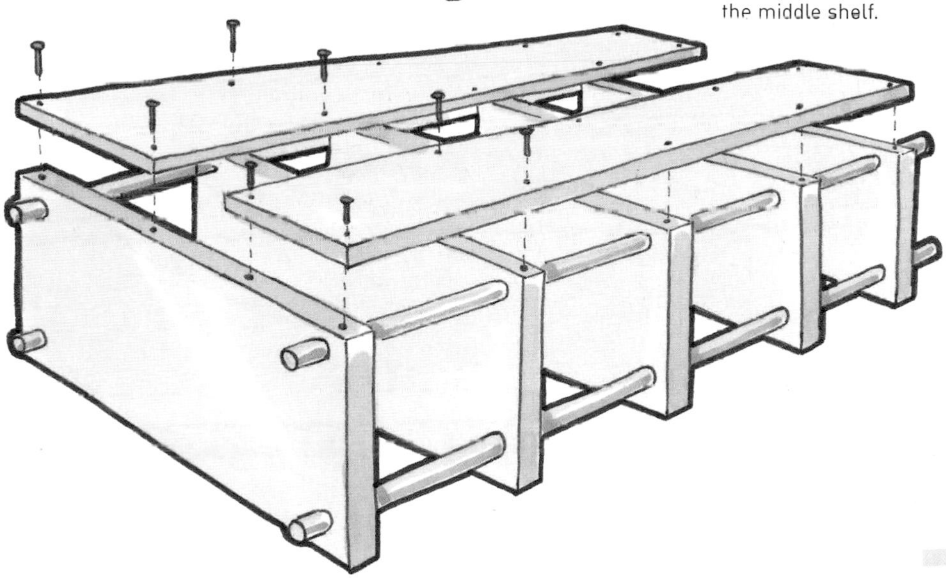

[THIS PROJECT STARTS OUT ALMOST DONE IF YOU USE THE PREFAB BOARDS FROM THE HARDWARE STORE. YOU CAN USUALLY FIND A FEW DIFFERENT FINISHES, FROM A MELAMINE LAMINATE TO AN OAK OR MAPLE VENEER. **IF YOU CHOOSE PLYWOOD, THOUGH, YOU CAN PAINT OR STAIN THE SHELVES ANY COLOR YOU WANT!**]

[paperboy] FILE CABINET

If you want a really complete work space, you'll need someplace to put all your papers — **from treasure maps to bills, multimillion-dollar business contracts to love letters.** The "Paperboy" can handle it all!

YOU'LL NEED

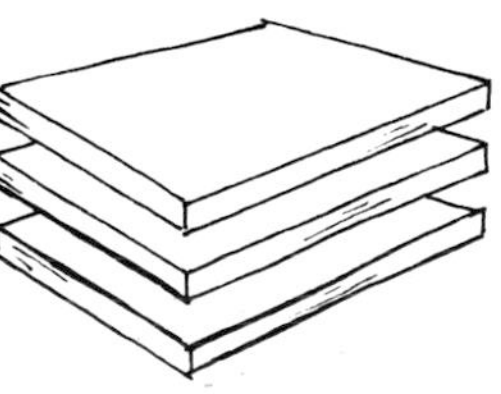

3 3/4" x 24" x 24" (19mm x 610mm x 610mm) pieces of plywood

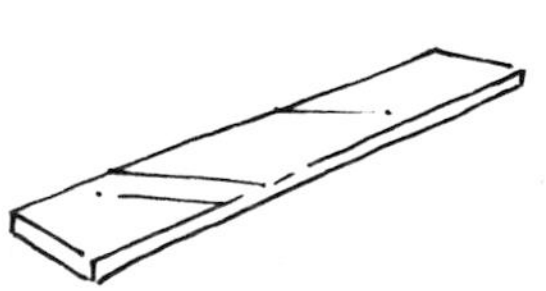

1 1/8" x 1" x 36" (3mm x 25mm x 914mm) steel strap

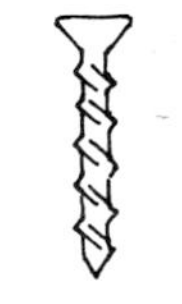

8 3" (75mm) wood screws

8 finish washers

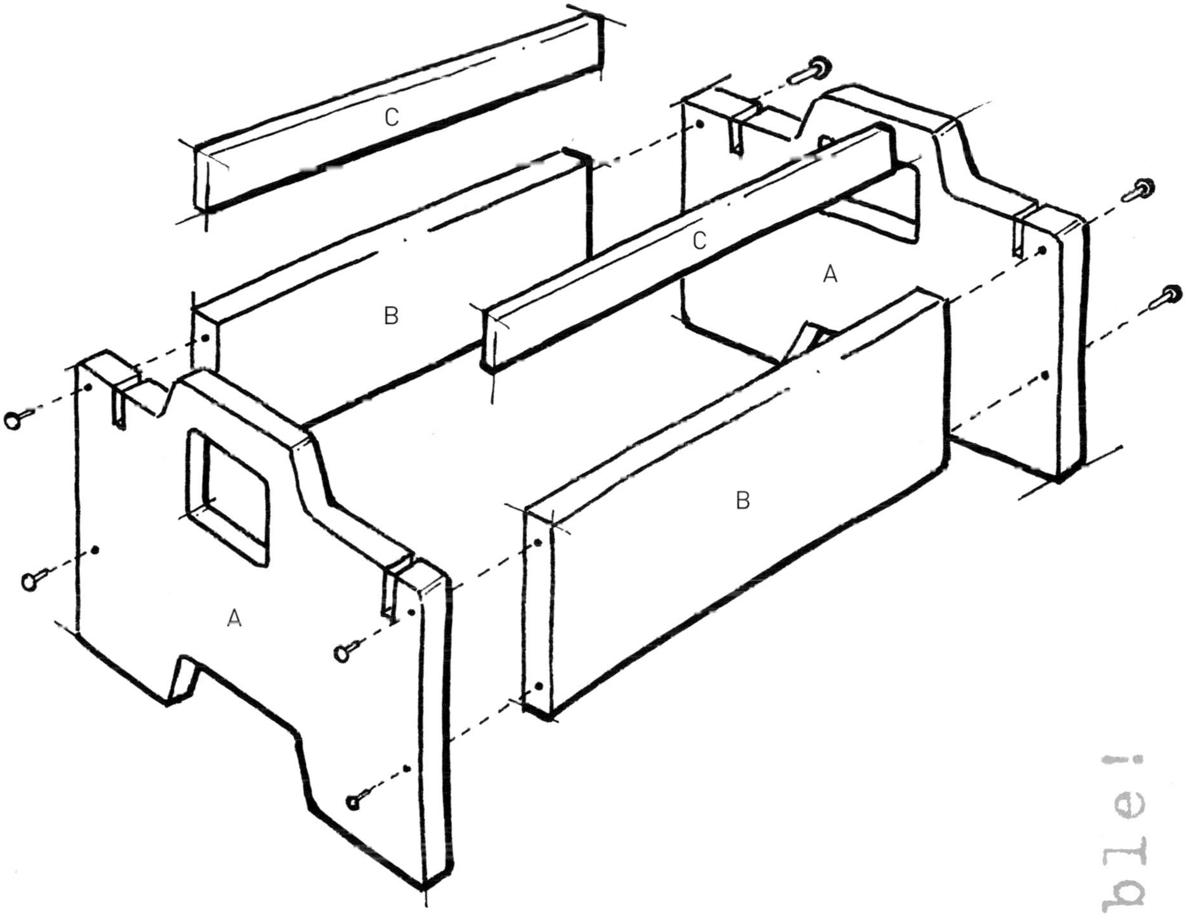

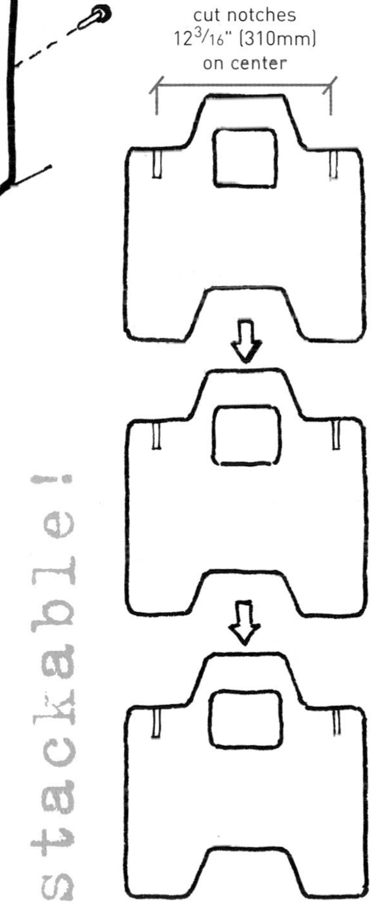

A B C C A B

cut notches 12 3/16" (310mm) on center

stackable!

cutting list

REF.	NO.	PART	STOCK	THICKNESS X WIDTH X LENGTH INCHES	MILLIMETERS
A	2	ends	plywood	3/4 x 17 x 17	19 x 432 x 432
B	2	sides	plywood	3/4 x 10 1/2 x 16 1/2	19 x 267 x 419
C	2	hanging rails	steel strap	1/8 x 1 x 18	3 x 25 x 457

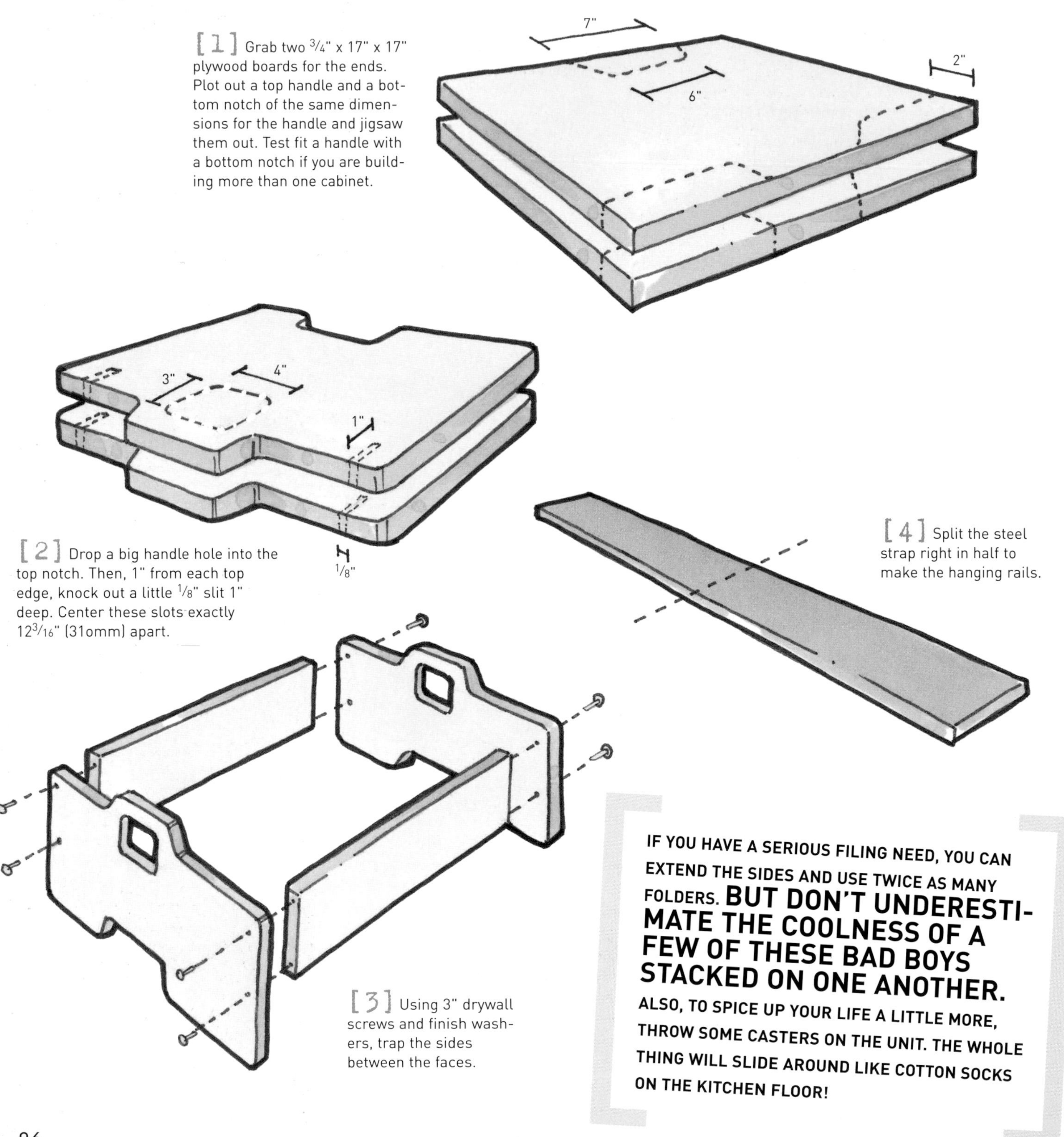

[1] Grab two 3/4" x 17" x 17" plywood boards for the ends. Plot out a top handle and a bottom notch of the same dimensions for the handle and jigsaw them out. Test fit a handle with a bottom notch if you are building more than one cabinet.

[2] Drop a big handle hole into the top notch. Then, 1" from each top edge, knock out a little 1/8" slit 1" deep. Center these slots exactly 12 3/16" (31omm) apart.

[3] Using 3" drywall screws and finish washers, trap the sides between the faces.

[4] Split the steel strap right in half to make the hanging rails.

IF YOU HAVE A SERIOUS FILING NEED, YOU CAN EXTEND THE SIDES AND USE TWICE AS MANY FOLDERS. BUT DON'T UNDERESTIMATE THE COOLNESS OF A FEW OF THESE BAD BOYS STACKED ON ONE ANOTHER. ALSO, TO SPICE UP YOUR LIFE A LITTLE MORE, THROW SOME CASTERS ON THE UNIT. THE WHOLE THING WILL SLIDE AROUND LIKE COTTON SOCKS ON THE KITCHEN FLOOR!

[5] Slide those two pieces of steel into the notches in the ends.

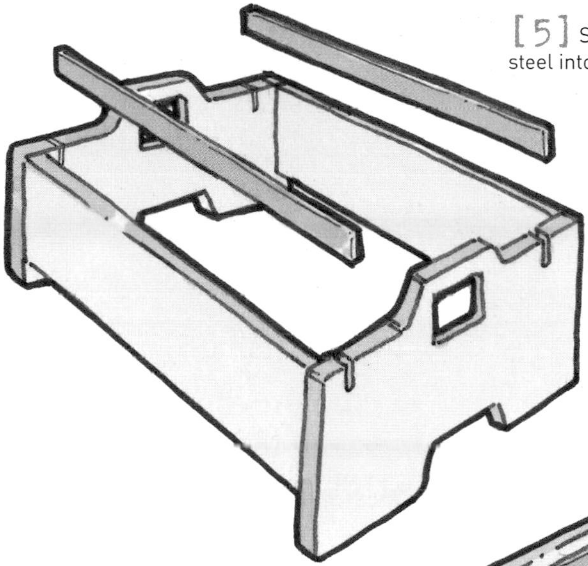

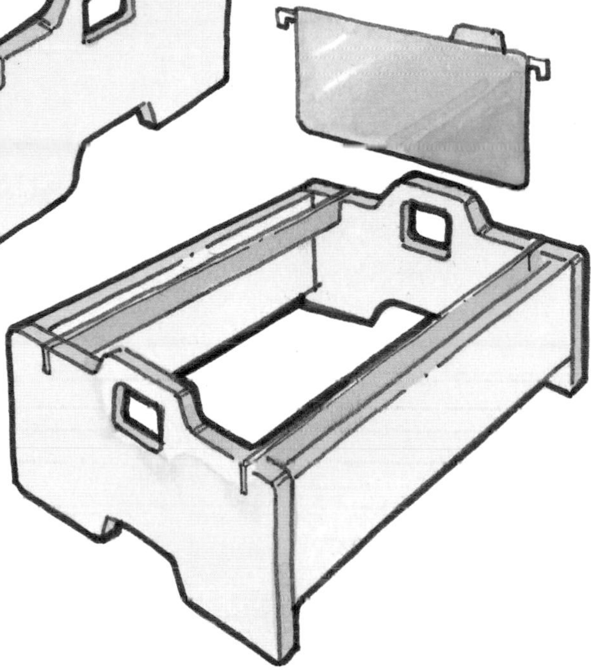

[6] Drop in your hanging files and fill 'em up with important documents.

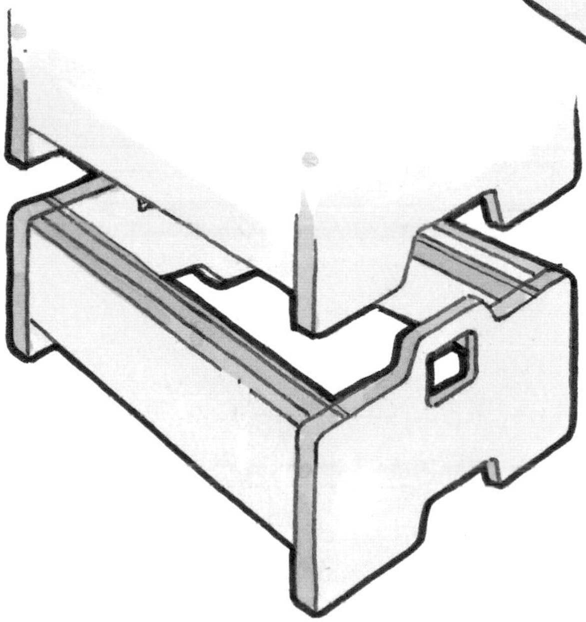

[7] If you're so important — or such a pack rat — that you fill up one file cabinet, build a second. It stacks right on top of the first!

[bonita]

TASK CHAIR

The "Bonita" chair is a beautiful task seat for the office. It is supportive, comfortable, warm and inviting. You'll be able to get so much done with the love this chair gives your body. It'll be there for you in good times and in bad. It'll always love you. It's a lot like my mom, Bonita.

This assembly requires some semi-hard-to-find hardware called drive anchors and pins. The local hardware guy might not have them, so you may need to look at woodworking stores, furniture-making stores or on the Internet. Trust me, it'll be worth the legwork to find them. They really make the chair.

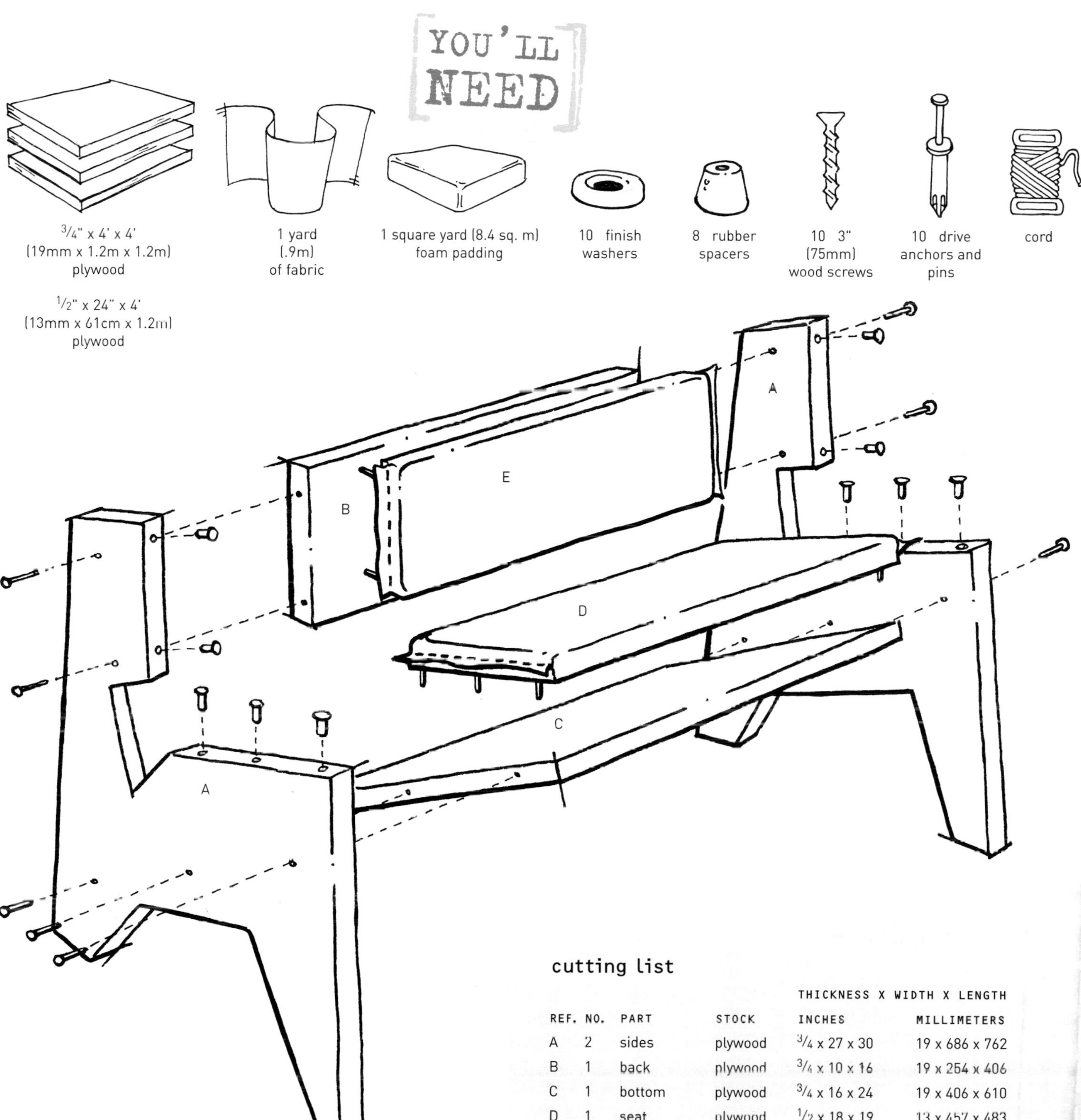

cutting list

REF.	NO.	PART	STOCK	THICKNESS X WIDTH X LENGTH INCHES	MILLIMETERS
A	2	sides	plywood	3/4 x 27 x 30	19 x 686 x 762
B	1	back	plywood	3/4 x 10 x 16	19 x 254 x 406
C	1	bottom	plywood	3/4 x 16 x 24	19 x 406 x 610
D	1	seat	plywood	1/2 x 18 x 19	13 x 457 x 483
E	1	back panel	plywood	1/2 x 10 x 19	13 x 254 x 483

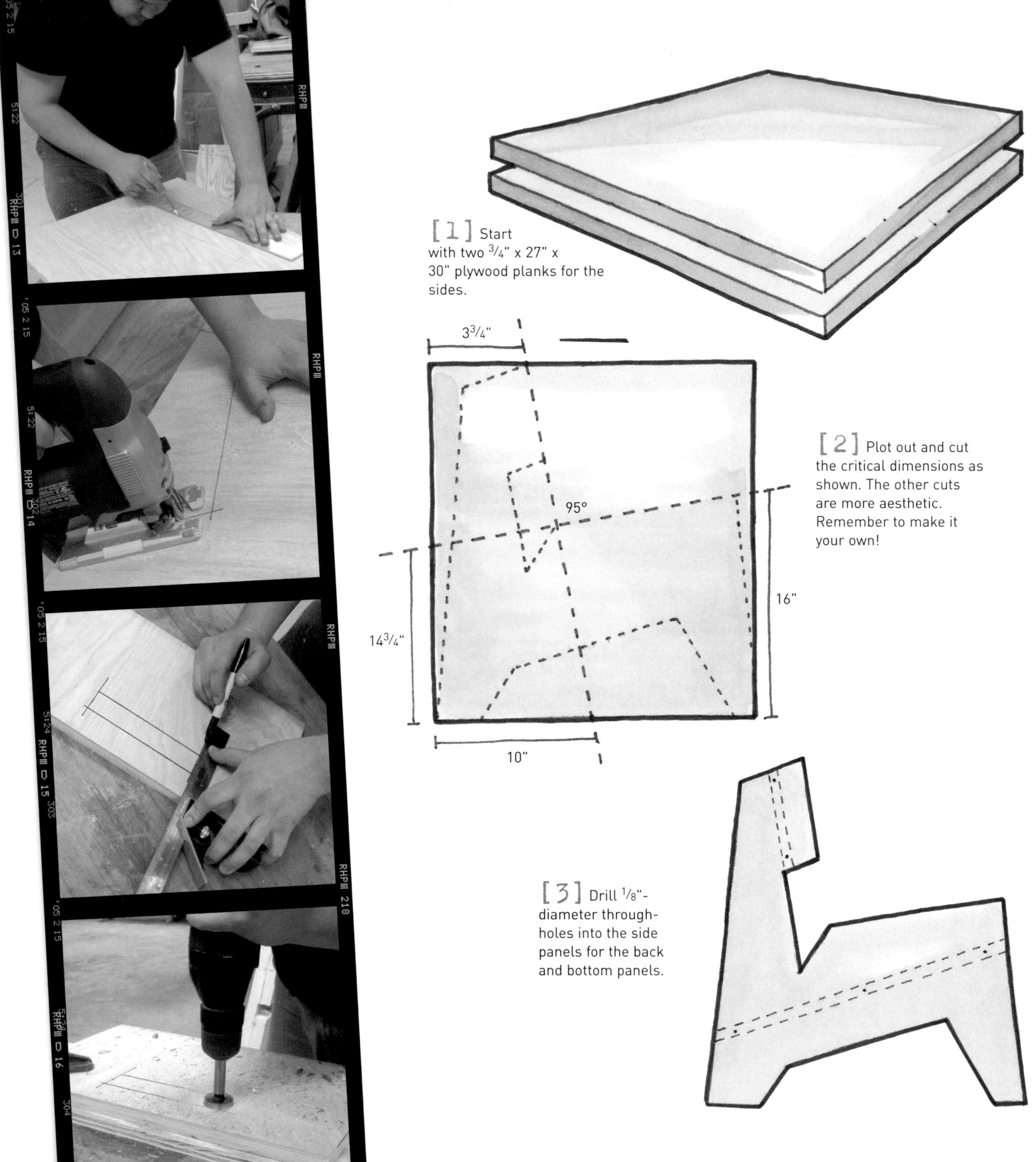

[1] Start with two 3/4" x 27" x 30" plywood planks for the sides.

[2] Plot out and cut the critical dimensions as shown. The other cuts are more aesthetic. Remember to make it your own!

[3] Drill 1/8"-diameter through-holes into the side panels for the back and bottom panels.

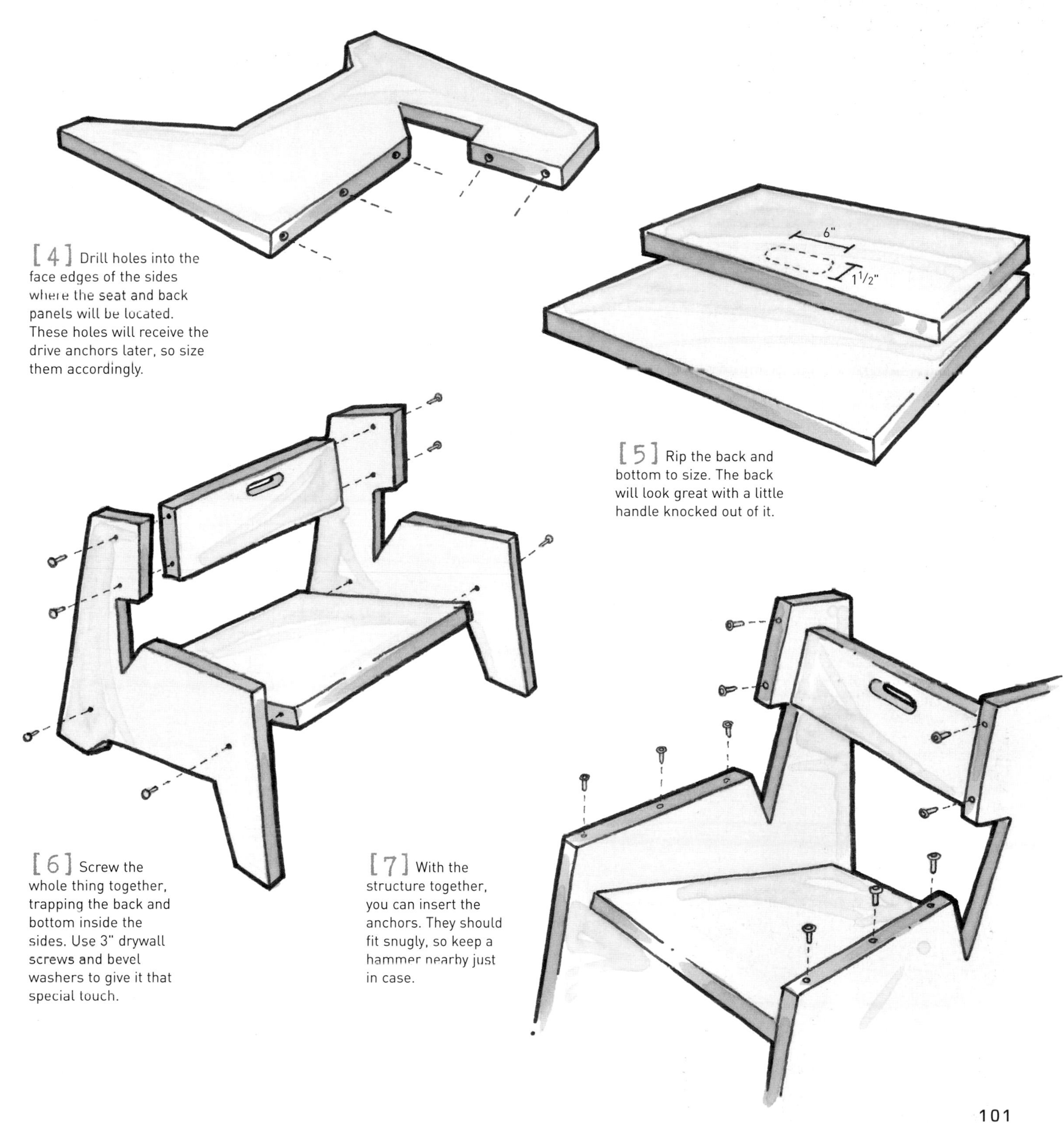

[4] Drill holes into the face edges of the sides where the seat and back panels will be located. These holes will receive the drive anchors later, so size them accordingly.

[5] Rip the back and bottom to size. The back will look great with a little handle knocked out of it.

[6] Screw the whole thing together, trapping the back and bottom inside the sides. Use 3" drywall screws and bevel washers to give it that special touch.

[7] With the structure together, you can insert the anchors. They should fit snugly, so keep a hammer nearby just in case.

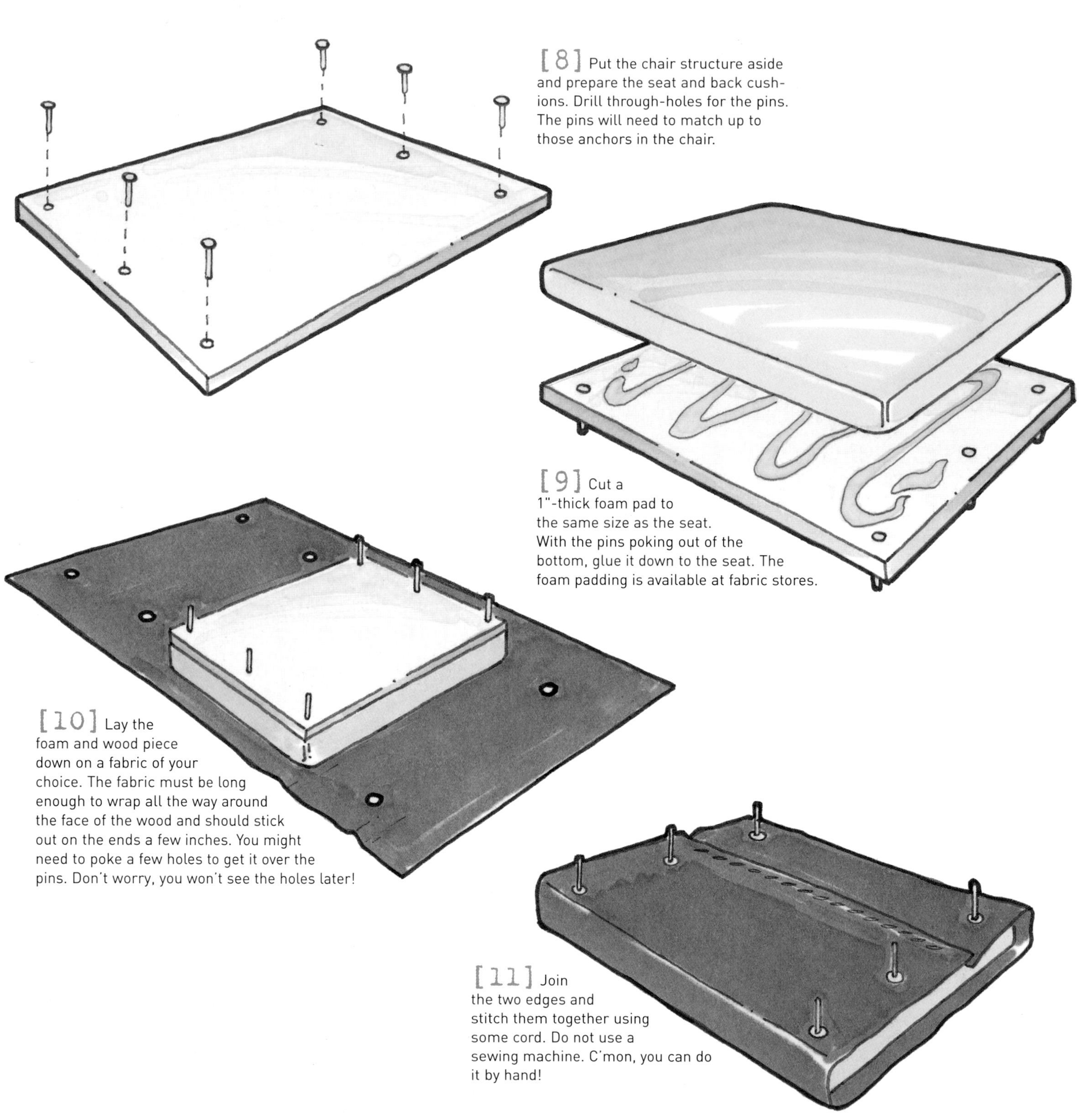

[8] Put the chair structure aside and prepare the seat and back cushions. Drill through-holes for the pins. The pins will need to match up to those anchors in the chair.

[9] Cut a 1"-thick foam pad to the same size as the seat. With the pins poking out of the bottom, glue it down to the seat. The foam padding is available at fabric stores.

[10] Lay the foam and wood piece down on a fabric of your choice. The fabric must be long enough to wrap all the way around the face of the wood and should stick out on the ends a few inches. You might need to poke a few holes to get it over the pins. Don't worry, you won't see the holes later!

[11] Join the two edges and stitch them together using some cord. Do not use a sewing machine. C'mon, you can do it by hand!

[12] Gather the ends and stitch them together. For a thick, visible stitch, use cording. Repeat steps 9-12 for the back cushion.

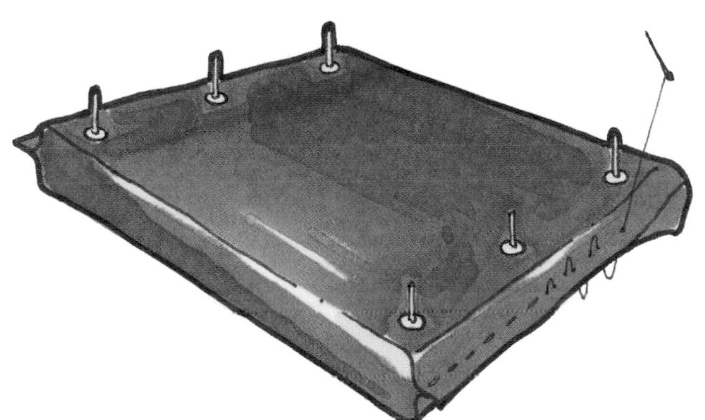

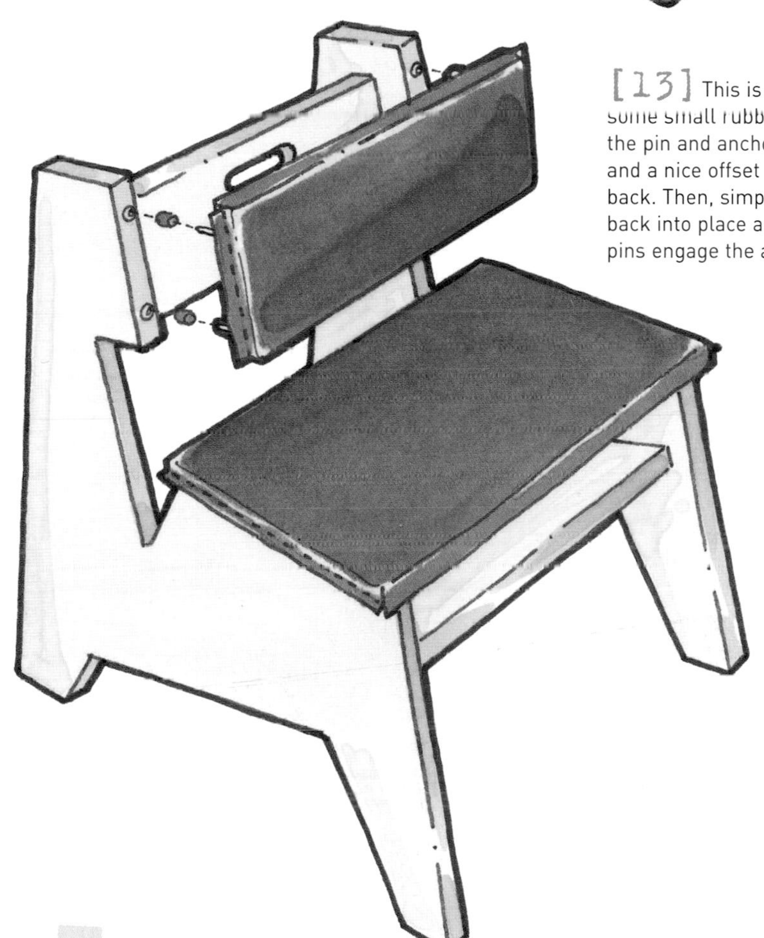

[13] This is the best part! Use some small rubber spacers between the pin and anchor for a little give and a nice offset look to the seat and back. Then, simply drop the seat and back into place and push until the pins engage the anchors.

YOU MADE IT! CONGRATULATIONS! THE ONLY THING LEFT IS TO NESTLE THE CHAIR UP TO YOUR DESK AND START WRITING SOME CREATIVE POETRY BEFORE THE SADE ALBUM RUNS OUT. OH, AND GO GIVE YOUR MOM A BIG HUG!

DESK ORGANIZER

[dr. dumpster]

I get lots of mail — pen pal letters, cool-guy club monthly newsletters and bills for my houses and cars. I find that the best way to make sure that the business in these mailers doesn't go unaddressed is to have them on hand and in front of me where I work. **"Dr. Dumpster" is the desk caddy that will do that for you.** The cable will no longer get shut off!

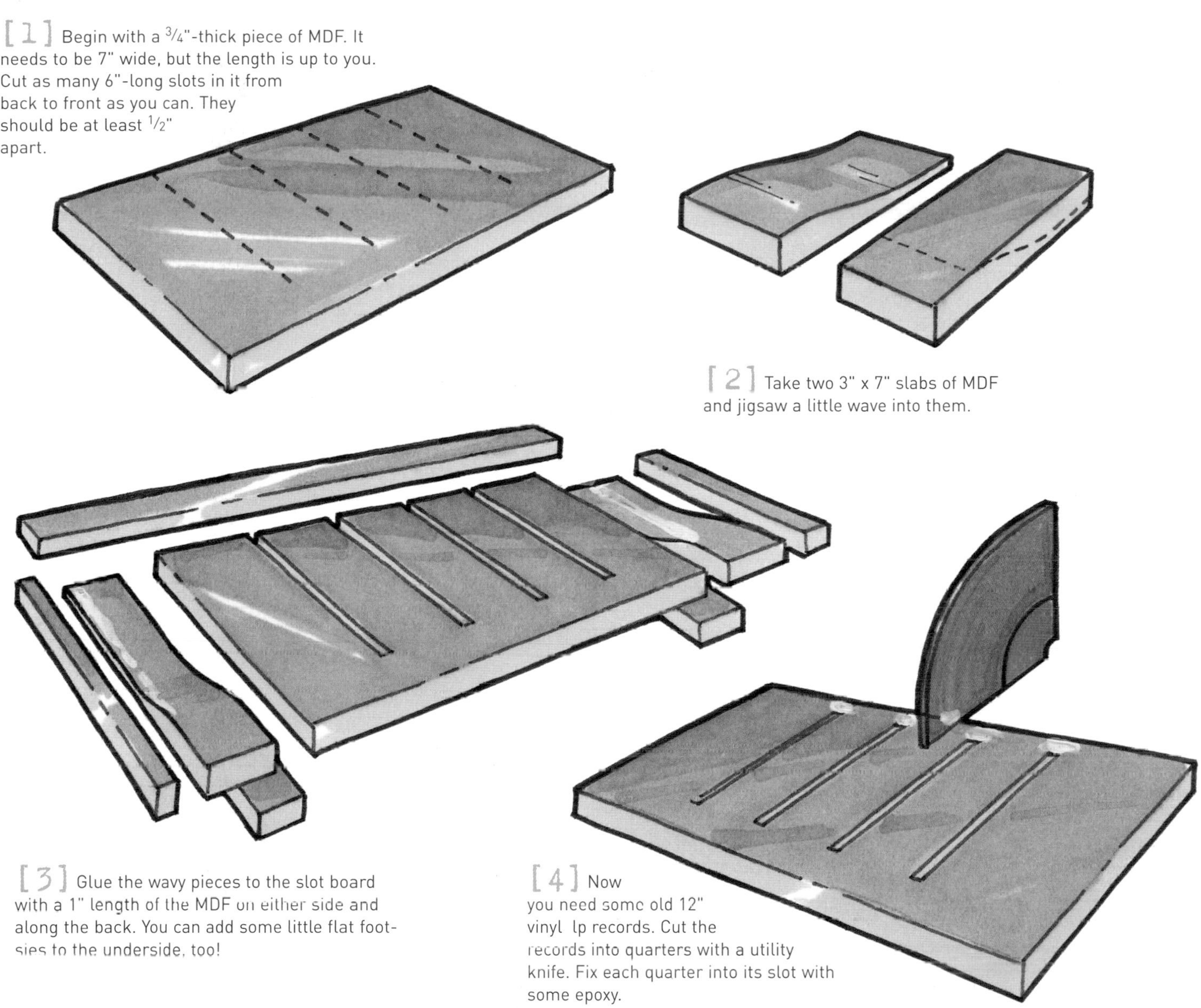

[1] Begin with a 3/4"-thick piece of MDF. It needs to be 7" wide, but the length is up to you. Cut as many 6"-long slots in it from back to front as you can. They should be at least 1/2" apart.

[2] Take two 3" x 7" slabs of MDF and jigsaw a little wave into them.

[3] Glue the wavy pieces to the slot board with a 1" length of the MDF on either side and along the back. You can add some little flat footsies to the underside, too!

[4] Now you need some old 12" vinyl lp records. Cut the records into quarters with a utility knife. Fix each quarter into its slot with some epoxy.

you'll need

3/4" (19mm) MDF

wood glue

12" vinyl lp records

epoxy

lacquer spray paint

PLACE THIS HIP LITTLE CADDY ON TOP OF YOUR DESK AND YOU'LL MARVEL AT HOW HANDY IT IS.

THE DIVIDERS HOLD ENVELOPES AND PAPERS AND THE LITTLE SLOPEY CUPS ARE PERFECT FOR PAPER CLIPS AND PUSH PINS. BEFORE YOU GLUE YOUR RECORD DIVIDERS INTO PLACE, HIT THE WHOLE THING WITH A LACQUER SPRAY PAINT OF YOUR CHOICE. AND DON'T FORGET TO DIG FOR COOL-LOOKING RECORDS TO CUT UP!

EAGLE

[KITCHEN]

AH, THE KITCHEN. **COULD THIS QUITE POSSIBLY BE THE BEST ROOM IN ANY HOUSE OR APARTMENT?** THERE ARE A LOT OF GREAT THINGS ABOUT THE KITCHEN. NAMELY, IT'S THE PLACE WHERE YOU CAN COOK UP SOME DELICIOUS GRUB. BUT WHILE YOU'RE STILL WAITING FOR YOUR MANSION IN THE HILLS TO BE BUILT, YOUR CURRENT KITCHEN MAY HAVE SOME SHORTCOMINGS. MOST KITCHENS ARE STRAPPED FOR SPACE AND ARE NOT TOO COMFY TO HANG OUT IN, SO THE PROJECTS IN THIS CHAPTER ADDRESS THOSE CONCERNS DIRECTLY. **AFTER THESE PIECES ARE FINISHED, YOU'LL HAVE A TERRIFIC PLACE FOR PREPARING AND ENJOYING ALL YOUR GREAT DISHES.** IF YOU CAN'T COOK, YOU CAN FIND LOTS OF DO-IT-YOURSELF BOOKS FOR THAT, TOO!

Every kitchen should have a table in it — either for chowing down a quick meal before heading out or for holding lots of mail, books, files and the occasional piece of Tupperware. **The "Diner" table is so much fun, though, you'll want to cozy up to it for a nice evening meal.** Now, I guess you gotta ask Mom for that meat loaf recipe!

[diner] KITCHEN TABLE

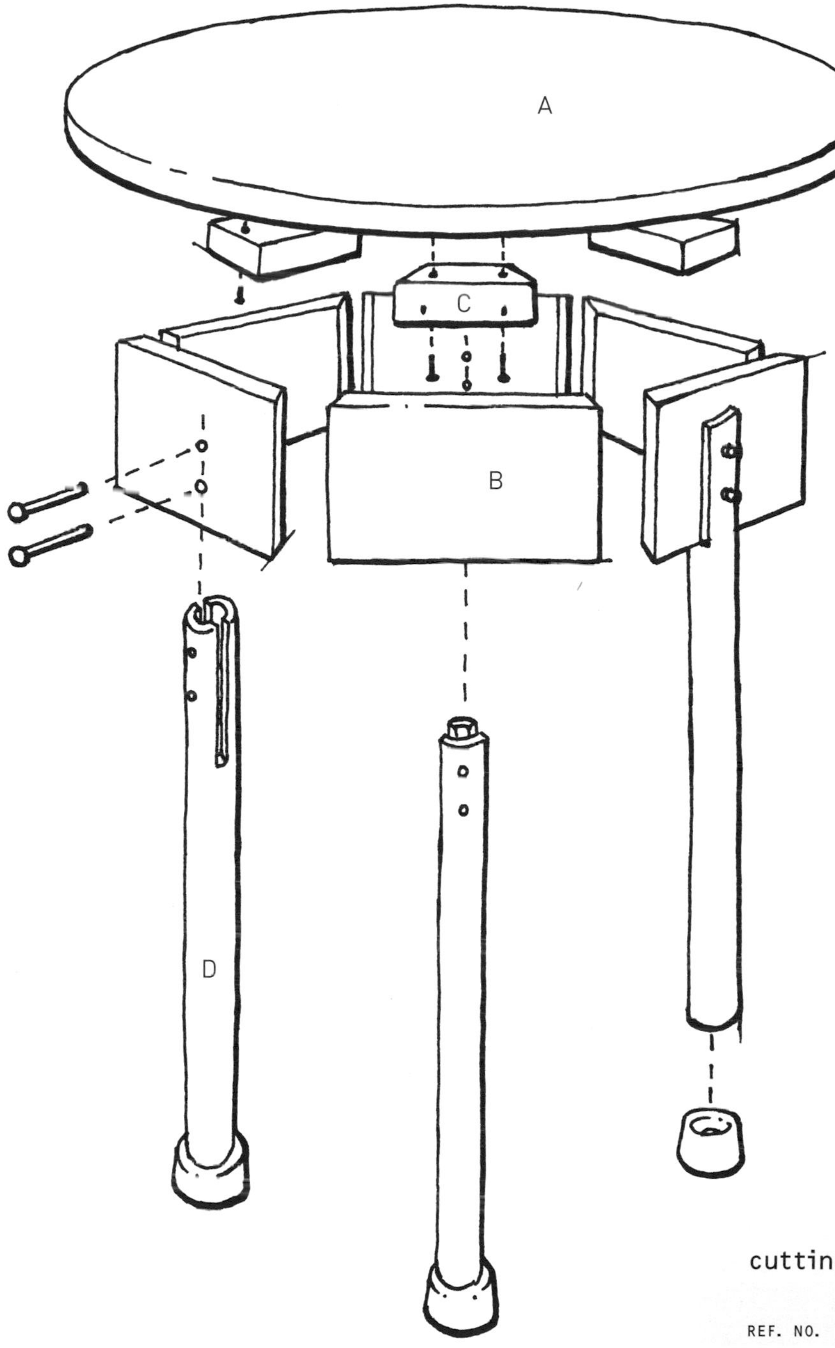

YOU'LL NEED

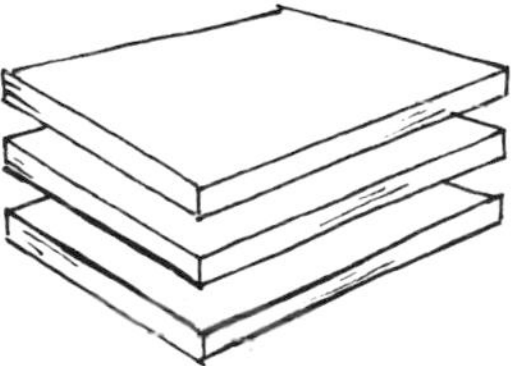

1 $^3/_4$" x 4' x 4' (19mm x 1.2m x 1.2m) plywood sheet

9 2" (50mm) drywall screws

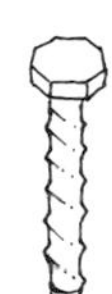

6 $^1/_4$"-20 x 2" (6mm x 50mm) hex bolts

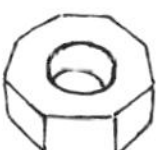

6 $^1/_4$"-20 (6mm) hex nuts

12 $^1/_4$" (6mm) flat washers

cutting list

				THICKNESS X WIDTH X LENGTH	
REF.	NO.	PART	STOCK	INCHES	MILLIMETERS
A	1	top	plywood	$^3/_4$ x 30 dia	19 x 762
B	6	apron rails	plywood	$^3/_4$ x 5$^1/_2$ x 11$^1/_2$	19 x 140 x 292
C	3	cleats	pine 2x4	1$^1/_2$ x 3$^1/_2$ x 10$^1/_2$	32 x 89 x 267
D	3	legs	steel	1$^1/_2$ dia x 36	38 x 914

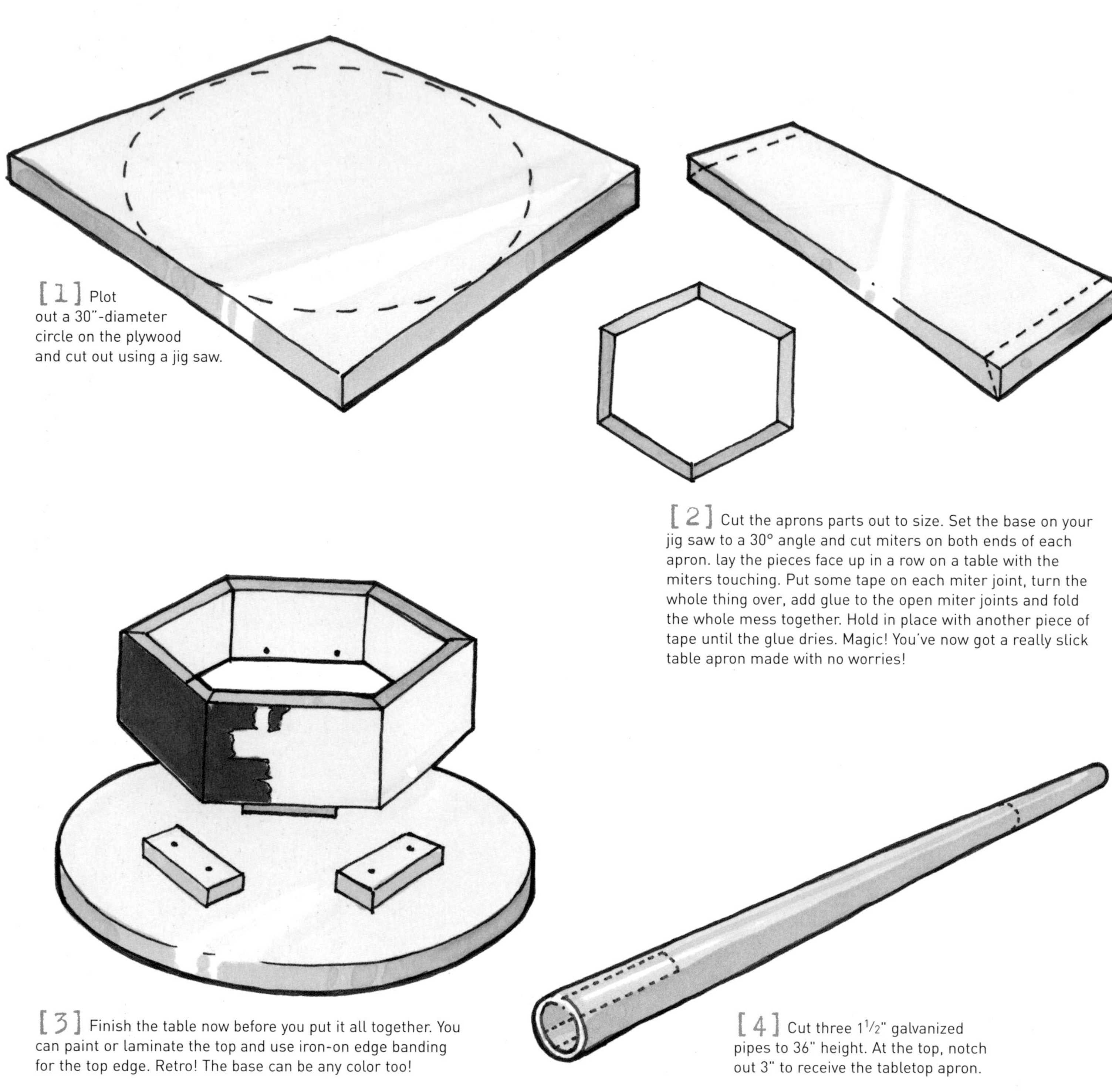

[1] Plot out a 30"-diameter circle on the plywood and cut out using a jig saw.

[2] Cut the aprons parts out to size. Set the base on your jig saw to a 30° angle and cut miters on both ends of each apron. lay the pieces face up in a row on a table with the miters touching. Put some tape on each miter joint, turn the whole thing over, add glue to the open miter joints and fold the whole mess together. Hold in place with another piece of tape until the glue dries. Magic! You've now got a really slick table apron made with no worries!

[3] Finish the table now before you put it all together. You can paint or laminate the top and use iron-on edge banding for the top edge. Retro! The base can be any color too!

[4] Cut three 1½" galvanized pipes to 36" height. At the top, notch out 3" to receive the tabletop apron.

[5] Two through holes here, at 2" and 4" should match up with those in the table body.

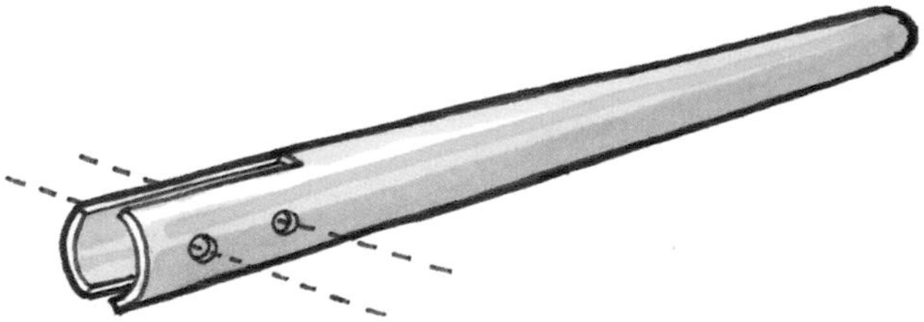

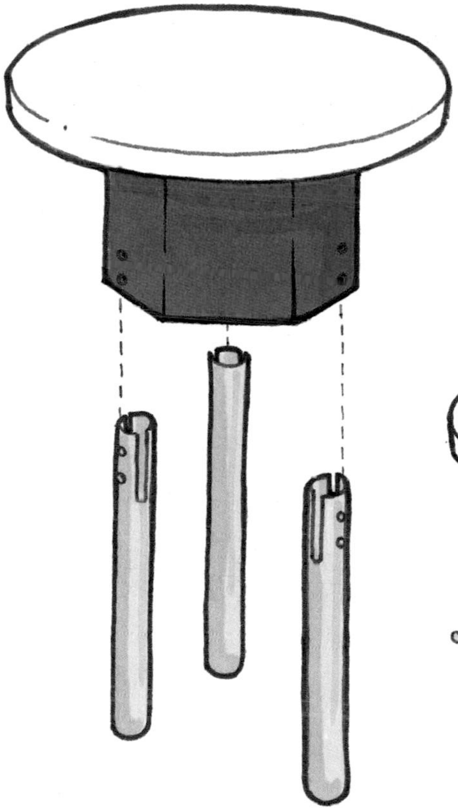

[6] Set the table on its top and slip the three table legs into place.

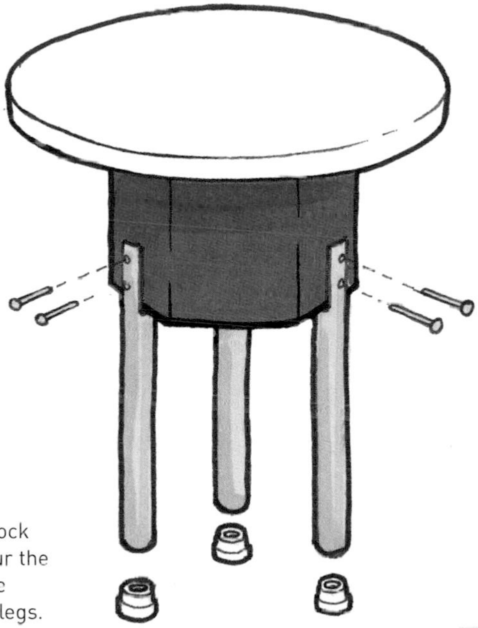

[7] Nuts and bolts lock the legs into place. Scour the hardware store for some nice rubber feet for the legs.

I FINISHED THIS TABLE IN A FUNKY, RETRO RED AND WHITE. I USED WHITE LATEX WALL PAINT FOR THE TOP AND RED LATEX WALL PAINT FOR THE BODY. YOU CAN BUY MELAMINE LAMINATE FOR THE TOP TOO. IT'S VERY EASY TO CLEAN AND IS RELATIVELY DIFFICULT TO DAMAGE. WANNA MIX IT UP EVEN MORE? **FIND SOME CRAZY RIBBON COLORS AND DESIGNS AT THE FABRIC STORE AND LAMINATE THEM TO THE EDGE WITH CONTACT CEMENT.** THEN, MATCH THE PAINT COLORS FOR THE TOP AND BODY TO THE RIBBON.

[m.f.d.] KITCHEN STOOL

You've just constructed a kickin' kitchen table to grub at, but that's not going to do you any good unless you have a stool or three to pony up to it. **This project utilizes some very industrial components that when put together create a very sleek, very legit bar stool.** I think this is one of the coolest, most fun projects in the book. You're going to want to take this baby along when you head to the corner pub.

cutting list

				THICKNESS X WIDTH X LENGTH	
REF.	NO.	PART	STOCK	INCHES	MILLIMETERS
A	1	seat	plywood	3/4 x 13 dia	19 x 330
B	1	base	plywood	3/4 x 18 dia	19 x 457
C	1	seat column	pine 2x4	3/4 x 1 1/2 x 22	19 x 38 x 559

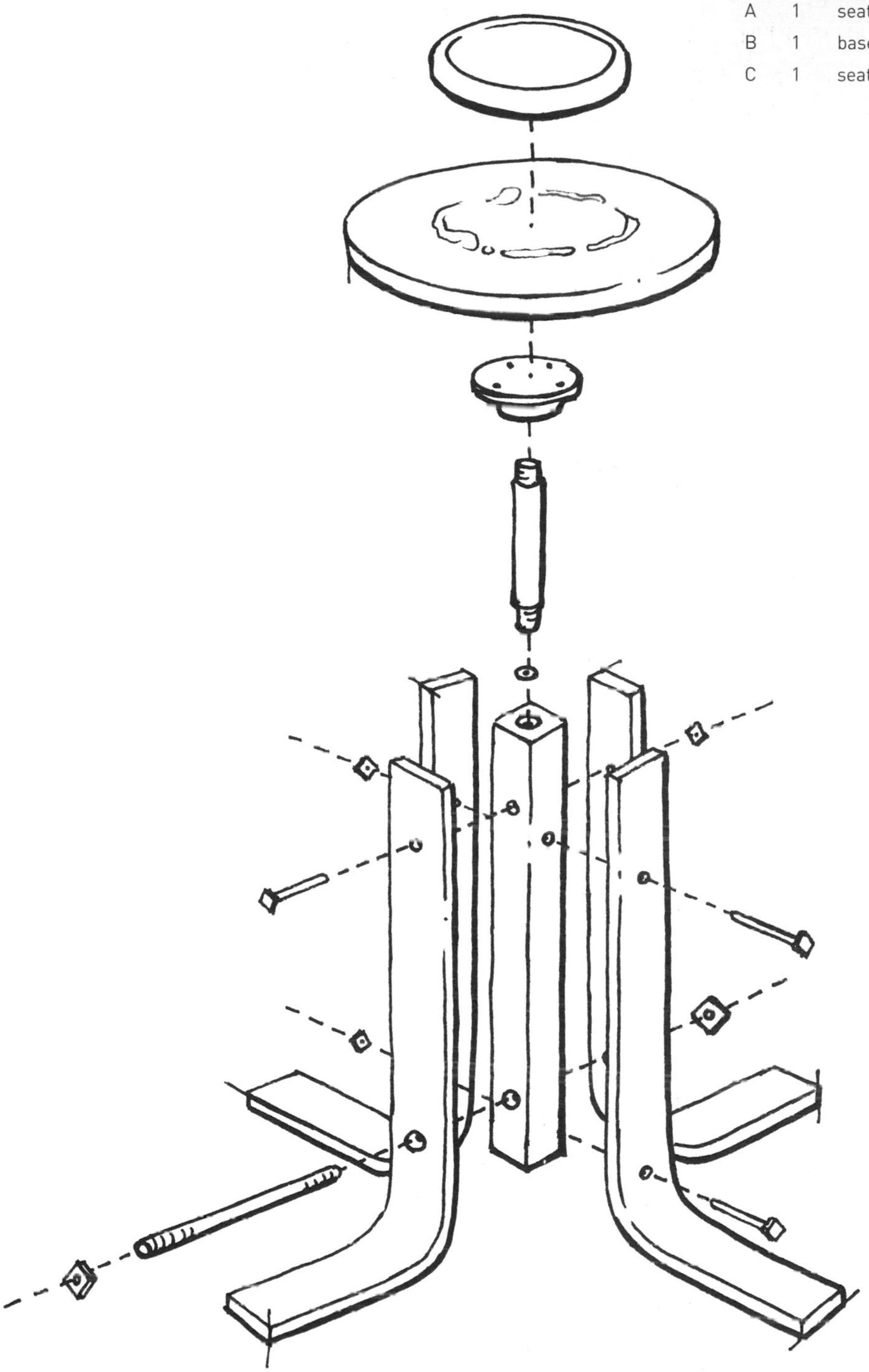

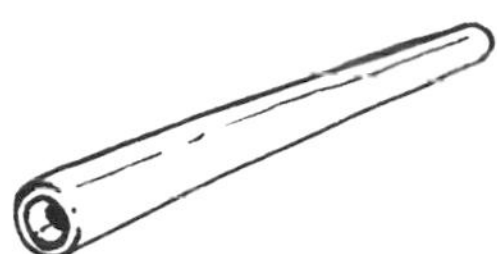

4 1/8" x 1" x 36" (3mm x 25mm x 914mm) steel bar

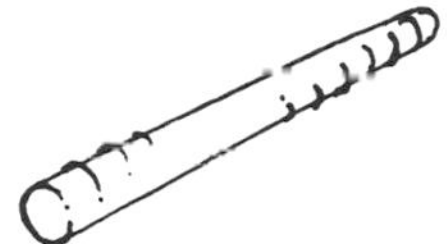

1 5/8" x 18" (16mm x 450mm) all-thread rod

2 5/8" (16mm) hex nuts

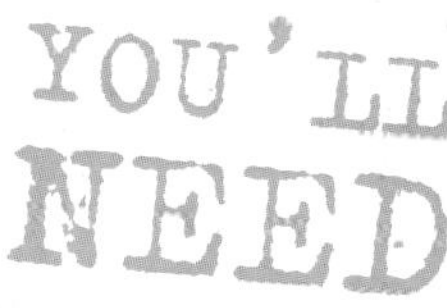

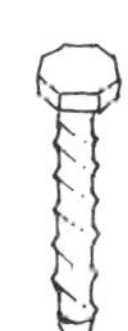

4 1/4"-20 x 2" (6mm x 50mm) hex bolts

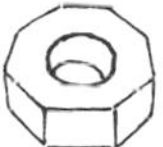

4 1/4" 20 (6mm) hex nuts

8 #14 x 3/4" (20mm) pan head sheet metal screws

1 1" (25mm) -diameter flat washer

1 1" x 8" (25mm x 200mm) pipe nipple

1 1" (25mm) floor flange

wood glue

[1] Kick this one off with two pairs of $1/8$" x $1\,1/2$" x 3' steel straps from the hardware store's metal supply.

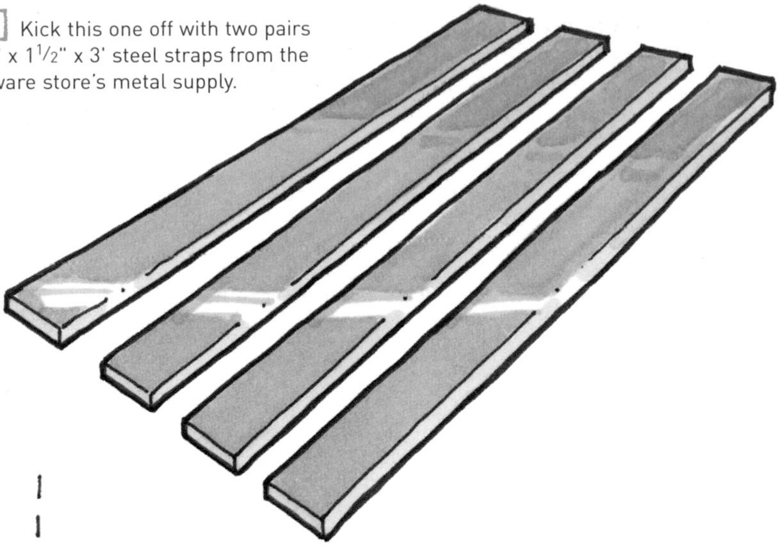

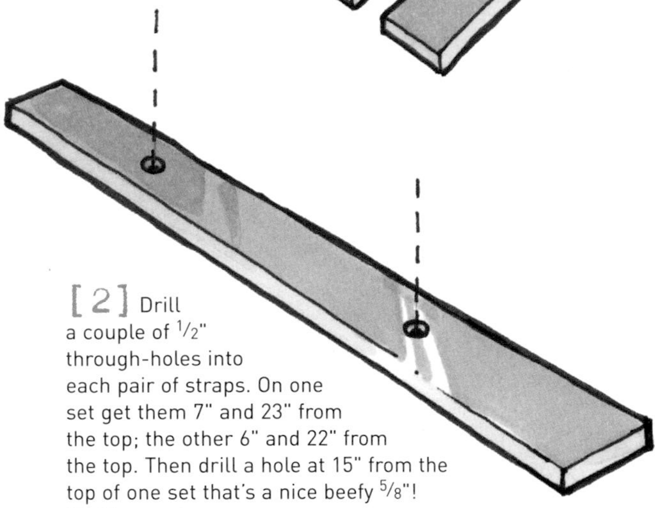

[2] Drill a couple of $1/2$" through-holes into each pair of straps. On one set get them 7" and 23" from the top; the other 6" and 22" from the top. Then drill a hole at 15" from the top of one set that's a nice beefy $5/8$"! You'll see why.

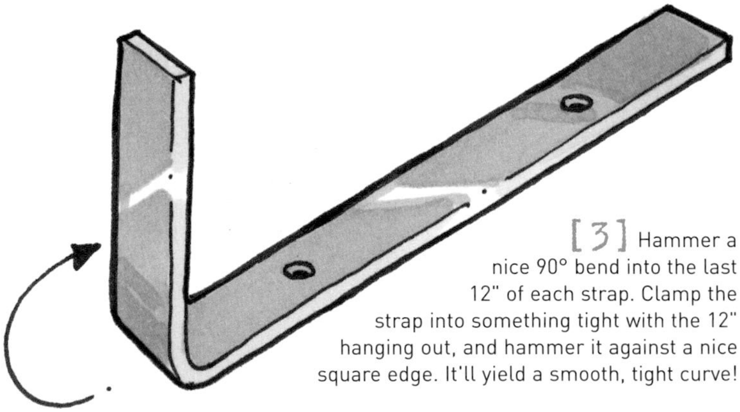

[3] Hammer a nice 90° bend into the last 12" of each strap. Clamp the strap into something tight with the 12" hanging out, and hammer it against a nice square edge. It'll yield a smooth, tight curve!

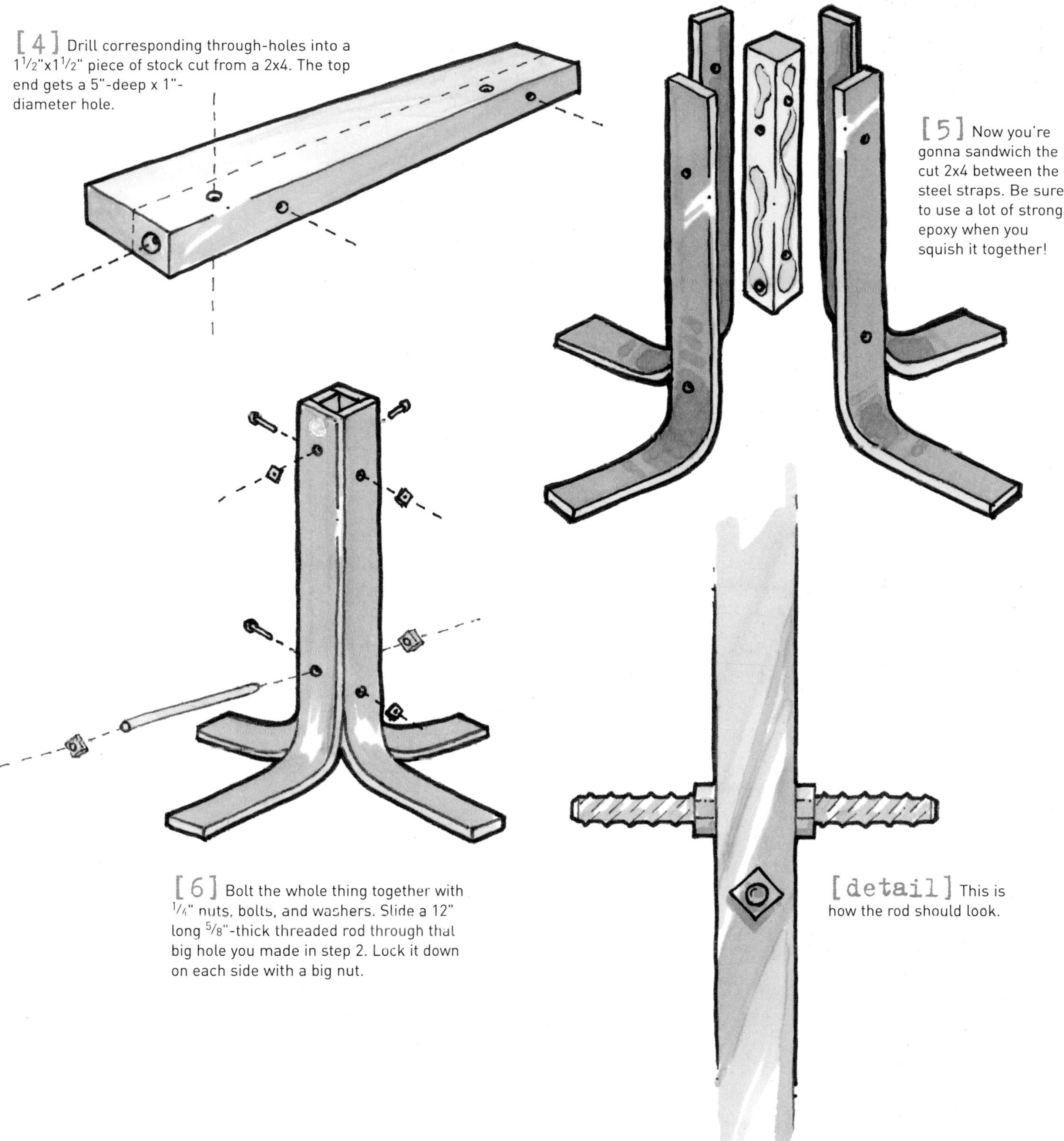

[4] Drill corresponding through-holes into a 1½"x1½" piece of stock cut from a 2x4. The top end gets a 5"-deep x 1"-diameter hole.

[5] Now you're gonna sandwich the cut 2x4 between the steel straps. Be sure to use a lot of strong epoxy when you squish it together!

[6] Bolt the whole thing together with ¼" nuts, bolts, and washers. Slide a 12" long ⅝"-thick threaded rod through that big hole you made in step 2. Lock it down on each side with a big nut.

[detail] This is how the rod should look.

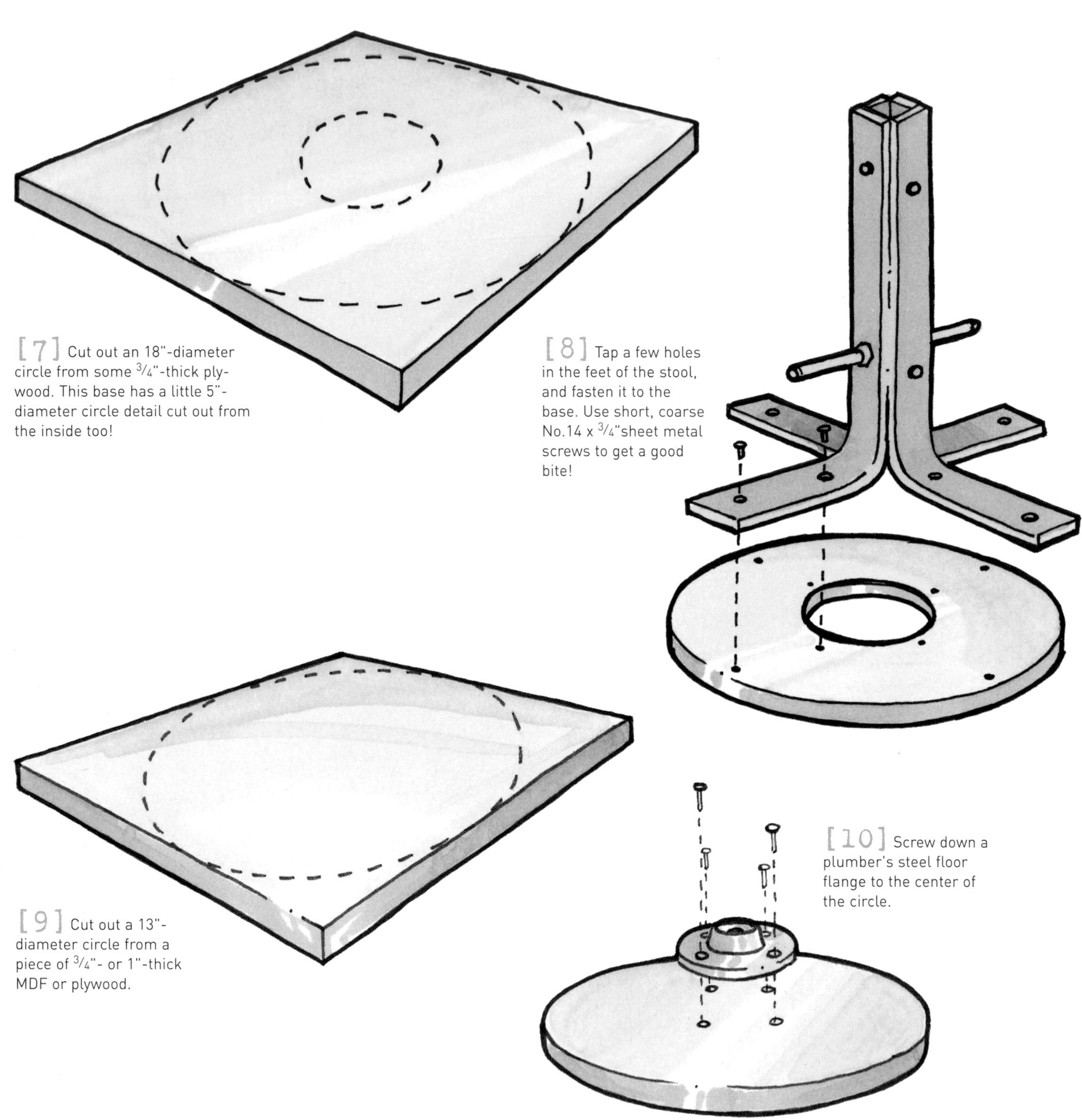

[7] Cut out an 18"-diameter circle from some 3/4"-thick plywood. This base has a little 5"-diameter circle detail cut out from the inside too!

[8] Tap a few holes in the feet of the stool, and fasten it to the base. Use short, coarse No.14 x 3/4"sheet metal screws to get a good bite!

[9] Cut out a 13"-diameter circle from a piece of 3/4"- or 1"-thick MDF or plywood.

[10] Screw down a plumber's steel floor flange to the center of the circle.

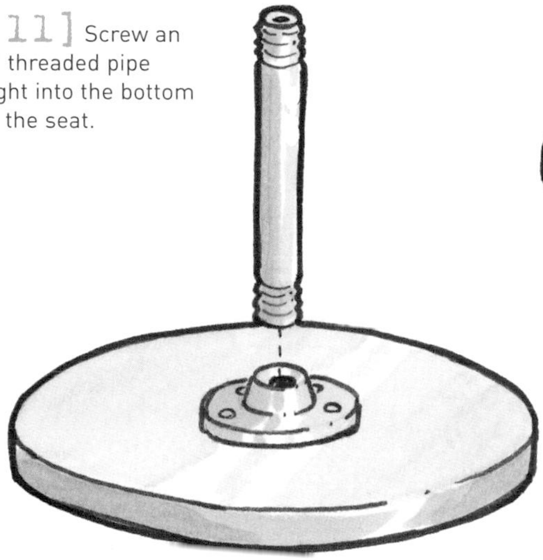

[11] Screw an 8" threaded pipe right into the bottom of the seat.

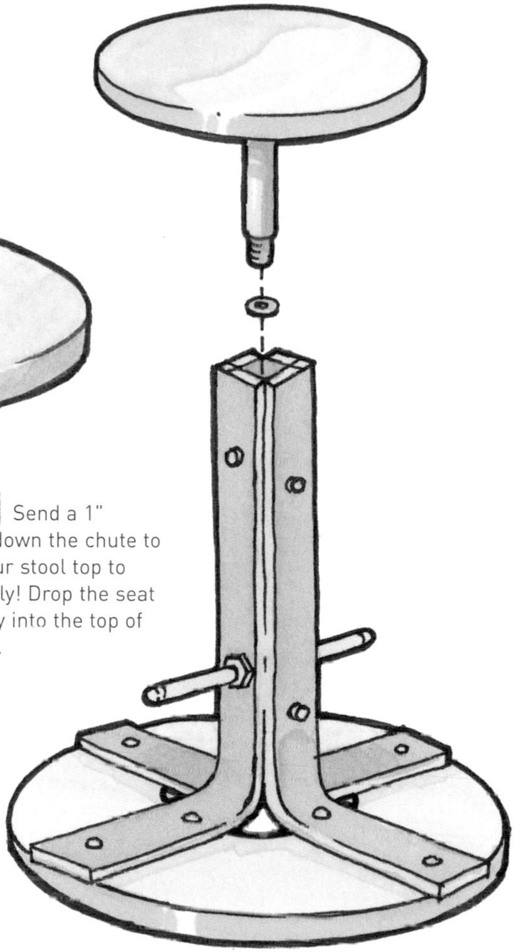

[12] Send a 1" washer down the chute to allow your stool top to spin freely! Drop the seat assembly into the top of the base.

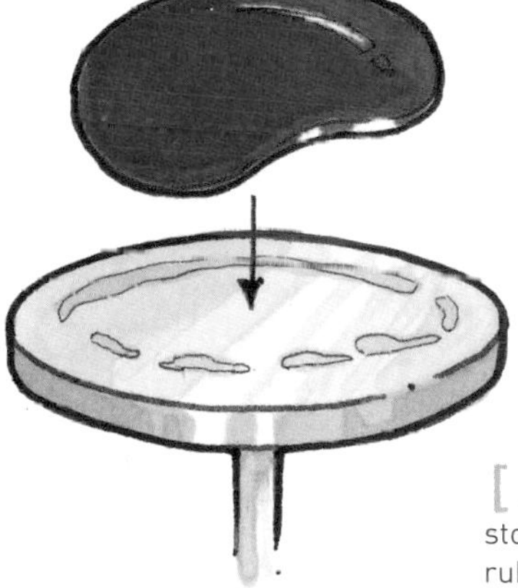

[13] Affix a little cushion onto the stool to make it comfy. A thin sheet of soft rubber or even a Frisbee would work!

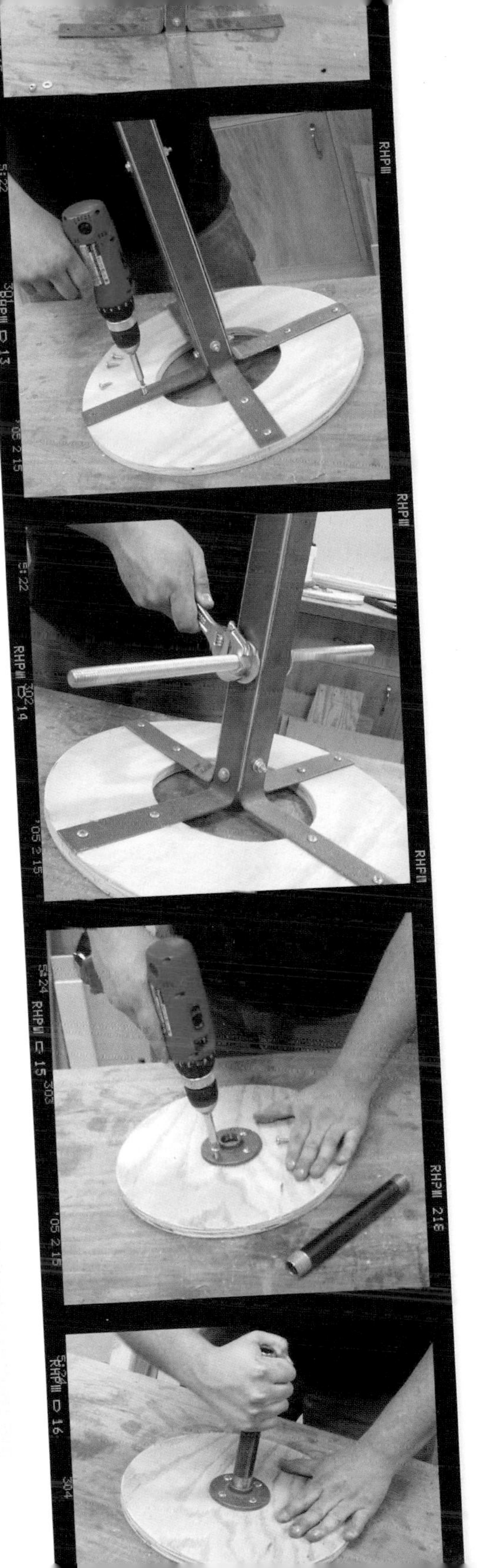

BE SURE TO COORDINATE THE COLOR OF THE STOOL TOP WITH THE COLOR OF THE TABLE AND THE REST OF THE ROOM. IF YOU DON'T LIKE SITTING ON CIRCLES, MAKE YOUR STOOL SQUARE, OVAL OR TRIANGULAR. SAME WITH THE SHAPE OF THE BASE. **CHOOSE A FABRIC TO COVER THE SEAT IF FLAT COLORS JUST DON'T DO IT FOR YOU.** GET THREE OR FOUR FINISHED AND YOU CAN PUT THEM ALL AROUND A TABLE OR LINE THEM UP IN FRONT OF A HOME BAR!

[nuke]

MICROWAVE CADDY

You won't know how you lived without this little caddy once you have it! Usually the microwave is butted up against a corner wall or fridge, trapping dust and kitchen gunk, and its top is too close to the bottom of the cabinets to really store anything. **This handy caddy will make usable space out of the area around your microwave like you never knew was possible!** You'll have a spice drawer, a cookbook slot and, oh yeah, a microwave shelf! This is a supercustomizable unit. Be sure to have the dimensions of your microwave on hand during the construction of this project.

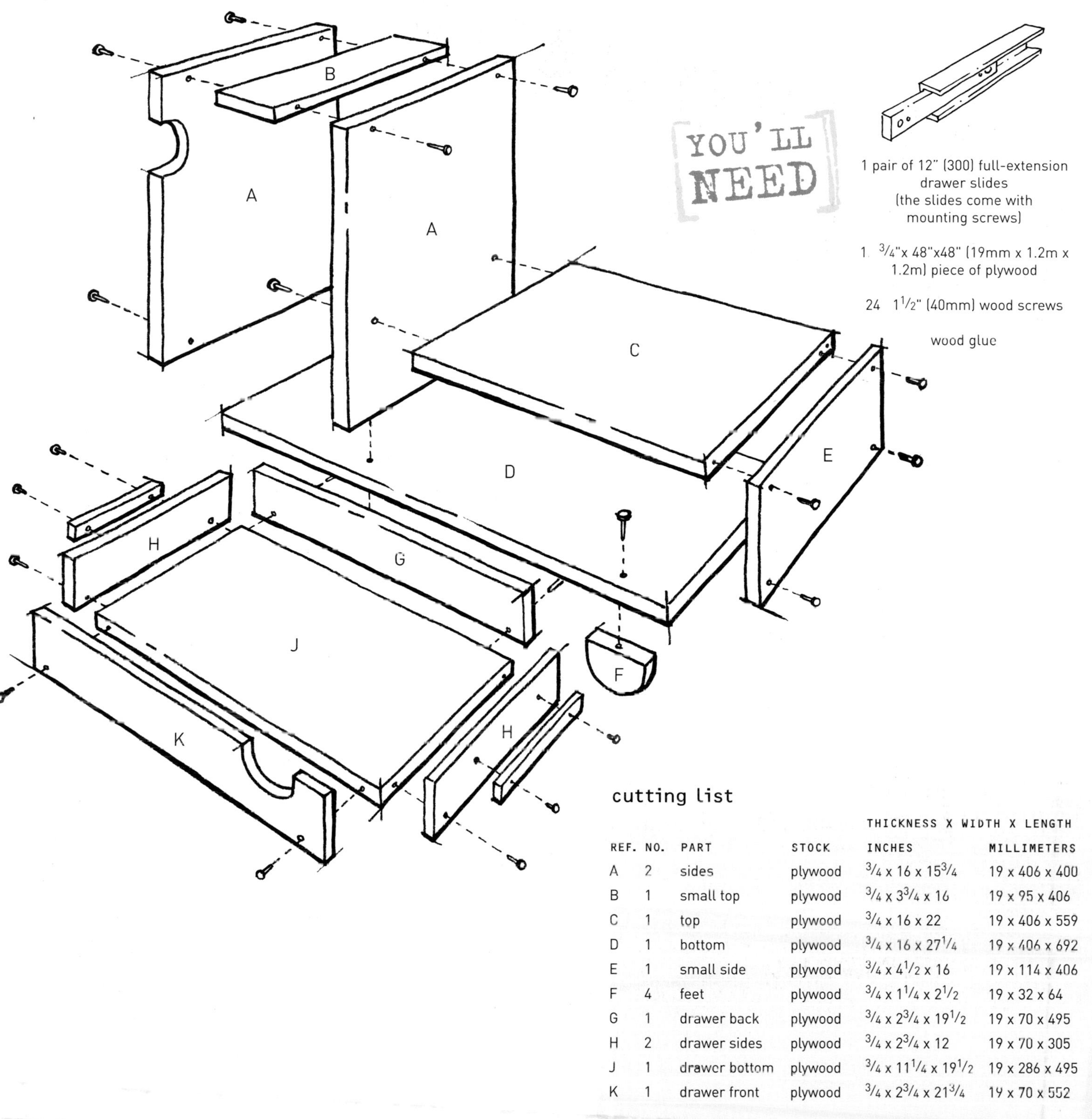

YOU'LL NEED

1 pair of 12" (300) full-extension drawer slides (the slides come with mounting screws)

1 3/4"x 48"x48" (19mm x 1.2m x 1.2m) piece of plywood

24 1 1/2" (40mm) wood screws

wood glue

cutting list

REF.	NO.	PART	STOCK	THICKNESS X WIDTH X LENGTH INCHES	MILLIMETERS
A	2	sides	plywood	3/4 x 16 x 15 3/4	19 x 406 x 400
B	1	small top	plywood	3/4 x 3 3/4 x 16	19 x 95 x 406
C	1	top	plywood	3/4 x 16 x 22	19 x 406 x 559
D	1	bottom	plywood	3/4 x 16 x 27 1/4	19 x 406 x 692
E	1	small side	plywood	3/4 x 4 1/2 x 16	19 x 114 x 406
F	4	feet	plywood	3/4 x 1 1/4 x 2 1/2	19 x 32 x 64
G	1	drawer back	plywood	3/4 x 2 3/4 x 19 1/2	19 x 70 x 495
H	2	drawer sides	plywood	3/4 x 2 3/4 x 12	19 x 70 x 305
J	1	drawer bottom	plywood	3/4 x 11 1/4 x 19 1/2	19 x 286 x 495
K	1	drawer front	plywood	3/4 x 2 3/4 x 21 3/4	19 x 70 x 552

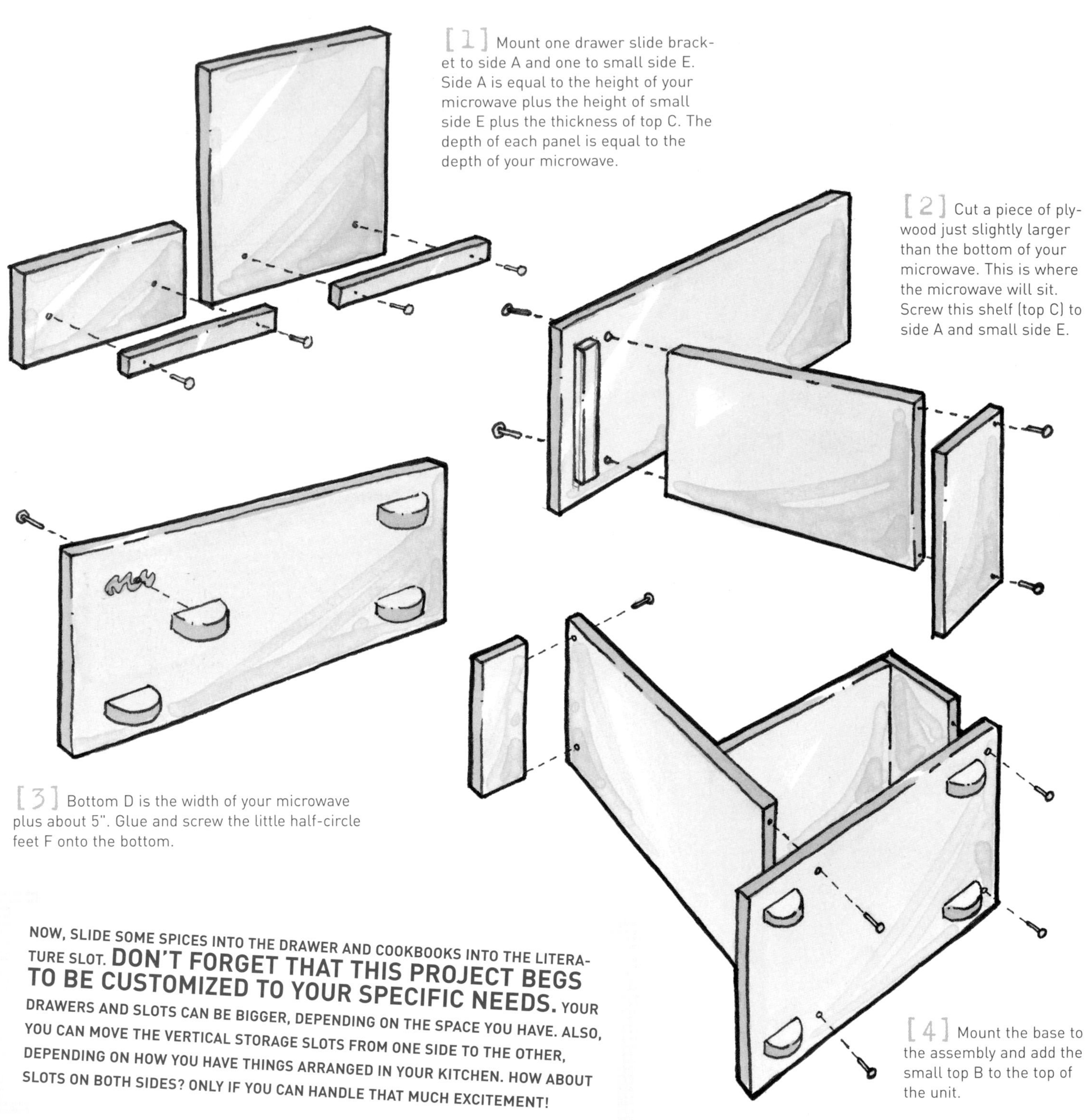

[1] Mount one drawer slide bracket to side A and one to small side E. Side A is equal to the height of your microwave plus the height of small side E plus the thickness of top C. The depth of each panel is equal to the depth of your microwave.

[2] Cut a piece of plywood just slightly larger than the bottom of your microwave. This is where the microwave will sit. Screw this shelf (top C) to side A and small side E.

[3] Bottom D is the width of your microwave plus about 5". Glue and screw the little half-circle feet F onto the bottom.

[4] Mount the base to the assembly and add the small top B to the top of the unit.

NOW, SLIDE SOME SPICES INTO THE DRAWER AND COOKBOOKS INTO THE LITERATURE SLOT. **DON'T FORGET THAT THIS PROJECT BEGS TO BE CUSTOMIZED TO YOUR SPECIFIC NEEDS.** YOUR DRAWERS AND SLOTS CAN BE BIGGER, DEPENDING ON THE SPACE YOU HAVE. ALSO, YOU CAN MOVE THE VERTICAL STORAGE SLOTS FROM ONE SIDE TO THE OTHER, DEPENDING ON HOW YOU HAVE THINGS ARRANGED IN YOUR KITCHEN. HOW ABOUT SLOTS ON BOTH SIDES? ONLY IF YOU CAN HANDLE THAT MUCH EXCITEMENT!

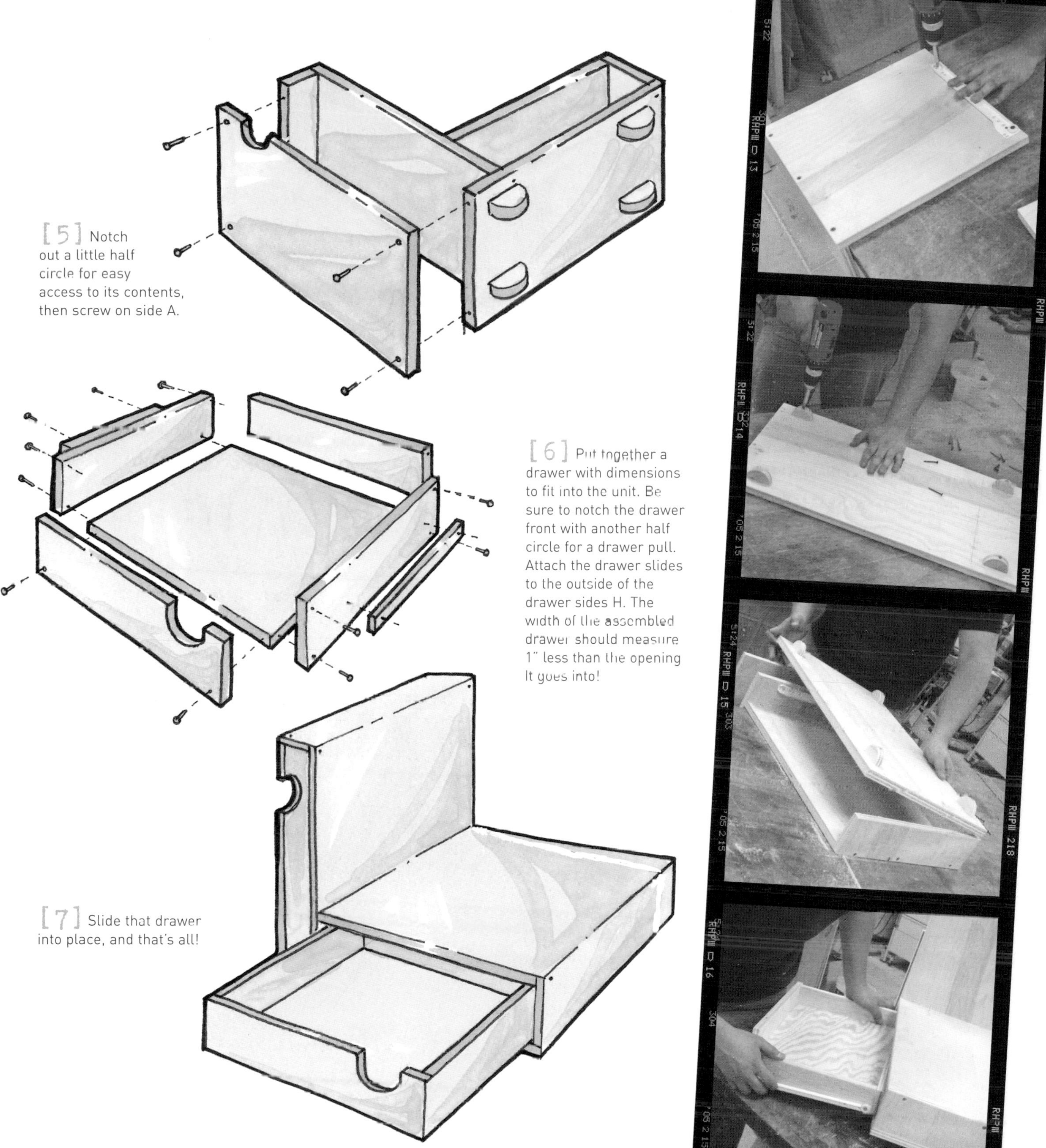

[5] Notch out a little half circle for easy access to its contents, then screw on side A.

[6] Put together a drawer with dimensions to fit into the unit. Be sure to notch the drawer front with another half circle for a drawer pull. Attach the drawer slides to the outside of the drawer sides H. The width of the assembled drawer should measure 1" less than the opening it goes into!

[7] Slide that drawer into place, and that's all!

[colony]

BOUQUET VASE

Everyone knows it's nice to get flowers. Even boys like to get flowers, although they probably wouldn't admit it. I know I hate them! The worst thing to do when you get flowers, though, is to shove them in a pitcher or pint glass or tin can full of water. **Look in the plumbing section of the hardware store for all the good stuff in this project,** and put together a fantastic home for your beautiful bouquets!

you'll need

PVC pipe

1 2" or 3" (51mm to 76mm) PVC coupling

1 3" (76mm) PVC cap

epoxy

lacquer spray paint

[1] Start with a long length of 1/2"-diameter PVC pipe. Cut it into six to eight different lengths anywhere from 3" to 8".

[2] Drop two little holes in the bottom of each pipe, and lop the top off at some angle that looks good. You can tell, I'm sure, that this will be a precise assembly.

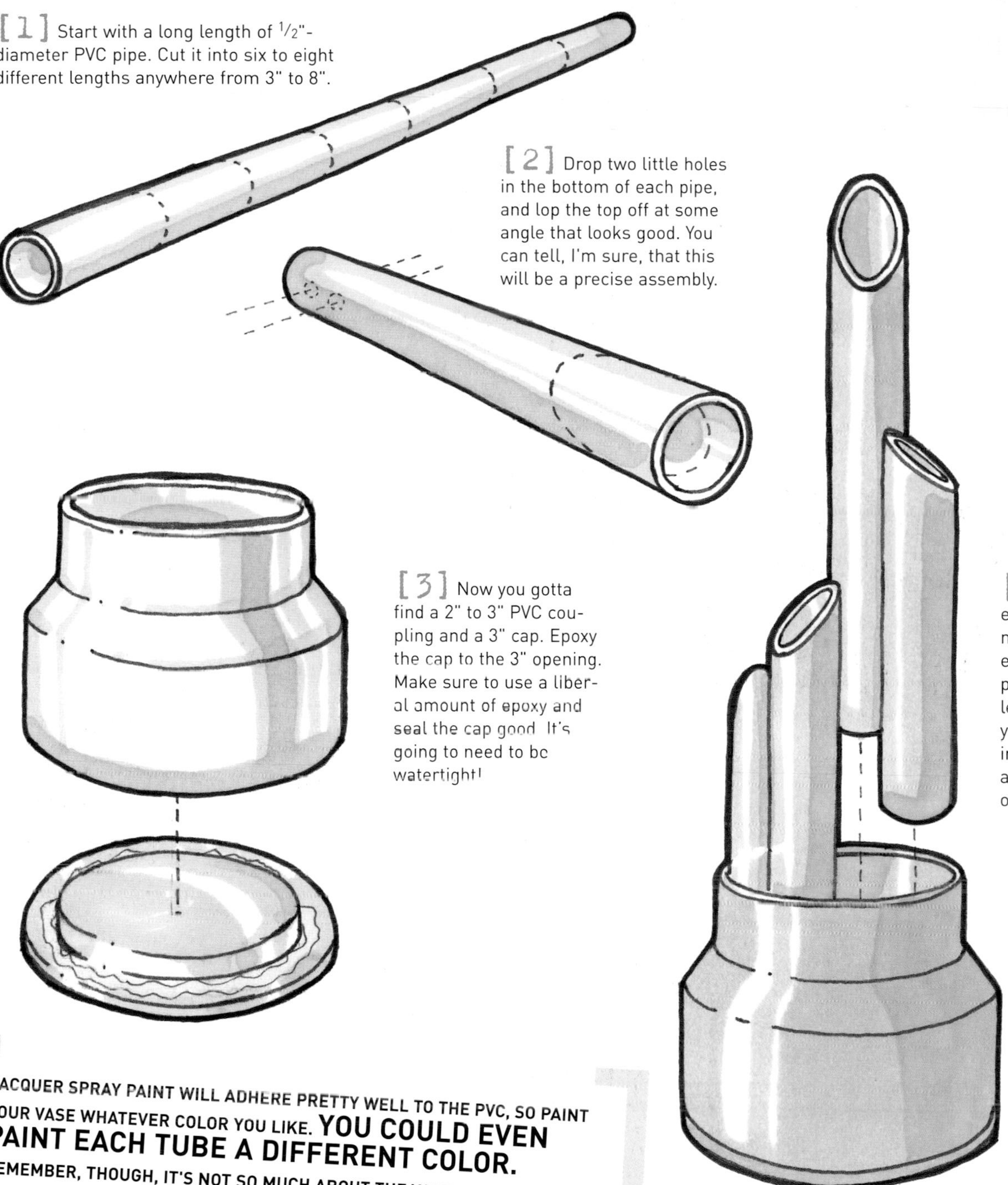

[3] Now you gotta find a 2" to 3" PVC coupling and a 3" cap. Epoxy the cap to the 3" opening. Make sure to use a liberal amount of epoxy and seal the cap good. It's going to need to be watertight!

[4] Now, drop the six to eight lengths in place. You might need a few drops of epoxy in some strategic places, depending on the lengths of the tubes. Be sure you don't cover up the holes in the bottom; those are to allow water to flow throughout the unit.

LACQUER SPRAY PAINT WILL ADHERE PRETTY WELL TO THE PVC, SO PAINT YOUR VASE WHATEVER COLOR YOU LIKE. **YOU COULD EVEN PAINT EACH TUBE A DIFFERENT COLOR.** REMEMBER, THOUGH, IT'S NOT SO MUCH ABOUT THE VASE AS IT IS THE BEAUTIFUL FLOWERS YOU PUT INSIDE. FIND A NICE BOUQUET AND TRY YOUR HAND AT ARRANGING, KEEPING IN MIND THE VARIATIONS OF COLORS, HEIGHTS AND TEXTURES OF ALL THE FLOWERS.

[keyhole] WINE RACK

A true sign of sophistication is when a bottle of wine joins the repertoire of adult beverages available at your house. If you're not there yet, this keyhole wine rack will definitely help you get there.

This little box is so beautiful and refined that you'll be racing to the store for a bottle of cabernet!

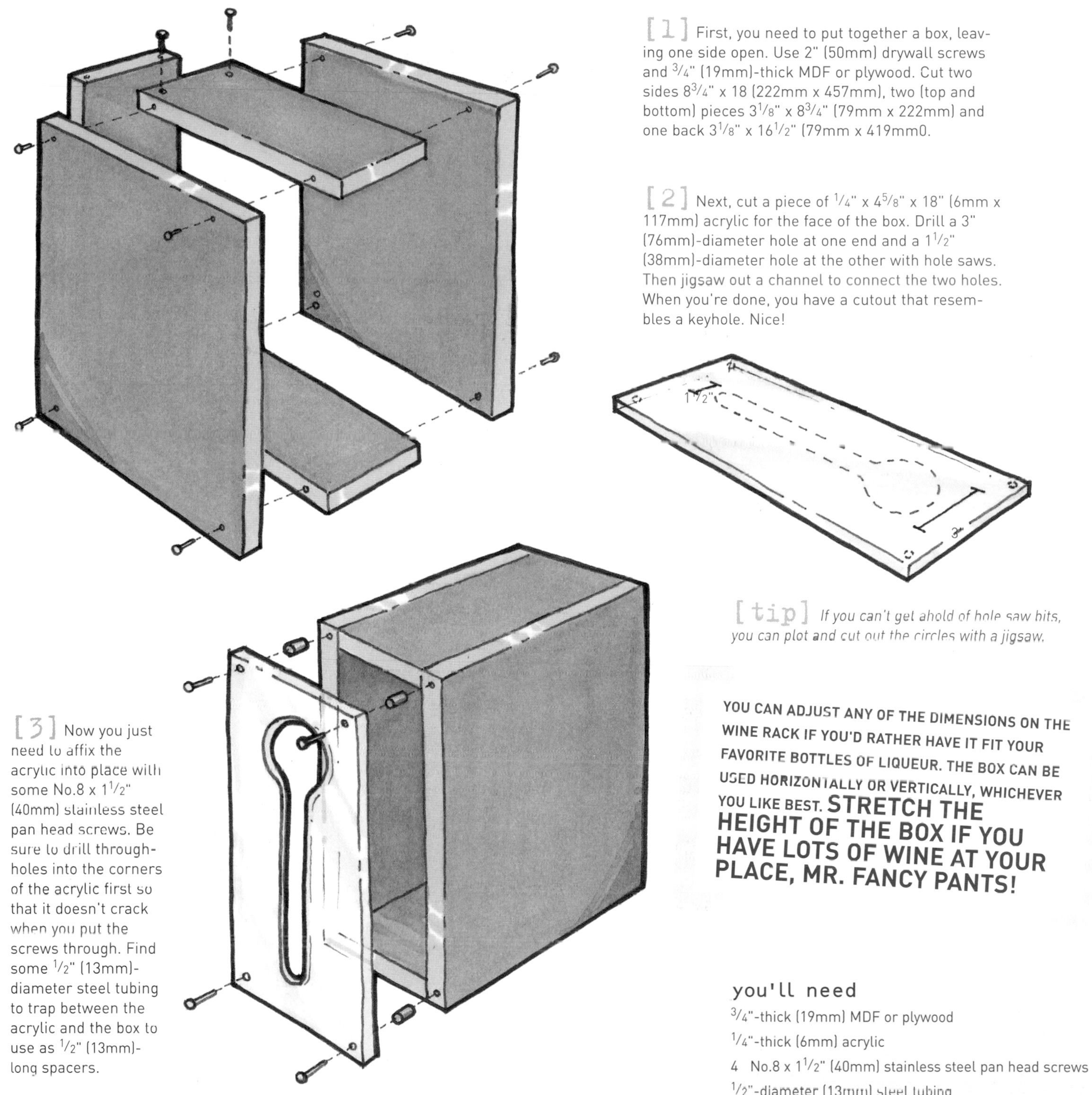

[1] First, you need to put together a box, leaving one side open. Use 2" (50mm) drywall screws and $^{3}/_{4}$" (19mm)-thick MDF or plywood. Cut two sides $8^{3}/_{4}$" x 18 (222mm x 457mm), two (top and bottom) pieces $3^{1}/_{8}$" x $8^{3}/_{4}$" (79mm x 222mm) and one back $3^{1}/_{8}$" x $16^{1}/_{2}$" (79mm x 419mm0.

[2] Next, cut a piece of $^{1}/_{4}$" x $4^{5}/_{8}$" x 18" (6mm x 117mm) acrylic for the face of the box. Drill a 3" (76mm)-diameter hole at one end and a $1^{1}/_{2}$" (38mm)-diameter hole at the other with hole saws. Then jigsaw out a channel to connect the two holes. When you're done, you have a cutout that resembles a keyhole. Nice!

[tip] *If you can't get ahold of hole saw bits, you can plot and cut out the circles with a jigsaw.*

[3] Now you just need to affix the acrylic into place with some No.8 x $1^{1}/_{2}$" (40mm) stainless steel pan head screws. Be sure to drill through-holes into the corners of the acrylic first so that it doesn't crack when you put the screws through. Find some $^{1}/_{2}$" (13mm)-diameter steel tubing to trap between the acrylic and the box to use as $^{1}/_{2}$" (13mm)-long spacers.

YOU CAN ADJUST ANY OF THE DIMENSIONS ON THE WINE RACK IF YOU'D RATHER HAVE IT FIT YOUR FAVORITE BOTTLES OF LIQUEUR. THE BOX CAN BE USED HORIZONTALLY OR VERTICALLY, WHICHEVER YOU LIKE BEST. STRETCH THE HEIGHT OF THE BOX IF YOU HAVE LOTS OF WINE AT YOUR PLACE, MR. FANCY PANTS!

you'll need

- $^{3}/_{4}$"-thick (19mm) MDF or plywood
- $^{1}/_{4}$"-thick (6mm) acrylic
- 4 No.8 x $1^{1}/_{2}$" (40mm) stainless steel pan head screws
- $^{1}/_{2}$"-diameter (13mm) steel tubing

[SUPPLIERS]

B&Q
B&Q Plc
Portswood House
1 Hampshire Corporate Park
Chandlers Ford
Eastleigh
Hampshire
SO53 3YX
0845 609 6688
www.diy.com
Tools, paint, wood, electrical, garden

HANCOCK FABRICS
One Fashion Way
Baldwyn, Mississippi 38824
877-322-7427
www.hancockfabrics.com
Fabrics, sewing supply

THE HOME DEPOT
2455 Paces Ferry Road, NW
Atlanta, Georgia 30339-4024
800-553-3199 (U.S.)
800-628-0525 (Canada)
www.homedepot.com
Tools, paint, wood, electrical, garden

JO-ANN STORES, INC.
5555 Darrow Road
Hudson, OH 44236
330-656-2600
www.joann.com
Fabrics, sewing supply

LOWE'S
P.O. Box 1111
North Wilkesboro, North Carolina
28656
800-445-6937
www.lowes.com
Tools, paint, wood, electrical, garden

MCMASTER-CARR
www.mcmaster.com
Anything you could ever want or need in tools, hardware and accessories

ROCKLER WOODWORKING AND HARDWARE
4365 Willow Drive
Medina, Minnesota 55340
800-279-4441
www.rockler.com
Woodworking tools and hardware

SMOOTH-ON
2000 Saint John Street
Easton, Pennsylvania 18042
800-762-0744
www.smooth-on.com
Liquid rubbers and plastics

WOODCRAFT
P.O. Box 1686
Parkersburg, West Virginia 26102-1686
800-535-4482
www.woodcraft.com
Woodworking hardware and accessories

****DON'T FORGET TO PATRONIZE YOUR INDEPENDENT NEIGHBORHOOD HARDWARE/D.I.Y STORES!****

INDEX

UNLEASH YOUR CREATIVITY WITH THESE TITLES FROM F+W PUBLICATIONS!

Creativity is more than just part of your job-it's your passion! Live it to the fullest with this resource book by Jim Krause designed to ignite your imagination and inventiveness through a wide variety of idea-sparking concepts, images and exercises.

ISBN 1-58180-438-5, hardcover, 312 pages, #32635-K

If working on deadline after deadline has left you feeling creatively zapped, this book will rejuvenate your imagination and give you new ideas and outlooks on your work and life as a designer. Find out what inspires forty top creatives and incorporate their insights into your world.

ISBN 1-58180-555-1, hardcover, 240 pages, #33011-K

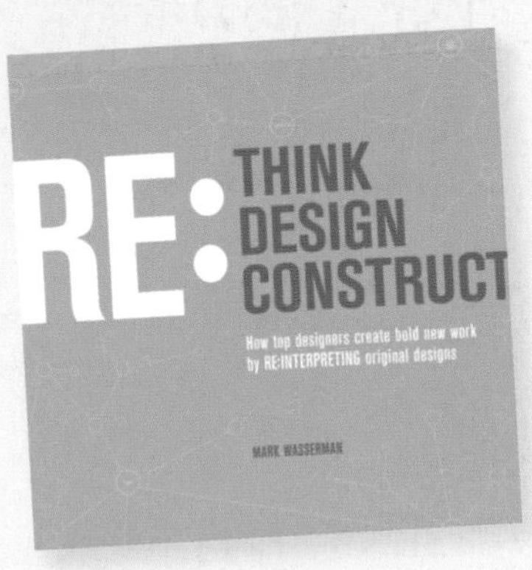

For every creative problem you encounter, there are several solutions-but what happens when you can't even think of one alternative? You pick up this book and study 37 print and electronic designs to see how other designers have reinterpreted original art, changed the design process, and come up with brilliant approaches that worked for them-and will inspire you.

ISBN 1-58180-459-8, hardcover, 192 pages, #32716-K

Begin thinking, planning and building furniture that is unique to your living space and lifestyle. Professional cabinetmaker Jim Stack helps you get your ideas down on paper and refined into a construction drawing and cutting list that will serve as a blueprint for your work.

ISBN 1-55870-613-5, paperback, 128 pages, #70555-K

THESE AND OTHER GREAT BOOKS ARE AVAILABLE AT YOUR LOCAL BOOKSTORE, ONLINE SUPPLIER OR BY CALLING 1-800-448-0915.